Patricia L. Kutzner

The use of imagery
in
Wolfram's «Parzival»

A distributional Study

Stanford German Studies

Edited by the Department of German Studies
Stanford University, California

Herausgegeben vom Institut für Germanistik
der Universität Stanford, Kalifornien

Vol. 8

Herbert Lang Bern
Peter Lang Frankfurt/M.

Patricia L. Kutzner

The use of imagery in Wolfram's «Parzival»

A distributional Study

Herbert Lang Bern
Peter Lang Frankfurt/M.

ISBN 3 261 01549 7

Herbert Lang&Cie AG, Bern (Schweiz)
Peter Lang GmbH, Frankfurt/M. (BRD)
1975. Alle Rechte vorbehalten.

Druck: fotokop wilhelm weihert kg, Darmstadt

CONTENTS

LIST OF TABLES

CHAPTER I

PURPOSE AND METHODOLOGY

To what ends did Wolfram apply the much discussed imagery of <u>Parzival</u>? How far can a consideration of that question proceed entirely from an empirically objective base established from within the text of the epic itself? These are the two questions to which this study addresses itself.

Wolfram discussions inevitably revolve around the question of possibilities, attempting to elevate one or the other into the realm of convincing probability. Many of the most stimulating studies rely heavily upon evidence from extra-textual factors, applied comparatively and conjecturally to Wolfram's works, factors relating to those many cultural or psychological phenomena which possibly (but not unquestionably) account for his thought or style. One line of inquiry deduces common speech styles and the Spielmann epic rather than courtly speech and literature as the prevailing influences. (1) Singer reaches the opposite conclusion and argues that a key feature of style, at least in <u>Parzival</u>, is emulation of the <u>trobar</u> <u>clus</u>, that esoteric, purposely obscure, highly self-conscious style of certain Provencal poets, of whom the legendary Kyot may have been one. (2) Dilthey is representative of those who stress Wolfram's untutored originality, (3) while others find him highly literate and following in the traditions of classical rhetoric. De Boor speaks for the compromise assumption, most prevalent today, that Wolfram was literate but probably only moderately so and lacking in much formal education. (4) Still, Brinkmann finds his most characteristic element of style as being a preference for features of the <u>ornatus difficilis</u>: "erzwungene Bildlichkeit, Umschreibung, andeutender Ausdruck, neuerungslustiger Wille zum Fremdartigen, Gekünstelten, Rätselhaften."(5) Bayer recognizes influences of the traditions of classical rhetoric as conveyed through medieval Church scholarship, but denies the <u>ornatus difficilus</u> as typical of Wolfram. He prefers to relate his style to that of the <u>sermo humilis</u> on the one hand and, on the other, to the arts of recitation going back to Greek antiquity, seeing in Wolfram the best example in medieval literature of a style reminiscent of Ovid's acclaimed teacher Kallimachus. (6) For Glunz the chief stylistic influence is the Scholastic conception of the poet's role as a creative channel for the divine Author (most apparent in <u>Willehalm</u>, to be sure). (7) Weber finds Wolfram's relationship to Christian tradition one of the main keys to both content and style, the other being his "germanic nature," to which Weber attributes the combining of the irrational with a thorough-going realism and the dominance of content over form. (8) Analogical thinking and the attitudes underlying the cult of worship of the Virgin Mary, the elevation of Minneglorification to a mystical level as seen in the Cluniac and Cistercian orders of the time are the twin forces which shaped <u>Parzival</u>, according to Schröder's analysis: (9)

> Der Typus Mensch, dem Wolfram angehört, hat sich um 1200 sonst nur im Minnesang, im lyrisch-kultischen Gedicht, dichterisch ausgelebt, nicht im Epos, das vielmehr dem moralisierenden, ästhetisierenden oder abenteuerfreudigen Sinn die rechte Form bot. Wolframs Einmaligkeit beruht darauf, dass er kultischen Minnepreis in

epischer Darstellung gab, d.h. den hymnischen Vollzug zum epischen umdachte.

Undeniably, each such study expands our imagination about Wolfram and our perspective of the cultural web of his times, reducing the temptation to formulate hasty and naive certainties.(10) However, amid "geistesgeschichtliche" conjecture, enriching though it is, facts about Wolfram's artistry remain scarce. Furthermore, few of the facts that have been established are of much help in accounting for either the internal organization or the effect of his style. As Sacker points out, while the many positivistic researches of the late 19th and early 20th centuries collected facts, they failed to relate them to the artistic whole; and until we have a clearer idea about "how Wolfram's style works, what all the bits add up to and how they function," comparing him with other writers and traditions leads in circles, providing little sure insight into his own artistry.(11) Lippka is sceptical about the validity of reaching any but fragmentary conclusions on the question of this artistry as long as the possibilities of a lost Kyot source must remain unresolved.(12) Nevertheless, even without being able to settle the question of what is unique to Wolfram and what he borrowed, it should still be possible to discover how the components of any single work interact within that work to produce the artistic effect of the whole.

Reporting on the state of research in 1954, Eggers laments the lack of serious investigations of language and style which could form a solid philological basis from which to approach other Wolfram questions. He specifies a need in the areas of "Sprachkunst, Stilgehalt, Symbolgehalt und Bildgehalt."(13) During the following decade several studies emerged in which structural analysis attempted to relate elements of form to content, but Jackson's research survey (through 1960) calls them superficial and mentions only two.(14) Sacker also deprecates the results of these studies, but he contends that, nevertheless, this is the methodology which might prove most promising for future scholarship.(15)

The genesis of the present study derived from three separate interests which converged in my speculations about Parzival. The first was a personal delight in Wolfram's style, without being able to say exactly what that was or why it affected me as it did. The second was an interest in the assumptions about metaphoric expression being put forth by critics, psychologists, and philosophers of language in our own day. The third was the question of ways in which the empirical rigorousness of linguistic analysis might be applied fruitfully to literary analysis. These three came together in a focus on the imagery in Parzival.

That there are striking differences in the frequency of poetic imagery in Parzival is apparent to the most casual reader just from the contrast between the 116 lines of the Prologue and the first 116 lines of the following Gahmuret episode. One is struck by the abundance of imagery in the former, some of it very obscure, which renders comprehension of the Prologue markedly more difficult than the following narrative which flows along easily with hardly a poetic figure in sight. Later portions of the narrative, however, again include much imagery of varying degrees of

10

obscurity. Why does frequency of imagery vary so widely in _Parzival_? If an analysis of the entire work were to reveal significant similarities between passages of high image frequency as contrasted with those passages of lowest frequency, it should be possible to suggest some answers to that question which would also contribute to our awareness of Wolfram's poetic craftsmanship. The hypothesis underlying this study is that it will in fact be possible to demonstrate a relationship between the frequency of imagery in a passage and the poetic function of that passage.

If an empirically objective basis for a discussion of the imagery in _Parzival_ is wanted, a methodology should be used which takes the whole of the epic into account, not just the passages or images that support one's hypotheses. Every instance of imagery should be considered from a standpoint which is consistent throughout in order to have a constant factor to which variables can be related. The hope of such work would be to discover and define recurring patterns within the initially amorphous mass of image occurrence. These patterns could then be examined for their similarities and differences in effect or function within the narrative or thematic environments in which they occur. The most valid theory for Wolfram's use of imagery would be the one which most wholly described the resulting picture.

Such has been the methodology attempted in this study. The factor selected to serve as the constant is the category of image frequency, expressed as a ratio of the number of images occurring within a certain number of lines. In order that literary significance might be represented in this ratio, the environments within which image frequency is thus measured have been defined according to theme or narrative event. This was felt to be more likely to reveal stylistic patterns which could be related to affective intent or consequence than a ratio reflecting the conventional division of the epic into 30-line sequences.(16) The entire epic is divided sequentially, therefore, into topically separated passages. What emerges is a schematic picture of the distribution of imagery throughout _Parzival_ relative to narrative content. This forms the empirical basis for subsequent discussion of Wolfram's style.

To speak of Wolfram's intent seems a natural corollary to speaking of what he does, but in so doing it is important to remember that there we are moving beyond factuality into the quite different realm of possibility, unproven and probably unprovable. As far as imagery is concerned, what can be shown with certitude is only what he did, not whether or not he did it consciously and deliberately. Nevertheless, what he did and "how it works" is the sort of style characterization we are after.(17)

The pre-existing collections of imagery, which will be discussed later, were neither comprehensive nor systematic enough to serve this method. Therefore, still another catalog of the imagery in _Parzival_ is added herewith to the literature. Every effort has been made to produce a complete listing of images in the order of their appearance. The chief difficulty, of course, has been in deciding whether or not a word or phrase was being used figuratively or in the commonly accepted meaning of the time. As Wehrli points out, there are few texts which resist adequate translation as stubbornly as do the Middle High German verse epics. This is attributed to semantic change. In some instances words have extended or contracted their meaning in modern German without any new equivalent having been developed for the MHG connotation. (18) What appears as metaphorical transference in the semantic context of modern German may well have been nothing of the sort in MHG. For example, the process of semantic development has narrowed the public meaning of the word dach, which was the MHG term for a covering in general, not just a roof, while the meaning of MHG liebe has expanded in modern German to include minne. As a more troublesome problem, Wolfram seems to use some words in connotations which are uniquely his own, yet he does it so often that one is apt to assume the usage is standard MHG. The verb lêren, for example, appears often with a dependent infinitive where the implication is similar to the function of modern German lassen, ie., to cause an action to occur, as in "schaden lêren" (P21, 18) or "sterben lêren" (P106, 14). Sometimes the accusative object is a noun instead of an infinitive, but the meaning is still closer to one of causation than of transmitting knowledge: "flust lêren" (P197, 14), "pîn lêren" (P385, 5), to cite just a few of the many instances. MHG zil is an even more difficult term, appearing in many contexts in which the modern German Ziel would make no sense at all, even by the widest stretch of metaphorical imagination. One of the connotations of zil common in Parzival seems also to have been Wolfram's invention. This is zil joined with another noun in the genitive to imply a superlative degree of the essence of that nominal concept, as in "dô saz diu maget an vreuden zil" (P190, 18), or "da erwarp iu swîgen sünden zil" (P316, 23) (19).

It has seemed best to consider any semantic usage which is unique to Wolfram as metaphorical, but this can not be the sole criterion. The power of an expression to call attention to itself through some incongruity with logic or with common speech habits and assumptions seems basically essential for the selection of literary metaphor. If we accept Auerbach's definition of a literary language as the spoken language of the educated classes, (20) we may assume that the more often an expression appears in the court epics in a certain connotation, the more likely that connotation is to be a standard, rather than figurative, usage. This can be only a rough guideline, however, because of the difficulty in discriminating between a faded or buried metaphor and a traditional one.

A faded metaphor is an expression which logic wants to call a metaphor but which has become such common currency in a language that no native speaker either perceives or uses it as figurative. The phenomenon ranges from what Wellek and Warren designate as the etymological metaphor (ie., "table leg") to what Hayakawa calls a metaphor which "has been so successful that it has passed into the regular language and died as a metaphor."(21) The latter is one of the most important means by which languages grow and change. A good example may be the phrase used above, "common currency." Does a contemporary native speaker of English notice the metaphorical transference involved, or does he grasp its meaning so smoothly from long familiarity that the expression has become devoid of imaginative impact? Surely the latter is the case.

PURPOSE AND METHODOLOGY

In attempting to avoid inclusion of dead metaphors in his catalog of Wolf-ram's imagery, Tapp excluded expressions which he found also in Old High German or in any ante-Wolfram Middle High German authors. (22) However, according to Lausberg, so many actual metaphors were preserved by rhetorical tradition among Latin writers that the poets of late antiquity rarely produced a truly original one. (23) Could these traditions have persisted to influence medieval writers, even Wolfram? Apparently so, for Singer's studies, as well as those of Glunz, Curtius, and Auerbach indicate that many expressions appearing in _Parzival_, though common-place, are more in the nature of traditional metaphors than dead ones. (24) They were probably still used for literary effect, however trite they may seem to us. Litera-tures in which the traditional metaphor plays a valid part do not subscribe to the modern view that a poet's expressions should be his very own and never merely borrowed from another poet. On the contrary, in such cultures the very familiarity of phrases and images is important in giving an appropriate background and tone to the poet's work. Hearing these commonplaces is part of the listener's pleasure. (25)

That some such esthetics may have been operative in Wolfram's time seems quite likely in view of the self-consciousness of the courtly culture. Therefore, nei-ther originality nor singularity has been the basis of metaphor selection, but rather simply the criterion of incongruity as described above. Where intuition has had to be the chief guide, the hope has been to err rather in the direction of including too many questionable metaphors than too few genuine ones.

Returning to the question of intent, numerous hypotheses can be put forward to account for Wolfram's use of imagery in general and of metaphor more particu-larly, in addition to the hypothesis of traditional metaphor just mentioned (which, incidentally, Parry claims to be especially strong in oral literatures). One of these would consider metaphoric thinking as a kind of perception which may be character-istic of a poet's mental processes. According to such an hypothesis, Wolfram would produce figurative language because it was most natural to him personally to per-ceive things in these terms. From this point of view, he would not be trying to im-press anyone with his images, there would be no intent to stylistic ornamentation, but rather, the images would flow out of his mind in response to the simple desire to express his intuitive perceptions.

Many who view the phenomenon of imagery in this way are most interested in what they see as the non-logical or a-logical aspect of "true" as distinguished from "merely ornamental" metaphor. The British critic Middleton Murry represents this school of thought when he says: (26)

> Metaphor, if regarded by a prosaic eye, or analyzed by a mind which
> has lost a certain keenness of intuition, does tend to look like ornament...
> My conviction is that true metaphor...has very little to do even with an
> act of comparison. Logically, of course, it is...But creative literature
> of the highest kind is not amenable to logical analysis...Metaphor be-
> comes a mode of apprehension.

In another discussion Murry refers to Aristotle's expressed admiration for the same phenomenon, as the one stylistic device that "cannot be learned from others, a sign of original genius, since a good metaphor implies the intuitive perception of the similarity in dissimilars."(27) The appeal of this view of metaphor would be obvious if one wished to emphasize Wolfram's originality and uniqueness both as thinker and as poet.

At one point in his Rhetoric, however, Aristotle touches upon the view that the use of metaphor, alone among the figures of speech, is common to all men, not just poets.(28) This aspect of metaphor has attracted much study by both psychologists and philosophers of language in this century, some of whom postulate metaphorical thinking as something rooted deeply within the human psyche, perhaps the prevailing mode of thought in pre-logical periods of both civilizations and of individual development.(29) As one recent discussion of creativity puts it:(30)

> Experience is largely reported in metaphorical terms, and its effective sharing with others has traditionally been the province of the poet and novalist. A child may do this well before his verbal expressions become emasculated by convention.

Such a perspective could support hypotheses favoring Wolfram's naturalness, his closeness to folk tradition and speech, his divergence from the more sophisticated courtly attitudes or expressions, his untutored, perhaps illiterate, background. In this view the possibility of original genius would not be discarded, but the emphasis would be on that about Wolfram which was essentially, timelessly human, Wolfram as free from "emasculation by convention," a most natural, "unspoiled" poet in contrast to the notion of Wolfram as a sophisticated highly literate poet.

The hypotheses considered so far have looked upon metaphorical expression as coming about in a relatively spontaneous fashion. Assuming the opposite, one could imagine metaphor and other forms of imagery being resorted to deliberately for a variety of purposes: to illustrate, to clarify, to enliven, to amuse, to emphasize, to express the otherwise inexpressible, or to give the impression of skill, wit, and a gift for poetics, which may have been what Wolfram had in mind in the self-characterization: "ich bin Wolfram von Eschenbach / und kan ein teil mit sange" (P114, 12-13). This standpoint runs counter to the trends of contemporary literary criticism as expressed by Wellek and Warren:(31)

> The whole series (image, metaphor, symbol, myth) we may charge older literary study with treating externally and superficially. Viewed for the most part as decorations, rhetorical ornaments, they were studied as detachable parts of the works in which they appear. Our own view...sees the meaning and function of literature as centrally present in metaphor and myth. There are such activities as metaphoric and mythic thinking, a thinking by means of metaphors, a thinking in poetic narrative or vision. All these terms call our attention to the aspects of a literary work which exactly bridge and bind together old

divisive components, "form" and "matter." These terms look in both directions; that is, they indicate the pull of poetry toward "picture" and "world" on the one hand and toward religion or Weltanschauung on the other.

Such a perspective, as well as those of Murry, Richards, Aristotle, and the psychologists and philosophers of language mentioned above, are essentially non-historical, devoid of historical relativism. The attempt is to establish theories which can be considered valid for poets and other men in all times.

A quite different approach is to try to view Wolfram's use of imagery from within the criteria of his own time, an approach no less current than the trends illustrated by Wellek and Warren, and, to judge from post-World War II publications, a trend growing steadily in strength, primarily on the continent. (32) In this approach attention is focused upon the fact that in Wolfram's time all lettered men were thoroughly schooled to an awareness of imagery as a rhetorical device in the very sense that Wellek and Warren deplore. Following on the heels of the revival of Latin in the 11th century as a medium of creative and personal expression came the revival of interest in the 12th century in the classical canons of rhetoric, viewing it in three functions: as a part of logic, as the art of stating truths certified by theology, and as the art of words in sermons, letters, and literature. (33) Glunz finds evidence that Cicero's rhetorical writings were considered the supreme authority for writers in some quarters; both Auerbach and Curtius stress Ovid's example as a primary influence. But was this rhetorical awareness limited to the scholarly clerics? Apparently not. Anything beyond the most rudimentary study of Latin would bring a student into contact with rhetorical models and stylistic ideals. Rhetorical theory as it pertained to literary style was an important part of the grammatical studies in the Trivium. Both of the most common Latin grammars in use all over Europe at the time, the Donatus Ars Maior and the Priscian Institutiones Grammaticae, were filled with examples from classical writers, especially Virgil. (35) Only the first step in Latin instruction, the Ars Minor of Donatus, omitted these illustrations.

Supposing, however, that Wolfram was not a lettered man, that he never got beyond his elementary Donatus, if indeed, he experienced even that, through what channels might classical models and ideals of literary expression have come to exert influence upon his own style? Veldeke's Eneit comes to mind immediately, of course. (36) The French Eneas upon which it was modeled had replaced Virgil's style with one more typical of later antiquity, a style which Auerbach describes as:

> eine Zerstörung der klassisch-vergilischen Vorstellung vom Erhabenen durch übermässige Verwendung rhetorischer Formen, zu denen auch die prunkvolle Beschreibung gehört,

characteristics which carried over into Veldeke's work, known and admired by Wolfram. (37) On the basis of Hartmann's pride in his literacy, it can be assumed that he had progressed beyond the Ars Minor, in which case his style, too, had been exposed to classical rhetoric. Indeed, the court epic form itself, as well as its predecessors in the heroic and national epic, was created by rhetorically schooled clerics who knew their ars and auctores. (38) Whether or not Wolfram knew Latin, these influences helped shape the literature to which he was exposed and must, therefore, have helped to shape his own concept of what literature should sound like.

The possibility of influence coming to him through the language and style of sermons should also be considered. While the overly rhetorical, highly ornamental style of which the Eneas is an example continued to be practised in the medieval Latin school tradition, a more moderate, less decorative style seems to have been the prevailing model for sermons of the time, the sermo humilis, a style to which Bayer specifically relates Wolfram's characteristics. (39) Horacek supports this view in her commentary on those features which most strongly suggest oral, rather than written, literature when she notes: (40)

> Die grosse Zahl von Gleichnissen und anschaulichen Bildern hat Wolf-
> rams Erzählkunst mit der mittelalterlichen Predigt gemeinsam. Manche
> primitiv theoretisierenden theologischen Partien (z. B. Wh218, 1ff) er-
> wecken überhaupt den Eindruck, dass hier nicht geistliche Literatur,
> sondern Predigtgut verwertet ist.

The sermo humilis was the style declared by Augustine to be most appropriate for the stories of martyrs and most similar to the Bible. Auerbach describes its characteristics as combining:

> das Zutrauliche und Einfache, zugleich Alltägliche und Wunderbare,
> zugleich Unterhaltende und Lehrende, aus dem Beliebigen und Ge-
> wohnlichen sich unmittelbar ins Ernsthafte und Hohe, Gute und Weise
> Erhebende. (41)

As for metaphor, from Aristotle onward teachers of rhetoric gave it special praise as a stylistic device, with only the reservation that it be used judicially and not to excess. Though Aristotle's Rhetoric and Poetics seem to have been actually read rather little during the medieval period, Quintillian's pedagogical treatise on style for both speaking and writing was widely known and used. (42) In this we find: "metaphor has been invented for the purpose of exciting the mind, giving a character to things, and setting them before the eye," a valuable adornment to any style unless used so frequently as to obscure the language and "render the perusal of it fatiguing."(43) How many of the metaphors passed along by rhetorical tradition might have come to Wolfram's ears, well-worn but still well-regarded, through sermons, the Eneit, or Hartmann, to mention only a few of his possible sources? In short, the influence of classical rhetoric either through formal study or indirectly through models absorbed into both church and secular, oral and written literature seems to have been so pervasive that it is hard to imagine that Wolfram's concept of style would remain unaffected.

If this is assumed to have been the case, one's hypotheses about Wolfram's intent with imagery would incline to agree with Brinkmann when he contends that the application of medieval literary concepts are more to the point and more productive in evaluating Wolfram's artistry than the concepts of modern literary theory with which this discussion of intent began. (44) However, it would surely be fallacious to assume that evidence of consciously rhetorical artistry, extending perhaps even to deliberate ornamentation in some passages or aspects of Parzival, precludes the presence also of poetic "naturalness" or spontaneity. The most complete grasp of Wolfram as poet is probably not to be found in an either-or attitude but in an assumption of both-and, both rhetorically traditional and spontaneously unique. Literary tradition is surely an essential part of the total picture, but the dynamics of the poetic creation still have their locus within the unique personality of the poet. As Bumke puts it:

> ...seine "dunkle" Stilmanier, die so stark auf die Nachahmer gewirkt hat, paart sich eigentümlich mit einer schlichten, unkomplizierten Ausdrucksweise, dass also verschiedene Stiltendenzen nebeneinander stehen, deren Wurzel offenbar nicht ein definierbares "Stilideal" ist (wie es für die gelehrten Dichter massgebend war), sondern die einmalige und widersprüchliche Individualität des Dichters. (45)

Furthermore, even the relationship to literary tradition must be viewed as an expression of individuality, for the critic must take account not only of the presence of traditional elements but also of the will of the poet to pick and choose from among the various traditional possibilities available to him, putting these elements to use in the service of his own stylistic concepts. (46) Therefore, both the hypotheses of contemporary literary theory as well as the perspectives of medieval standards need to be kept in mind in attempting to account for the essence and functioning of Wolfram's style.

The risks of anachronistic interpretation are everpresent, of course. We must agree with Kuhn that it is inherently impossible for modern critics to see through the eyes or hear through the ears of medieval audiences and poets. Because of the vast differences which have accrued to our manner of thinking, Kuhn insists that the best we can do to guard against prejudiced distortions is to define scrupulously the basis from which we establish the factuality of our "facts."(47) Applying this to an analysis of Wolfram's style, we would reiterate a point made earlier, that while poetic intent may elude our criteria of certainty, poetic acts need not. It should be possible to show as fact where his imagery occurs. What the effect of its occurrence is on listener or reader is only slightly more conjectural. Whether or not Wolfram intended it to have that effect is most conjectural of all and actually has little to do with the critical objective of trying to account for what all the stylistic bits and pieces add up to and how they function within the whole. In examining the studies of Wolfram's imagery which preceded this one, therefore, the conclusions they reached will be of interest; but the process used to reach those conclusions and the assumptions underlying the processes will be the primary concern.

PURPOSE AND METHODOLOGY

Notes

(1) Oskar Jänicke, De dicendi usu Wolframi de Eschenbach (Diss., 1861). See also the critique by Franz Pfeiffer of the Jänicke and Lachmann position, "Ueber das Parzival und Wolframs Sprachgebrauch," Germania: Vierteljahrschrift für deutsche Altertumskunde, 6(1861), 239-245. Friedrich Dahms deals particularly with the Spielmann influence in Die Grundlagen für den Stil Wolframs von Eschenbach (Diss., Greifswald, 1911).

(2) Samuel Singer, "Wolframs Stil und der Stoff des Parzival," Wiener Sitzungsberichte, 180, 4. Abh. (1916), 1-127; also Neue Parzival-Studien (Zurich: Max Niehaus, 1937).

(3) Wilhelm Dilthey, "Die Ritterliche Dichtung und das Nationale Epos," Von Deutscher Dichtung und Musik (Leipzig: B.G. Teubner, 1933), 107-130. This position has been defended more recently by Herbert Grundmann, "Dichtete Wolfram am Schreibtisch?" Archiv für Kulturgeschichte, 49 (1967), 391-405.

(4) Helmut de Boor, Geschichte der deutschen Literatur, Vol. II Die höfische Literatur (Munich: Beck, 1953), 91-92.

(5) Hennig Brinkmann, Zu Wesen und Form mittelalterlicher Dichtung (Halle/ Saale: M. Niemeyer, 1928), 101. See also Traugott K. Reiber, Studien zu Grundlage und Wesen mittelalterlich-höfischer Dichtung. Unter besonderer Berücksichtigung von Wolframs dunklem Stil (Diss., Tübingen, 1954).

(6) Hans J. Bayer, Untersuchungen zum Sprachstil weltlicher Epen des deutschen Früh- und Hochmittelalters (Berlin: Erich Schmidt, 1962), 201 ff.

(7) Hans H. Glunz, Die Literarästhetik des europäischen Mittelalters (Frankfurt/ Main: Vittorio Klostermann, 1963), 295 ff.

(8) Gottfried Weber, Wolfram von Eschenbach: Seine dichterische und geistesgeschichtliche Bedeutung, Vol. I (Frankfurt/Main: Moritz Diesterweg, 1928), 3 and 249 ff.

(9) Walter Johannes Schröder, "Grundzüge eines neuen Wolframbildes," Forschungen und Fortschritte, 26 (1950), 178.

(10) Heinrich Lausberg explains the purpose of his Handbuch der literarischen Rhetorik: eine Grundlegung der Literaturwissenschaft (Munich: Hueber, 1960), 7 in these terms: "Die Phänomen-Breite der Antike erlaubt einen wurzelhaften Einbau auch nach-antiker Detail-Phänomene, auf die der Interpret mittelalterlicher und neuzeitlicher Literatur stossen wird. Jedenfalls befindet sich der Interpret, wenn er die Antike als Ausgangsbasis wählt, auf sicherem Boden." See also E.R. Curtius, Europäische Literatur und lateinisches Mittelalter (Bern: Francke, 1948) and E. Auerbach, Literatursprache und Publikum in der lateinischen Spätantike und im Mittelalter (Bern: Francke, 1958).

18

(11) Hugh Sacker, An Introduction to Wolfram's Parzival (Cambridge: University
      Press, 1963), 175 ff.

(12) Erwin Lippka, "Zum Stilproblem in Wolframs Parzival: Bericht über den
      Stand der Forschung," Journal of English and Germanic Philology, 62 (1963),
      609. He draws particular attention to the great number of Provencal docu-
      ments which must have been destroyed in the Albigensien wars.

(13) Hans Eggers, "Wolframforschung in der Krise? Ein Forschungsbericht,"
      Wirkendes Wort, 4 (1953-54), 274-290. Three other research reports ignore
      style altogether: Ralph Lowet, Wolfram von Eschenbachs Parzival im Wandel
      der Zeiten (Munich: Pohl, 1955); Werner Schröder, "Zum gegenwärtigen
      Stande der Wolfram Kritik," Zeitschrift für deutsches Altertum und Litera-
      turgeschichte, XCVI (1967), 1-29, discussing only document research; and
      Heinz Rupp, "Das neue Wolframbild," Deutschunterricht, V (1953), 82-90.

(14) W.T.H. Jackson, "Medieval German Literature," The Medieval Literature of
      Western Europe, a Review of Research 1930-1960, John H. Fisher, ed. for
      Modern Language Assoc. (New York: N.Y. University Press, 1966), 213.

(15) Sacker, loc.cit.

(16) Despite Eggers ingenious analysis of the architectonics of Parzival, I do not
      find the 30-line grouping truly significant in the dramatic unfolding of the
      narrative. See Hans Eggers, "Strukturprobleme mittelalterlicher Epik dar-
      gestellt am 'Parzival' Wolframs von Eschenbach," in Wolfram von Eschen-
      bach, Heinz Rupp editor (Darmstadt: Wissenschaftliche Buchgesellschaft,
      1966), 158-172.

(17) For a fuller treatment of this point see W.K. Wimsatt, Jr. and M.C. Beards-
      ley, "The Intentional Fallacy," in Essays in Modern Literary Criticism, Ray
      B. West, editor (New York: Holt, Rinehart, Winston, 1962, reprinted from
      1952), 174-189.

(18) Max Wehrli, "Wolfram von Eschenbach: Erzählstil und Sinn seines Parzival,"
      Deutschunterricht, VI (1954), Heft 5, 17.

(19) Karl Kinzel, "Zur charakteristik des Wolframschen stils," Zeitschrift für
      deutsche Philologie, V (1874), 27 ff.

(20) Auerbach, op.cit., 187.

(21) Rene Wellek and Austin Warren, Theory of Literature (New York: Harcourt,
      Brace, 1956), 186; and S.I. Haykawa, Language in Thought and Action,
      (New York: Harcourt, Brace, 1949), 124.

(22) Henry Tapp, An Investigation of the Use of Imagery in the Works of Wolfram
      von Eschenbach (Diss., Yale, 1954), 34.

(23) Lausberg, op.cit., 288

(24)   Glunz, op.cit., 62; Singer, Curtius, Auerbach, op.cit., passim.

(25)   Milman Parry, "The Traditional Metaphor in Homer," Classical Philology,
        XXVIII (1933), 30-43.

(26)   John Middleton Murry, The Problem of Style (London: Oxford University
        Press, 1922), 12-13. I.A. Richars says much the same thing: "There are
        few metaphors whose effect, if carefully examined, can be traced to the lo-
        gical relations involved." in Principles of Literary Criticism (London: Rout-
        ledge and Kegan Paul, 1949, 240. See also Richards, "Metaphor," The
        Philosophy of Rhetoric (N.Y.: Oxford Univ., 1936), 89-138.

(27)   J.M. Murry, "Metaphor," Countries of the Mind: Essays in Literary Criti-
        cism (London: Oxford University Press, 1931), 3. The reference is to the
        Poetics, chapter 22, page 1459a, line 4, in the Bekker edition numbering.

(28)   Artistotle, Rhetoric, book III, chapter 2, page 1404b, lines 32-35, translated
        by W. Rhys Roberts (New York: Random House, 1954).

(29)   Among the major treatments should be mentioned: Owen Barfield, Poetic
        Diction: A Study in Meaning (London: Faber and Gwyer, 1928); Kenneth
        Burke, "Four Master Tropes," Grammar of Motives (N.Y.: Prentice-Hall,
        1945), 503-517; Susanne K. Langer, Mind: As Essay on Human Feeling,
        Vol. I (Baltimore: Johns Hopkins, 1967); Hermann Pongs, Das Bild in der
        Dichtung, Vol. I: Versuch einer Morphologie der metaphorischen Formen
        and "Das dichterische Bild und das Unbewusste," in Vol. II: Voruntersuchun-
        gen zum Symbol (Marburg: Elwert, 1960, 1963); Heinz Werner, Die Ur-
        sprünge der Metapher, Heft 3 of Arbeiten zur Entwicklungspsychologie, Felix
        Krueger, editor (Leipzig: Engelmann, 1919).

(30)   Frederick Perls, R.E. Hefferline, Paul Goodman, Gestalt Therapy: Excite-
        ment and Growth in the Human Personality (New York: Dell, 1965), 25.

(31)   Wellek and Warren, op.cit., 182. See also John V. Hagopian, "Symbol and
        Metaphor in the Transformation of Reality into Art," Comparative Literature,
        XX (Winter, 1968), 45-54.

(32)   Singer, 1916 and 1937; Brinkmann, 1928; Bayer, 1962; Glunz, 1937 and
        1963; Lausberg, 1960; Curtius, 1948; Auerbach, 1958; Reiber, 1954;
        Schwietering, 1925 and 1957, to mention only the works referred to in this
        study. A forerunner of the trend was Konrad Burdach, "Nachleben der grie-
        chisch-römischen Altertums in der mittelalterlichen Dichtung und Kunst," a
        paper delivered at the Kölner Philologenversammlung, 1895, but not published
        until 1925 in Vorspiel I (Halle/Saale: Max Niemeyer), 49-100.

(33)   Auerbach, op.cit., 206. See also Richard McKeon, "Poetry and Philosophy
        in the Twelfth Century, the Renaissance of Rhetoric," Modern Philology, 43
        (May, 1946), 217-234; and "Rhetoric in the Middle Ages," Speculum, 17
        (January, 1942), 1-32.

(34)   Glunz, op.cit., 230-231; Auerbach, op.cit., 157; Curtius op.cit., 388.

(35)   Wayland Johnson Chase, The Ars Minor of Donatus (Madison: University of
       Wisconsin Studies in the Social Sciences and History, No. 11, 1926), 4, 5,
       15. Also Auerbach, 148; Curtius, 50.

(36)   This is the view of Wolfram's access to classical influence held by Julius
       Schwietering, "Typologisches in mittelalterlicher Dichtung," in Vom Werden
       des deutschen Geistes, Ehrismann Festschrift (Berlin: de Gruyter, 1925),
       40 ff.

(37)   Auerbach, op.cit., 142.

(38)   Curtius, op.cit., 387-388, 60 ff.

(39)   Bayer, op.cit., 201 ff.

(40)   Blanka Horacek, "Ichne kan deheinen Buochstabe," Festschrift für Dietrich
       Kralik (Horn, N.-Ö: Berger, 1954), 137. Wolfram's much-discussed bow
       image (P241, 1-30 and 805, 14-15) may well show clerical influence, for
       example, according to comparison made with medieval Biblical exegesis of
       Old and New Testament in terms of a bow, an hypothesis presented before
       the Modern Language Association in New York, 1970, in an unpublished paper,
       "Wolfram's Bow Metaphor and the Poetics of 'Parzival'" by Arthur B. Groos,
       Jr.. See also the discussion of P115, 27 in terms of traditional Augustinian
       exegesis of Psalm 70: Hans Eggers, "Non cognovi litteraturam," Festschrift
       Pretzel (Berlin: Erich Schmidt, 1963), 162-172.

(41)   Auerbach, op.cit., 76; also 29-30 and 53.

(42)   Curtius, op.cit., 72.

(43)   Marcus Fabius Quintilian, Institutes of Oratory: Education of an Orator,
       Vol. II, translated by John S. Watson (London: Bell, 1876), 14 and 19.

(44)   Brinkmann, op.cit., 101.

(45)   Joachim Bumke, Wolfram von Eschenbach (2nd edition, Stuttgart: Metzler,
       1966), 15.

(46)   Paul Böckmann, Formgeschichte der deutschen Dichtung, Vol. I: Von der
       Sinnbildsprache zur Ausdruckssprache (Hamburg: Hoffman und Campe,
       1949), 164. Wehrli expresses a similar view, op.cit., 26.

(47)   Hugo Kuhn, "Zur Deutung der künstlerischen Form des Mittelalters,"
       Studium Generale, 2 (1949), 116. See also W.J. Schroder, op.cit., 175.

CHAPTER II

IMAGERY RESEARCH

Of all the components of Wolfram's style, his imagery has been the subject of more research than any other single factor. Kinzel began the process in 1874 when he compared Wolfram and Hartmann relative to: 1) types of negation; 2) the usage of zil, site, kraft, and name; 3) periphrasis of persons; 4) personification; and 5) images in which abstractions are depicted in concrete terms, such as "schame ist ein slôz ob allen siten" (P3, 5) or "manec wîbes schoene an lobe ist breit" (P3, 11).(1) In this he worked chiefly from Parzival and Titurel with only brief incursions into Willehalm, making no claim to an exhaustive treatment, but merely contributing more concrete data to a definition of the differences between the two poets, a question receiving much attention among the philologists of the time. Usually he found the difference to be a matter of degree, but in some instances it seemed a matter of exclusive usage by Wolfram. Following Lachmann's theory about courtly and un-courtly words Kinzel denoted certain of Wolfram's metaphors as related to the Volksepos or Heldenepos. Other of Wolfram's expressions he designated as simply not appearing in Hartmann's works without judging their degree of courtliness. In this Kinzel also initiated the study of Wolfram's originality in imagery, though to a very limited degree since the range of comparison was so narrowly restricted.

In the same year that Kinzel's work appeared Förster produced the first catalog of Wolfram's images.(2) The images are organized according to the experiential referent from which they derive and comprise an admittedly incomplete list. His focus was primarily upon a list of referential categories and only secondarily upon a list of images. His three main categories, human life, animal and plant life, and other natural phenomena, are divided and subdivided into fifty different referents, with the location cited for each exemplifying image. No attempt is made to examine the literary context in which the images or the categories appear nor to draw conclusions from the fact that the presence of these particular fifty categories can be demonstrated. Neither did he consider whether or not the failure of other categories to appear in Wolfram's work might have some significance. The list is presented as part of a broader enumeration of syntactical and semantic elements in Wolfram's style without attempting, as Kinzel did, to demonstrate the degree to which these were specific to Wolfram. That purpose might have been expected, however, in view of a statement in his introduction to the effect that the real key to the peculiarities of Wolfram's style should be sought in his use of language.(3) His section on imagery is prefaced by the assertion that "Bilder und Vergleiche sind weitaus eins der bedeutendsten Momente der gewaltigen Meisterschaft Wolframs," and apparently he considered the variety of referent an indication of this mastery for he adds "ihr Bereich ist fast unübersehbar."(4) He must have had some unstated assumptions about artistry in mind for the selection of images was neither merely consecutive nor random, and criteria other than referential category entered into his choices. At the end of his categorization he remarks that, since he had attempted to consider "die bezeichnendsten Bilder" and since he found most of them in Willehalm, his results support the Lachmann judgment that Willehalm is "in der Form reicher und feiner ausgebildet als der Parzival."(5) He gives no indication of the criteria for "bezeichnendst."

Like Kinzel and Förster, Bötticher includes imagery in his work as only one among a number of aspects of Wolfram's language, the others being: 1) Bavarian elements such as dropping the final /e/, loss of /e/ in a final syllable, certain pronunciations apparent in rhyme patterns, and a few specific terms; 2) popular, ie., un-courtly, warrior terms; 3) apokoinu; 4) shifting from indirect to direct discourse; 5) anacoluthia; and 6) ellipses.(6) His discussion of imagery is actually an elaboration upon the work of Kinzel and Förster. In reference to the former he discounts the theory that Wolfram's language was less courtly than Hartmann's, adds to his list a few more instances of imagery unique to Wolfram (ie., not found in Hartmann), and develops especially the demonstration of imagery which lends concrete reality to abstractions. This treatment Bötticher extends beyond a consideration of abstract terms to attempt to show a thrust for the most vividly graphic, sensory, concrete depiction possible as a ubiquitous element and probably the greatest strength in Wolfram's style, his "Gabe zur Veranschaulichung."(7) Förster's praise of the extensiveness of the referential categories included in the imagery is echoed by Bötticher with the assumption underlying such praise more fully articulated:(8)

> Wir sahen nun oben in einigen Einzelheiten, wie sein angebornes Streben nach möglichster Sinnlichkeit in der Darstellung ihn ganz von selbst zur metaphorischen Redeweise führte. Er hätte es aber zu solcher Originalität auf diesem Gebiete nicht bringen können, wenn ihm nicht auch ein Reichtum von Anschauungen, ein Gefühl für die unendliche Fülle der Natur angeboren gewesen wäre, das fast an orientalische Phantasie erinnert.

Bötticher sees little value in referential categorization, however. To cast light upon Wolfram's use of language, the need is rather to observe how he applies his images, how he introduces them, how he carries them out, and where his choice of image is conspicuously apt or original.(9) Bötticher then examines a number of images containing syntactical confusion or passages where confusion results from the clustering of images, and remarks a fondness of Wolfram's for unusual, even bizarre, comparisons. His observations modify Förster's evaluation of Willehalm. He finds that epic to be free of the confusion in syntax or allusion which occurs in Parzival, but he does not find the imagery superior in any way, whether in vividness, variety, or originality. As far as methodology is concerned, basic assumptions are articulated more carefully in Bötticher's work than in the previous two treatments of imagery. The processes followed from these to his evaluative statements, however, can make no greater claim than they to having considered all the available data.

Image categorization by means of referent was used also by Bock in 1879 as a prelude to conclusions about the degree of Wolfram's uniqueness.(10) His work considered only Parzival and there only images which expressed terminology applied to the emotions of joy and sorrow. He did not concern himself with situations of joy and sorrow and the expressions used within them, but only with what Wolfram says about these emotions. The focus is upon Wolfram's language and upon whether or not similar portrayals can be found in the work of other Germanic poets. The range of his comparison extends from <u>Beowulf</u> to Hartmann, but it hardly seems possible that the comparison can have been sufficiently thorough to account for all occurrences of the description of joy and sorrow. Nor is it clear that his goal was aided by the process of referential categorizing. To the extent, however, that he notes similar usages in other works, he shows that Wolfram was not alone in depicting joy and sorrow as: 1) persons engaged in knightly pusuits or relationships; 2) persons experiencing other, more general, human fates; 3) participating in activities or conditions typical of plants; or 4) as inanimate objects. No attempt is made to relate his findings to Förster's. It might have been interesting to speculate upon the relatively limited range of categories found for metaphoric description of these two emotions as compared with the full extent of referential categories Förster noted in Wolfram's imagery as a whole. (Bock finds no references to animals, for example.) However, Bock does not address himself to this question. The most interesting conclusion proceeding from his examination of the expressions for joy and sorrow is that Wolfram turns all description into action, "dass er teils die Gegenstände handelnd, wirkend einführt, teils die Personen, die sie wahrnehmen, bei dieser Tätigkeit uns vorführt." (11) Although Bock does not provide enough evidence to extend this characterization to "all" description, it nevertheless offers more insight into the workings of Wolfram's style than the process of categorization might have been expected to contribute. Bock's conclusions as to the sources of influence on Wolfram include Hartmann most of all of his direct predecessors, and more indirectly then Hartmann's predecessors, the Spielmann poets, Minnesang, and the allegorical tendencies of clerical poets and preachers. (12) The assumption seems to be that if something in Wolfram also appeared before him, his usage must derive from that influence. Why Hartmann is held to have been more influential than Veldeke is not mentioned. One suspects that the reason has to do with the general prejudice of Bock's time which related all standards to Hartmann.

Following these four studies appearing all between 1875 and 1879, a decade was to pass before anything further was added to the discussion of Wolfram's imagery. What appeared then was the first half of Ludwig's ambitious undertaking to give a full accounting not only of the location, referent, and nature of each of Wolfram's images, but also of the stylistic aspects of his figurative mode of expression. (13) The latter part of the project was never executed to the point of publication. More than any of his predecessors in this pursuit, Ludwig is explicit about the assumptions underlying his work. The objective of his collection and categorization is "um der dichterischen Phantasie in ihren Quellen nachzuspüren und die beiläufigen Grenzen ihres Fluges zu bestimmen." (14) His concept of poetic imagination is stated in terms that place him squarely in the ranks of the non-historical, psychologizing theorist of metaphor: (15)

> Die Bilder Wolframs sind unbewusste Offenbarungen seiner Dichter-
> phantasie, er dichtet nicht, um seine Zuhörer durch die Kühnheit seiner

Bilder zu überraschen, sondern er überrascht damit, sobald er dichtet. Bilder und Gleichnisse quellen ihm gleichsam unter dem Füsse auf, wohin er auch im Reiche der Dichtung seine Schritte lenken mag. So drängt ihn Schritt für Schritt eine Gedankenfülle, die erstaunlich ist, und ohne viel Ueberlegen, ohne Engherzigkeit und Ziererei greift er das Nächste, Beste aus jener Gedankenfülle auf, wenn es nur seinem poetischen Drange genügt, alles plastisch, lebendig zu gestalten, lieber Handlung als Beschreibung zu bieten.

Ludwig's essential agreement with the evaluation of Bötticher, Förster, and Bock is readily apparent. What distinguishes his work from theirs, besides the fuller articulation of assumptions and inferences, is its goal of complete statements and the degree to which it achieves this. It is true that Ludwig does not claim to have included every single image, merely every single type of image formation, by which he specifies the personification of abstractions, proverbial-type images, and metaphor and simile combined under the single term "Bild." The total number of examples cited for all of his categories is so great, however, that one has the impression very few images could have escaped his attention. The rather random ordering of his categories with the scarcity of logical restructuring among and within them adds to this impression. It seems that the categories grew out of the images themselves as he encountered each one in sequence, rather than categories having been established logically and images then sought to demonstrate them, as one almost suspects was the case in Förster's neat work. Ludwig's loose organization does render his catalog very awkward as a reference tool, however, whether one is seeking a particular category or information about a given image. He uses at least thirty-three categories, possibly more; from his presentation it is often hard to distinguish subdivisions from independent categories, nor is alphabetization employed as an aid. This clumsiness is all the more regrettable because buried among his listings is much edifying commentary on specific images, information on the degree of commonplaceness of a usage at the time; on possible sources from legend, proverb, or other allusion; on similarity to metaphoric or proverbial expressions alive in 19th century German; or on medieval customs, knowledge of which is helpful to an understanding of an image. Some of this commentary is in the nature of educated guesswork, no doubt, and some of it has been supplanted by later discoveries, especially by Singer. Mainly, however, later work seems to have complemented Ludwig's commentary rather than to render it obsolete. The following examples may suffice to indicate the nature of this commentary and the way it might be useful to a newer student of medieval German literature:(16)

Vergleiche mit dem Weibe und dessen Eigenschaften, welche das Verglichene erniedrigen, begegnen bei Wolfram ausserordentlich selten... Die Vorstellung vom 'Weib' im Volke weicht hier (P450, 5) eben ganz der höheren Auffassung von 'Frau' in den ritterlichen Kreisen, die im Gegensatz zum Volke nicht des weiblichen Geschlechts Ohnmacht und Schwäche, sondern überall dessen Uebermacht und siegreiche Stärke anerkennen.

Der Ausdruck 'schanze' ist zwar so allgemein und häufig gebraucht, dass er in den meisten Fällen schon in die allgemeine Bedeutung 'Wechselfall, Glücksfall, Wagnis' übergegangen ist...doch ist an einigen Stellen die Uebertragung noch fühlbar: P60, 21; 494, 3; 747, 17.

Würfelspiel ist das Gebiet des Spieles, aus dem die ganze mhd. Kunstpoesie mit Vorliebe ihre Bilder entlehnt.

The frequency of images drawn from aspects of plant life had been noted also by Ludwig's predecessors, while those from the animal kingdom were far rarer, so much so that in Bock's study, as we have seen, animals could be excluded as a category entirely. In regard to plant life Ludwig contends that the great number of metaphors derived from this area reveal how unconscious and how natural the comparison with plants was for Wolfram. Many of the images could have been borrowed from common speech practice with no conscious regard for their semantic transference. Plant imagery was as ready to Wolfram's mind as knightly terminology. (17) With animals it was quite different, probably because, Ludwig asserts, he would view them primarily from the point of view that was closest to the life of a knight, namely in terms of hunting or of a knight's experience with horses. (18) The following conclusion is then drawn: (19)

Jene sinnige Auffassung...mit der der Dichter sich in das Leben der Pflanzenwelt versetzt und seinen körperlichen und geistigen Organismus unter dem Bilde des vegetabilischen erblickt, vermag er natürlich nicht auf die Tierwelt zu übertragen, und daher der auffallend geringe Gebrauch metaphorischer Wendungen, die dieser entlehnt sind...

Why it should be more natural for a knight to identify with plants than with animals he really hasn't explained. If Wolfram's plant metaphors are mainly commonplaces within the standard language which he uses without awareness of their transference, it seems irrelevant to speak of a "sinnige Auffassung."

Because of the wealth of plant metaphors and because Ludwig assumed many to be inconsequential clichés, he did not cite all of them. Instead, he limited his selection to "nur die auffallenderen, für Wolfram charakterischen Uebertragungen." These, he contends, are typically images with ethical implications. (20) Most of those he then cites by location do describe ideal qualities in human character, but it is not clear that this usage is more particularly Wolfram's than that of others of his time.

Ludwig's openly expressed assumptions often seem sufficiently full of insight to warrant further reflection. However, there also seems to be little attempt on his part to substantiate many of his statements, amounting at times to a rather breezy indifference to the distinctions between fact and opinion. One final illustration of this tendency may be taken from his summation. After defining the basic nature of a poetic image as the "sinnliche Veranschaulichung irgend einer Vorstellung: das Besondere steht für das Allgemeine, das Bekannte für das Entfernte," he contends that the external world is naturally much closer and more obvious to man than his internal experiences, and that therefore poetic imagination necessarily draws upon the external world for its images. The only exception he allows is the phrase "the speed of thought."(21) His certainty in this matter is perhaps not surprising for the view he expresses has been widely held. Alternative hypotheses to account for the apparently concrete nature of much metaphoric imagery have been raised only quite recently. (22) The point here is not to contest Ludwig's hypothesis but rather to point out that he himself seems unaware that it is, or logically should be, an hypothesis.

Ludwig's work seems to have remained the final word on Wolfram's imagery for a long time. Nothing more appeared until Singer's first major treatment in 1916 except Rogozinski's study of Titurel. (23) As part of his stylistic analysis the images there are compared with those revealed by Förster and Bötticher in Parzival and Willehalm in order to identify which are to be found only in Titurel. Of the latter Rogozinski attempts to discriminate which are entirely Wolfram's own invention from those which have counterparts elsewhere. The basis of comparison is not defined. He discusses the only four instances for which he found similar usages outside of Wolfram, and apparently assumed the others to be original. A glance at his list of the latter suggests that his range of search was inadequate for his intentions, for the list includes such words with frequent metaphorical transference as blüete and brief, both of which appear metaphorically in Parzival. More important than his conclusions about the images themselves is the assumption with which he prefaces his examination of imagery, namely, that the use of an original or rare image reflects a greater degree of personal involvement by the poet in the substance of what he is saying than he feels in those passages where his imagery is more commonplace. (24) Here there appears for the first time the question of how one might use imagery to ascertain variations in the degree of Wolfram's own interest in his work. As will be seen, this question formed a major thesis of Jensen's extensive study in 1927 and also of Mackensen's in 1955. (25)

Singer's work, of course, throws the entire question of Wolfram's originality into a new light. (26) The many similarities he demonstrates between certain stylistic features in Parzival and various 12th century French and Provencal works raise important questions, whether or not one accepts his thesis that they prove Wolfram's use of a missing French or Provencal Perceval version in addition to Chrestien's. His work does not prove that, of course, so long as any other possible explanation for these similarities exists. However, the similarities are so numerous (as regards metaphor, startlingly so) that, at the very least, one must wonder about the likelihood of Wolfram having been exposed to a far greater variety of literary models, whether from hearing or reading, than just the Middle High German possibilities and Chrestien that previous research has assumed. Among the images for which Singer has found parallels are some of Wolfram's seemingly most novel ones: the counterfeit heart (P3, 12); the shorttailed cow (P2, 20); the magpie's coloration (P2, 6); the "fliegende bispel" (P1, 15); and the epic's "fliehen unde jagen" (P2, 10); the spears numerous as a forest (P66, 23); pulling hair in the palm of the hand (P1, 26); the shield with a hem sewn by the blows of a sword (P245, 9); the lady slender as a rabbit on a spit (P409, 26); the strange tale of Adam's daughters producing the race of Cundrie and Malcreatiure (P518, 11), and many more. (27) Such parallels could be coincidental, just as two people can come up with the same idea independently of one another, but a more interesting possibility is the question of whether certain images, a sort of common fund of them, might not have been shared by poets throughout medieval Europe to a far greater degree than most Wolfram scholarship prior to Singer had considered likely. He pioneered a trend which has gained momentum only since 1945, the attempt to view MHG literature from a broader perspective than that of German development; to view it as medieval European literature, focusing upon the typically medieval rather than the typically German or typically French characteristics. (28)

Jensen's study, as noted above, concerns itself neither with the question of originality nor of "Germanness" but rather with that of Wolfram's personal involvement, his emotional participation in Parzival. The purpose of the research is to answer these three questions: (29)

1) wodurch und worin äussert sich Wolframs Anteilnahme? 2) sind Pathos oder Lyrik die Kennzeichen von Wolframs Stil? 3) wem gilt sein Mitfühlen, wem vielleicht mehr und wem weniger?

In answering them he hoped to contribute to a fuller understanding and appreciation of Wolfram not only as a poet but, more importantly to Jensen, as a great man: "Das Allgemein-menschliche bleibt das Wesentliche, an Wolfram wie an Parzival." (30) As he approaches the data appropriate to his three questions in a very systematic, well-defined order he touches upon so many of the more conspicuous rhetorical and linguistic features of Parzival that the finished study seems encyclopedic. Naturally, in a work of such breadth, no single element can be treated exhaustively, and the reader must try to content himself at times with very inadequate evidence for a given conclusion and only Jensen's claim that it is actually based upon far more data than time and space permit him to present.

Of all the many topics in the study only the treatment of imagery concerns us here. His hypothesis is clear: (31)

Das Bild ist natürlich besonders geeignet, uns zu sagen, wo tiefere Teilnahme des Dichters zu suchen ist; wird er doch im Grossen und Ganzen nur solche Stellen mit ihm schmücken, die ihm lieb oder wichtig und lebendig sind.

The assumption of a consciously decorative use of imagery is in direct contrast to Ludwig's thesis of unconscious spontaneity, though Jensen shares with him the belief that Wolfram reveals a strongly personal element through imagery. While for Ludwig this revelation is to be seen in the types of imagery and the sheer abundance of it, Jensen looks to the location of the imagery for its personal significance. The quantity of "bedeutungsvoller" images (he does not say which these are) is first examined relative to each of the books of Parzival. This produces the result that Books

III, IV, V, VI, and IX have the greatest amount, then Books II and VII, followed by XIII and XV. Only two of these, he notes, are Gawan narrative, a very important point for the theme he has been developing gradually in the preceding parts of the study, namely, that the answer to his third question (ie., "to whom does Wolfram extend his personal interest?") is definitely Parzival, emphatically not Gawan. When he examines the distribution of all images, not just the "more significant" ones, his results have a slightly different rank order (VI, II, III, V, VII, IX, XIII, XV, IV) with another book, Book XII, now also becoming prominent. These changes do not materially alter the evidence for Wolfram's exhibiting preference for Parzival through his imagery. Curiously, Jensen does not mention that of the six books which do not rate at all in his two lists, one is a Parzival book, XVI, and in another, Book XIV, Parzival is at least as important a protagonist as Gawan. Gahmuret is not mentioned at all. Attention is called also to various other comparisons, all of which he claims support this conclusion as to preference, with no examination of whether they really do or do not, and little explanation of why they do. The reader is directed to consider: 1) the differences in treatment of Books I and II and of the scene of Cundrie's accusation of Parzival as opposed to Kingrimursel's accusation of Gawan; 2) four scenes of lament in which imagery is particularly plentiful; 3) fifteen depictions of beauty (none is of Gawan's beauty); fifteen images using bluome in descriptions of various persons other than Parzival (one image is for Gawan), and, without reference to the actual instances, we are told to consider that by far the most frequent use of this image applies to Parzival. The unfortunate impression left by Jensen's treatment is that an interesting approach to the question of function for Wolfram's imagery has been undermined in its execution by prejudice as to the desired outcome. Whether or not a strictly objective, thorough application of the study of distribution of imagery would support the same conclusion of preference for Parzival cannot be determined from the data he presents here.

Two studies in the next decade which trace a particular situation throughout MHG courtly literature touch upon Wolfram's imagery for these situations: Kohler's examination of the metaphor "Liebeskrieg" and Frenzen's study of images and gestures of grief. (32) Without explaining why, Frenzen picks only two situations in Parzival, Herzeloide's grief for Gahmuret and Gahmuret's grief for his brother. The remainder of the instances for Wolfram come from Willehalm. His entire treatment seems more appropriate as an essay than as research, with images selected only to illustrate his views. He asserts that images and forms are important to Wolfram only as expressions of an inner attitude, and that his significance lies in the depths of his personality and in an heroic bearing, which expresses itself in admonitions to control grief which are more prevalent in Wolfram's work than in that of his contemporaries. He asserts further that these admonitions have to do with the value placed upon "stolzer Männlichkeit," not with the social ideal of mâze. (33) The desire to see Wolfram's value as resting upon his quality as a person, which was apparent in Jensen's summation, seems here to have become so magnified as to render research for the purpose of discovering facts impossible.

Kohler's work does not suffer so noticeably from this problem. As she examines the "Liebeskrieg" images from Veldeke through Hartmann, Gottfried, and Wolfram, she addresses herself to all the actual instances of the metaphor and tries to let these instances speak for themselves. Noting that for Wolfram the metaphor appears primarily in the Gawan scenes, especially P532, 1 ff., she observes that Wolfram uses the cupid's bow variation of the image only once and proceeds there to criticize both this concept and the Venus mythology. Normally his images for "Liebeskrieg" are drawn from referents within the environment or activities of a knight (as in Gottfried's work, also), thereby changing the figure of Minne from its Ovidian form to something more deeply anchored within the medieval courtly culture. (34) She also remarks his tendency to give Minne a more ethical aspect than Veldeke had done, although he still views it as largely a power external to the individual. In summary she says: (35)

> Hartmann gibt den ersten Anstoss zur Eindeutschung des Bildes, Gottfried erweitert es durch viele plastische Prägungen, die er alle der ritterlichen Sprache entnimmt, und Wolfram verinnerlicht bewusst den Grundgedanken der Metapher. Er hat den 'Liebeskrieg' vollends seines letzten antiken Hauchs entäussert und gibt ihm die ernsthaft-sittliche Tiefe...

A new effort to find significance in a study of Wolfram's imagery by means of referential categories is represented by Tapp's research in 1954. (36) As Ludwig had done, Tapp accompanies his listing of images with whatever information he has on meaning, source, or degree of originality. His catalog seems to be more complete than any previous ones, although, as noted in the previous chapter, he attempted to omit any images which had already been established as metaphor in older usage. His citations are more immediately useful for the reader because he gives the entire clause or sentence in which they appear, not just the line reference as all the other listings had done. In Tapp's case the categorization is only a necessary step to the main purpose of his research which is an examination of the differences between direct discourse and narrative in terms of the kinds of imagery they contain. This produces a tabulation of his forty categories (similar but not identical to Förster's and Ludwig's) divided between narrative and dialog passages, both as a total for all works combined and also for each work separately, with the Lieder considered collectively as one work. He also establishes ratios of image frequency for each of the works: for the Lieder, 1 in every 21 lines; for Titurel, 1 in every 6 lines; for Parzival, 1 in every 21 lines; and for Willehalm, 1 in every 19 lines. (37) The discovery of less imagery in Parzival than anywhere else seems ironic in view of the exuberance with which this work's plenitude of imagery has often been greeted.

His resulting data indicate that the single largest category of images is that of arms and fighting, the second largest being plants and trees (supporting Ludwig's remarks). Since the range of referential categories appearing in at least three of the works is very wide, Tapp concludes that no preference for any particular category on Wolfram's part can be established. (38) However, some marked differences do appear relative to the division into narrative and dialog passages. Nine categories appear three times more often in narrative than in dialog: music, bathing, clothing, smithing and tanning, birds, jewelry, fire and artificial light, weather and water. Two categories, on the other hand, appear twice more often in dialog than in narrative: theft and thieving, and captives or capture.(39) When he compares the situation in the individual works, he discovers six categories which appear in both dialog and narrative in Parzival but only in narrative in Willehalm: sleep, reading and writing, smithing and tanning, jewelry, fire and artificial light, and earth or terrain.(40)

Attempting to find some significance in his statistics seems to occupy Tapp rather fruitlessly. The most interesting observation he makes is that most of the instances of those six image categories which appear in dialog in Parzival but not in Willehalm occur in scenes of emotional stress. From this he infers that there may have been something about these categories which made the images unsuitable for people of the social station Wolfram portrays:(41)

> If Wolfram himself then realized that these were images ill-befitting
> his characters but permitted them to use them in moments of emotional
> distress, by their very use in dialog he would convey to his hearers the
> degree of emotion which the characters were experiencing. His boldness
> in such procedure may have been part of the criticism directed at
> Parzival (cf. Wh 4, 23 ff.) and as a result of this in Willehalm and
> Titurel he consciously modified his 'modus operandi'.

It is a novel concept, but he has no evidence to either support or refute it. This attempt to derive information of literary significance from referential categorization of Wolfram's imagery has been largely futile. The main value in Tapp's work is contained within the information of the very extensive catalog itself.

Mackensen's work, published a year later, is the most comprehensive treatment to date of the imagery in Parzival.(42) Like Jensen and Tapp he uses image distribution rather than comparison with factors outside the epic as his tool for uncovering significance. New, however, is the attempt to relate image distribution to narrative content. To do this, Mackensen divides Parzival into what he feels to be its most important episodes, numbering 34 in all, ranging in length from 43 lines, "Conclusion," to 1800 lines, "Obilot" (comprising the whole of Book VII). For the constant relationship by which image frequency can be compared among passages of such differing lengths he defines frequency in terms of the number of images per 100 lines, interpolating arithmetically to arrive at this figure for passages shorter than that. This relationship, which he calls the frequency index, is found to be approximately 3 for the epic as a whole (omitting 190 lines of material which did not fit into his 34 passages and which he considered merely rhetorical, often bridging narrative gaps, but contributing nothing to the meaning of the epic).

In his distributional examination he includes not only distribution by referential category (knighthood, everyday life, and nature, each with a few subdivisions) but also distribution in terms of the manner in which the images are executed; that is,

whether the imagery is contained in one word, in a phrase, or in a more fully elab-
orated extension. He sees the significance of such distinctions to be in their implications for Wolfram's degree of personal involvement with the subject of the image,
the extended image being assumed to show the greatest degree of both poetic imagination and feeling, the single word image showing the least. For the epic as a whole
he finds these three types of image to bear a proportionate relationship of 9:6:2, ie.,
nine single word images for six phrase images for two extended images. Wolfram's
degree of involvement is assumed to be only moderate in a passage which shows
these same proportions in its imagery; to the degree that the proportion of extended
images exceeds this norm, personal interest is assumed to have been high. On the
basis of this type of calculation, Mackensen reaches the conclusion, for example,
that Wolfram's real emotional involvement in the Prologue was actually only slight
regardless of the excessive frequency of imagery there, because in form its imagery
maintains the proportions typical of the epic as a whole. The style is considered to
be one of rhetorical showmanship. The similarly discursive passage at the end of
Book II, on the other hand, is judged to have touched Wolfram's own feelings more
closely because its imagery shows a preponderance of the extended forms. (43)

Mackensen includes both simile and metaphor in his definition of image, as
well as various other types of vivifying periphrase. The key to a "genuine" image for
Mackensen, in contrast to abstract conceptualizing by means of metaphoric transference, is its ability to invoke concrete sensory perception. Therefore, not every
actual metaphor was included in his analysis. Commonplace metaphors were included, however, so long as it seemed that they retained their concretely sensory quality
in the context and manner in which Wolfram was using them. (44) Since Mackensen
quotes only a few of the actual images included in his statistics and gives only the
location of the others, it would be very tedious to examine his selection of images,
even more tedious to try to note which ones he excluded. He assumes that the relationships uncovered by his analysis would remain fairly stable even if slightly different criteria for images resulted in different totals. (45)

He finds overt comparison to be more prevalent in Wolfram's work than metaphor, but the formal differences between them are held to be unimportant in terms
of his particular inquiry, which he states as an examination of the imagery for
"Bildkraft, Phantasie, gegenseitige Zuordnung bestimmter Inhalte zu bestimmten
Bildvorstellungen und die Häufigkeit und Anordnung der Bildvorstellungen."(46) By
"Bildvorstellung" he means the referential category of an image, not the particular
image itself. For each of his 34 passages he calculates the number and percentage
of images for each major referential category, the number of images in each of the
three forms of image-execution, and the number of times a mixed image, or a dual-
image, or a cluster of images appears in the passage. These latter types of combined imagery he assumes to be more deliberate and intentional, less intuitive or spontaneous, than images which are simpler in their composition. Mackensen makes an
interesting distinction in his assumptions about Wolfram's type of personal involvement in passages marked by such combined imagery: (47)

Da sie beabsichtigt sind und verstärken wollen, gehören sie mehr auf die Seite des dichterischen Könnens als auf die Seite der Intuition. Wo sie auftreten, darf auf Punkte hervorragenden Interesse für den Dichter--oder die Hörerschaft--geschlossen werden, kaum aber auf eine unmittelbare innere Bewegtheit Wolframs.

The significance of an examination of image referents is stated to be its aid in identifying those associative tendencies which are characteristic of a particular poet. A poet is assumed to reveal more of his individuality in imagery than in the form or content of the narrative, since, as Mackensen assumes, the latter is bound to tradition in a way that imagery is not. (48) He also assumes that the tendency to draw images from particular categories for particular situations is largely unconscious.

His analysis of Wolfram's categories and the frequency and type of imagery within them produces a few conclusions which contradict the findings of earlier research. The impression that Wolfram "verrittert die Welt" with his imagery, a generalization which had gone unchallenged since Bock's statement in 1879, is modified by the discovery that the images divide themselves fairly evenly among the categories of knighthood, everyday life (ie., not limited to a knight's experiences), and nature. As Mackensen points out, Wolfram depicts the world of knighthood just as much with images from everyday experience and nature as vice versa. (49) Of the three main categories, the imagery from nature is livelier and shows more intimate appeal to Wolfram, from Mackensen's point of view, in that singleword images are in the minority compared with phrase images and extended images combined, a situation which is reversed in the other two categories. Even more curious, in view of the dearth of animal imagery in Bock's and Ludwig's work, is the fact that animal imagery figures prominently in Mackensen's nature category; though not as numerous as plant imagery, it has a far greater proportion of phrase- and extended images, and is therefore qualitatively more important. (50)

The question of Wolfram's originality is first raised in the discussion of nature imagery. There Mackensen believes that he finds enough evidence of clear borrowing from tradition and cultural stock to cast doubts also upon the degree of originality in the other categories, knighthood and everyday life, where borrowing was not so obvious. He draws the assumption from this that the lesser margin of error would lie in assuming derivation from the collective cultural stock rather than from personal observation, except where evidence for the latter was very clear. In that Mackensen fails to cite the evidence from which he deduces that certain images are definitely not from Wolfram's experience, his argument is weakened. One thinks immediately of the allusions to mythical creatures, of course, but these make up only a small part of the entire imagery. Nevertheless, subsequent conclusions are worth noting, namely, that other than biographical interest, the question of image source has little to do with an analysis of Wolfram's artistry, since here the significant matters are the quality of the execution of the image, the variety and distribution of the image referents, and the function of the image in the whole structure of the epic. In this regard he notes that no matter whether Wolfram derives an image from "allgemeinem Bildungsgut" or from personal experience, he uses it only if it carries genuinely vivid concreteness for him; "er überschaut ihre Vielfalt und hat sie genügend angeeignet, um sie in ungezwungener Buntheit und Lebendigkeit darstellen zu können."(51)

In any event, Mackensen remains interested in Wolfram's choice of referential category and the indications of a greater or lesser quality of personal feelings involved in the categories. As criteria for the latter he consistently applies the form of image execution. On this basis he concludes from his statistics that the referential categories which most frequently revealed a deeper response from Wolfram are hunting, personal observation in everyday life, animals, and the category of artisans or handworkers. He then examines the frequency of extended images from these categories within the following narrative themes: references to style and epigrammatic utterances; descriptions of action or scenery; reference to persons; pain and joy; mockery; minne; and battle. From this he deduces that Wolfram tends to use extended images from hunting for descriptions of action or scenery but not at all in battle scenes. For the latter he draws upon personal observation from everyday life and also upon imagery from Handwerk. Animal imagery is especially developed in reference to persons, but is also noticeable in descriptions of action and scenery, as well as in mockery. Extended images from personal experience predominate in reference to minne, with very little use of the other three favorite categories. (52)

When Mackensen applies this criterion of image execution to the three chief protagonists, he reaches the curious result that Wolfram seems to have brought more genuine feeling more often to his images in the Gahmuret scenes than in those concerned with Parzival and Gawan, though the differences between Gahmuret and Parzival are very slight.(53) The percentages of single word images for the three are respectively 44 %, 49 %, and 61 %. This Mackensen assumes to be the least valuable type of image, the most trite. The most valuable type, the extended image, composed 16 % of Gahmuret's imagery, 14 % of Parzival's, and only 7 % of Gawan's. The next most valuable type, the phrase image, composed 40 % of Gahmuret's imagery, 37 % of Parzival's and 32 % of Gawan's. Mackensen seems to ignore the implications of his theories here regarding Wolfram's preference for Gahmuret over Parzival, yet it is arresting to note the degree to which these statistics, coupled with Mackensen's assumptions about imagery, support Jensen's contentions about Wolfram's lack of interest in Gawan.

When Mackensen turns from his statistics to an examination of the function of imagery in selected scenes his discussion becomes less consistent and the criteria of significance which he has attempted to establish for image-type seem to become unimportant to him. This is surprising in view of the pains he has taken with the foregoing. The subsequent discussion of scenes could have occurred in its given form without any of the preliminary analysis. The scenes are chosen in terms of narrative significance, taken out of Wolfram's sequence and rearranged according to thematic logic, by which, for example, Parzival's grail-related scenes are discussed as a group and then his grail-independent knighthood scenes. Such examination has obvious value, but since the statistical data were assembled on a division of the material which differs from this, it becomes impossible to relate the two findings in an exact way. The thread of Mackensen's work breaks down at this point, as if he had done two entirely different studies and combined them without coordination. The patterns of image distribution he had discovered are not clearly related to his analysis of content, although to some extent they seem to remain present in the back of his mind, for some of his ultimate conclusions about Wolfram's use of imagery suggest a synthesis of his two approaches. One can only wish he had demonstrated the synthesis more clearly.

Nevertheless, his conclusions about the use of imagery contain several observations which, if somewhat lacking in consistent substantiation, certainly merit further consideration and offer generally new perspectives in the evaluation of Wolfram's work. He assumes both a deliberate and an intuitive artistry. Imagery is said to be usually lacking where the listener's emotional involvement in a scene and his perception of its significance could be expected from the action alone, or where a scene had no other significance than to relate a number of facts. Images serve to call special attention to that which they mark, just how much attention varying according to either the quantitative or qualitative force of the imagery. A quantitative emphasis is used at places where a certain pathos is wanted or significance is to be emphasized without sincerely felt involvement of the poet. As Mackensen puts it:(54)

> Es handelt sich also um Abschnitte, in denen der Dichter einen stärkeren
> rhetorischen Aufwand betreibt als gewöhnlich, er ist intensiver bei der
> Sache, aber weniger mit dem Herzen dabei. Die ausgesprochen repräsen-
> tativen Szenen, deren Wirkung betont werden soll, finden sich in dieser
> Reihe. Abschnitte feinerer seelischer Empfindung sind nicht darunter.
> Die Absicht überwiegt, die innere Beteiligung ist geringer.

The qualitative emphasis is achieved, as said before, through a single but more extended and "natural," ie., uncontrived image, and is assumed to reflect Wolfram's own feelings. The use of imagery in regard to persons seems to stand between these two, which Mackensen calls the exaggerated and the organic application of imagery. Entrances of new characters or the reappearance of previous ones are always accompanied by imagery to the degree of their significance in the epic. Significance may be indicated either quantitatively or qualitatively. Furthermore, the specific imagery used often indicates the person's coming role in the ensuing action. (55)

A few studies of imagery in Hartmann, Proust, and Shakespeare have also been examined for methodology. (56) With very few exceptions the questions raised and the methods employed have been the same as for Wolfram. The attempt to deduce information about a poet through the distribution of his imagery into referential categories was carried out by Spurgeon's work with Shakespeare to the ultimate possible extent for this method and drew critical ridicule for the method's basic fallacy, namely, the assumption that images are present in a poet's mind only from personal experience with the referent of the image. (57) A more useful outcome of referent study may be the identification of a poet's habitual categories, especially his tendency to cluster certain categories together. Armstrong has demonstrated how this fact might be used to establish authenticity of authorship as between Shakespeare and Marlow, a detective work reminiscent of Lachmann's rejection of Wolfram's authorship of the Jüngere Titurel.

Only Clemen's work on Shakespeare and Graham's with Proust introduce methodology or questions not yet applied to Wolfram. Both of them are dealing with the literary function of imagery. Clemen demonstrates how the function of Shakespeare's imagery changed over the period of his work. It evolved from an essentially decorative style with little or no dramatic significance in the early histories to become an increasingly integral element of dramatic effect in the later tragedies, until imagery became so organically a part of the structure of a play as to be wholly essential to the works's art and meaning. As the function of his imagery changed, so did its form. Simile was used less and less, being replaced by metaphor which, in turn, became more and more condensed and mixed, more subtly suggestive and less amenable to logical analysis.

The significance of a poet's preference for simile or metaphor seems to have been discussed so far by no one but Clemen. Curiously, the dominance of metaphor noted for Shakespeare's work is reversed by Proust, who apparently used many more similes than metaphors. (58) Grimm noted more simile in Tristan than in Parzival, but there seems to have been no further attention given to this aspect of Wolfram's style, aside from Mackensen's passing remark on the greater number of similes than metaphors. (59)

Graham's work with Proust uses referential categorization in a new way. Starting with the demonstration that Proust draws upon certain referential categories in a consistent relationship with various moods or themes he attempts to show how imagery functions as a pattern of unification within the novels. It appears to operate as a third structural element along with plot and characterization, but more subtly than these, almost subliminally, as it were.

Whether or not a similar function could be demonstrated for Wolfram's use of imagery is open to question, but it seems doubtful. Though Mackensen found some tendencies to link a few referential categories with specific themes, they were far from being exclusive relationships. The same categories also appeared in other themes and many categories were too evenly spread to reveal any tendency at all.

For Clemen's comparative method a long period of stylistic evolution must be present, such as is certainly the case for Shakespeare but far less so for Wolfram. Stylistic differences between Parzival and Willehalm and between both of these compared with Titurel are apparent, of course. To what extent the differences are related to changes in the types or uses of imagery has not been the subject of research, probably because differences in imagery are not sufficiently conspicuous to have attracted critical attention.

Summary

Spread throughout the chronology of the investigation of Wolfram's imagery certain questions have been considered repeatedly, questions about the form of the images, how they are executed, whether metaphor or simile and what kind of metaphor (Kinzel, Ludwig, Bötticher, Mackensen); about the referents of the images (Förster, Bock, Ludwig, Kohler, Tapp, Mackensen); about the sources of the images, whether unique to Wolfram or not (Kinzel, Bötticher, Ludwig, Rogozinski, Singer, Kohler, Tapp, Mackensen); about the function served by them (Kinzel, Bötticher, Jensen, Tapp, Mackensen); and about the ethical implications, either of the imagery as a whole or of particular ones (Jensen, Kohler, Frenzen). The question of function has been viewed as related to the stylistic ideal of heightened liveliness and vividness in general (Kinzel, Bötticher); in terms of revealing Wolfram's personality, his interests, preferences, background, or values (implied in all the categorizing studies but most articulately considered by Jensen, Kohler, Frenzen, and Mackensen); in regard to differences between passages of dialog as opposed to those of narrative (Tapp); and in regard to differences in emphasis for various passages (Mackensen). Tapp's was the first effort to treat imagery as one structural feature related to another.

Up to Jensen the methodology of all the studies had consisted of varying mixtures of the same three factors: collection and categorization of images, comparison of Wolfram's images with those of others, and speculation based upon the personal reactions of the investigator. With Jensen a fourth element entered into the methodology, that of image distribution. This seemed to offer the possibility of a fully internal analysis of a work, replacing the method of external comparison (ie., with other writers) as an approach to describing Wolfram's style. As we have seen, the first two attempts to apply this new element of methodology, Jensen's and Tapp's, have been disappointing in their results, in the one case because of deficient objectivity and in the other because of an apparently unfortunate assumption that the referent for an image would be a factor having literary significance. The next one, Mackensen's, was more successful in uncovering significant data even though a shift in methodology mid-stream tended to weaken the force of his conclusions.

Critical commentary on Wolfram's imagery extends, of course, far beyond the number of investigations discussed in this survey, but other than these, such commentary occurs in essay rather than research form. It is based upon a more general body of impressions about Wolfram's work, and while not without usefully suggestive insight, it does not present conclusions resting upon demonstration from collected data and has, therefore, been omitted from consideration here. To the extent that such commentary is relevant to the findings of the present study it will be discussed later.

Notes

(1)   Karl Kinzel, "Zur charakteristik des Wolframschen stils," Zeitschrift für deutsche Philologie, V (1874), 1-36.

(2)   Paulus Traugott Förster, Zur Sprache und Poesie Wolframs von Eschenbach (Diss., Leipzig, 1874).

(3)   Ibid., 1.

(4)   Ibid., 45.

(5)   Ibid., 69.

(6)   Gotthold Bötticher, "Ueber die Eigenthümlichkeiten der Sprache Wolframs," Germania, XXI (1876), 257-332.

(7)   Ibid., 303.

(8)   Ibid., 315.

(9)   Loc. cit.

(10)   Ludwig Bock, Wolframs von Eschenbach Bilder und Wörter für Freude und Leid (Strassburg: Trübner, 1879).

(11)   Ibid., 12.

(12)   Ibid., 34-35.

(13)   Karl Ludwig, Der bildliche Ausdruck bei Wolfram von Eschenbach (Programm des K.K. Staats-Ober-Gymnasium, Mies, 1889-90).

(14)   Ibid., 7.

(15)   Ibid., 5.

(16)   Ibid., 53, 47, 46.

(17)   Ibid., 15.

(18)   Ibid., 19.

(19)   Ibid., 20.

(20)   Ibid., 15.

(21)   Ibid., 60-61.

(22)   Langer, op.cit., 62-63, 193 ff.; Barfield, op.cit., 40-41, 71 ff.

(23)   Paul Rogozinski, Der Stil in Wolfram von Eschenbachs Titurel (Diss., Jena, 1903; published in Thorn: Francke.)

(24)   Ibid., 54.

(25)   Harro Dewet Jensen, Wolfram und sein Werk, der Stil des Parzival als Aus-
       druck der Persönlichkeit Wolframs und seiner Anteilnahme am Geschehen
       der Handlung. Ein Versuch. (Diss., Marburg, 1927); and Rainer Mackensen,
       Das Bild und seine Funktion im 'Parzival' (Diss., Tubingen, 1955).

(26)   Singer, op.cit., 1916 and 1937.

(27)   All but Adam's daughters are op.cit., 1916. It is in 1937.

(28)   One of the most valuable of such studies, in addition to the work of Curtius,
       Auerbach, and Schwietering, is by Hildegard Emmel, Formprobleme des
       Artusromans und der Graldichtung (Bern: Francke, 1951).

(29)   Jensen, op.cit., 3.

(30)   Ibid., 90.

(31)   Ibid., 19. All following data is from pages 19-21.

(32)   Erika Kohler, Liebeskrieg. Zur Bildersprache der höfischen Dichtung des
       Mittelalters, (Tübingen germanistische Arbeiten 21; Stuttgart: Kohlhammer,
       1935); Wilhelm Frenzen, Klagebilder und Klagegebärden in der deutschen
       Dichtung des höfischen Mittelalters (Bonner Beiträge zur Deutschen Philo-
       logie 1; Würzburg: Triltsch, 1936).

(33)   Ibid., 37.

(34)   Kohler, op.cit., 99.

(35)   Ibid., 100.

(36)   Henry Tapp, An Investigation of the Use of Imagery in the Works of Wolfram
       von Eschenbach (Diss., Yale, 1954).

(37)   Ibid., 216.

(38)   Ibid., 218.

(39)   Ibid., 220 ff.

(40)   Ibid., 241 ff.

(41)   Ibid., 248.

(42)   Rainer Mackensen, Das Bild und seine Funktion im 'Parzival' des Wolfram
       von Eschenbach (Diss., Tubingen, 1955).

(43)   Ibid., 30.

(44)   Ibid., 17.

(45)   Ibid., 20. His total for the epic is 699 images.

(46)   Ibid., 14.

(47) Ibid., 32.

(48) Ibid., 33.

(49) Ibid., 36.

(50) Ibid., 52.

(51) Ibid., 177.

(52) Ibid., 61.

(53) Ibid., Anhang, Uebersicht 5.

(54) Ibid., 30.

(55) Ibid., 180.

(56) Carl Schmuhl, Beiträge zur Würdigung des Stiles Hartmanns von Aue (Halle: Programm der Lateinischen Hauptschule, 1881); Victor E. Graham, The Imagery of Proust (London: Barnes and Noble, 1966); Caroline F.E. Spurgeon, Shakespeare's Imagery and What it Tells Us (N.Y.: Macmillan, 1935); Wolfgang H. Clemen, The Development of Shakespeare's Imagery (Cambridge: Harvard Univ., 1951); Edward A. Armstrong, Shakespeare's Imagination: A Study of the Psychology of Association and Inspiration (Lincoln: Univ. of Nebraska, 1963).

(57) Lillian Herlands Hornstein, "Analysis of Imagery; A Critique of Literary Method," PMLA, 57 (1942), 638-653.

(58) Graham, op.cit., Appendix 3.

(59) Wilhelm Grimm, "Gleichnisse im Ossian und Parzival," Kleinere Schriften, I (Berlin, 1881), 48-57.

CHAPTER III

THE IMAGES IN PARZIVAL

The concept of image is used broadly here to include both figurative periphrase and any comparison drawn from outside the actual epic matter at hand which
Wolfram invokes directly or implicitly in the process of describing or interpreting.
The images collected in the Table of Images which forms the main part of this chapter are listed in their order of appearance in the epic and are divided into two categories: metaphors, indicated by "M", and all other images, catalogued under "O".

The "other" category includes similes, of course, explicit comparisons in-
troduced by als ("ein maere in stichet als ein dorn"), sô ("liute vinster sô diu naht"),
denne ("ist iht liehters denne der tac / dem gelîche niht diu künegin"), or nach ("nach
rabens varwe was ir schîn"). Also among the types of images included are those
created by raising a hypothetical situation for illustration. These images are usually
hyperbolic in nature, such as the fisherman's disdainful rejection of the boy Parzival:
"ich engaebe iu ein halbez brôt / niht ze drîzec jâren" (P142, 23-24), or the description of the grail castle:

ob si suochten elliu her,
si engaeben vür die selben nôt
ze drîzec jâren niht ein brôt (P226, 20-22).

Another prominent type of image among the non-metaphoric category is the
allusion to literary, Biblical or folk lore likely to be known to a court audience of
the time. The following reference to Hartmann's Iwein may serve as an example of
a literary image; Wolfram helps describe the character of Sigune's grief for Schionatulander by saying:

dô nazten diu ougen ir die wât.
ouch was vroun Lûneten rât
ninder dâ bî ir gewesen. (P253, 9-11)

Singer has traced the amusing picture of the inadequacy of a false man's triuwe as
being like a cow whose tail is too short to kill the third fly (P2, 20-22) to a fabel
written by an Anglo-Norman satirist and known in a Latin version. (1) An apparent
allusion to folklore of the time, perhaps a lost proverb, is the passage in which
Wolfram speaks of Parzival's aimless wandering in a trackless forest in terms of
his coming upon plenty of "signs of the hammer":

genuoge hânt des einen site
und sprechent sus, swer irre rite
das der den slegel vünde:
slegels urkünde
lac dâ âne mâze vil,
suln grôze ronen sîn slegels zil. (180, 9-14)

Folkloristic images also appear in references to the supposed characteristics of such animals as lion, unicorn, pelican, and turtledove.

Images based upon a pun have been included in the non-metaphoric group. An example is the following description of Gahmuret's fate and his coat of arms:

> sîne anker heten niht bekort
> ganzes landes noch landes ort:
> dâ enwâren si ninder în geslagen.
> der herre muoste vürbaz tragen
> disen wâpenlîchen last
> in manegiu lant, der werde gast,
> nâch dem anker disiu mâl (14, 30-15, 5).

The pun just cited is also a metaphor, but the practice followed here has been to reserve the metaphor category for images which are only metaphors. The distinction drawn has often been a very fine one and may seem rather arbitrary, as, for example, when the image "der unstaete geselle hat die swarzen varwe gar" (1, 10-11) is considered an instance of color symbology rather than a metaphoric use of black. The assumption is that such a moral connotation for black was standard in the language, one of the accepted meanings of the word. The image helps to elaborate and develop the metaphor in:

> gesmaehet und gezieret
> ist swâ sich parrieret
> unverzaget mannes muot (1, 3-5)

but it is felt to be a familiar use of black as a moral symbol rather than a metaphor in itself. Therefore it is included in the "other" category.

An ironic expression such as "rewarding someone with death" (106, 8), although metaphoric in some aspects, is closer to being a bitter pun, it seems, and not a metaphor strictly speaking. Therefore, such instances have been included as "other." Non-ironic periphrase has also been so catalogued, images such as "the one people paint as a lamb" (105, 22), meaning Christ; or "an intimate honor" (44, 23), meaning sexual intercourse. These are metaphorical in the sense of substitution but they do not contain the element of logical incongruity which is the chief criterion for metaphor used in this study.

The non-metaphoric category also includes images which are simply implicit illustrations of Wolfram's meaning. They fit the definition of image given above in that they are examples which he draws from material outside the epic itself in order to illuminate a particular point or to heighten interest, but they do not involve any of the previously described forms of comparison or figurative use of language. Some of them are allusions to actual people or circumstances known to Wolfram personally, for example, the hungry mouse in his house (185,2) or the trampled vineyards at Erfurt (379, 18). Others are strictly imaginative, such as "wer roufet mich da nie dehein har / gewuohs, innen an miner hant?" as an image of impossibility (1, 26-27). Sometimes these figures help develop a metaphor as in the following:

> zin anderhalp an dem glase
> gellchet und des blinden troum,
> diu gebent antlitzes roum,
> doch mac mit staete niht gesln
> dirre trüebe lihte schln (1, 20-24)

The quality implied by the metaphor of the layer of cream on top of a pan of milk used to modify <u>antlitz</u> is clarified by other examples of this same quality in the images of the metal coating on the back of a mirror and the blind man's dream. These latter two images are illustrations, and strikingly imaginative it seems, but they are not metaphors.

The term metaphor has been reserved for images in which not only is a word or concept transposed from its normal or "literal" usage to either a novel or clearly figurative application without punning and without any qualifying "like", "as", or "as if", but in which also the element of logical incongruity is present. "Common sense" protests that hearts do not have neighbors (1, 1), a human countenance is not a pan of milk (1, 23), behavior is not a stone arch and cannot have a keystone (3, 5) a state of mind cannot be a form of weather, let alone a hailstorm (2, 17-19), and so on. The concept of "novel application" is a highly risky one because it involves making assumptions about the common meanings of Wolfram's time which may have to be revised with further evidence. This problem has already been discussed at greater length (p. 11 ff.). Examples of conventional courtly metaphor abound in <u>Parzival</u>, especially when some fair lady or noble knight is being described. Although literary commonplaces, these expressions are nonetheless true metaphors and were probably not common usage in mundane speech or prose writing.

When an image in the following Table of Images is considered to be a metaphor, the word or words in the citation which are the core of the metaphoric transference of meaning are underlined. Sometimes a citation given as one meaningful unit contains more than one image. Where such is the case an apostrophe is used to divide the images. The following lines from the prologue illustrate both of these cataloguing devices:

> diz <u>vliegende</u> blspel
> ist tumben liuten gar ze snel: '
> si enmugens niht erdenken,
> wande ez kan vor in <u>wenken</u> '
> rehte alsam ein schellec hase. (1, 15-19)

Three images are noted here: two metaphors, <u>vliegende</u> and <u>wenken</u> as applied to a lively or quickly changing figure, and a simile in the explicit comparison with a hare. Personification is also present in the idea of an image "behaving" this way. Personification of itself is not included in this study, however, and no images which involve only personification as the figurative element are listed.

In listing the images sequentially the epic has been divided into passages according to thematic unity. In Book I, for example, there are seven Gahmuret episodes following the prologue. Therefore the images of Book I appear in eight groups. The total number of images collectively and of metaphors specifically has been obtained for each passage group and finally, also, for each book. This information is summarized in Table II: Thematic Passages in Sequence.

Occasionally a thematic passage coincides with the thirty-line sectioning found in the manuscripts, but this is exceptional. The seven Gahmuret episodes of Book I vary in length from 89 lines (Gahmuret in the service of the Baruch) to 371 lines (Gahmuret received at Belacane's court). None of them appear in lengths which are multiples of thirty lines. The irregular length of thematic passages is typical for all of the sixteen books of the epic. At the end of each group of images in Table I the length of the passage is given.

The data contained in the Table of Images and in the summaries of Table II form the basis of all subsequent analysis of Wolfram's use of imagery. Unless otherwise stated the text is that of Leitzmann's seventh edition. In the Table of Images "M" refers to metaphor; "O" to other images; and "T" to total images.

THE IMAGES IN PARZIVAL

TABLE I: TABLE OF IMAGES

BOOK I

Prologue	1, 1-4, 26	M	O	T

		M	O	T
1, 1-2	Ist zwîvel herzen nâchgebûr, daz muoz der sêle werden sûr.	1	.	1
1, 3-6	gesmaehet und gezieret ist swâ sich parrieret unversaget mannes muot, ' als agelstern varwe tuot.	1	1	2
1, 10-14	der unstaete geselle hât die swarzen varwe gar ' und wirt ouch nâch der vinster var: ' sô habet sich an die blanken der mit staeten gedanken	.	3	3
1, 15-19	diz vliegende bîspel ist tumben liuten gar ze snel: ' si enmugens niht erdenken, wande ez kan vor in wenken ' rehte alsam ein schellec hase.	2	1	3
1, 20-25	zin anderhalp an dem glase gelîchet ' und des blinden troum, ' diu gebent antlitzes roum, doch mac mit staete niht gesîn dirre trüebe lîhte schîn: er machet kurze vreude alwâr.	1	2	3
1, 26-28	wer roufet mich dâ nie dehein hâr gewuohs, innen an mîner hant? der hât vil nâhe griffe erkant.	.	1	1
1, 29-30	spriche ich gein den vorhten och, daz gelîchet mîner witze iedoch.	.	1	1
2, 1-4	wil ich triuwe vinden aldâ si kan verswinden als viur in dem brunnen ' und daz tou an der sunnen?	.	2	2
2, 5-14	ouch erkande ich nie sô wîsen man er enmöhte gerne künde hân welher stiure disiu maere gernt und waz si guoter lêre wernt.			

47

dar an si nimmer des verzagent,
beide si vliehent unde jagent,
si entwichent unde kêrent,
si lasternt und êrent. '
swer mit disen schanzen allen kan,
an dem hât witze wol getân.   1 1 2

2, 17-19   valsch geselleclîcher muot
ist zuo dem helleviure guot
und ist hôher werdekeit ein hagel.   1 . 1

2, 20-22   sîn triuwe hât sô kurzen zagel
daz si den dritten biz niht galt,
vuor si bî bremen in den walt.   . 1 1

2, 23-24   dise maneger slahte underbint
iedoch niht gar von manne sint:
vür diu wîp stôze ich disiu zil.   1 . 1

3, 5   schame ist ein slôz ob allen siten.   1 . 1

3, 7-10   diu valsche erwirbet valschen prîs.
wie staete ist ein dünnez îs
das ougestheize sunnen hât?
ir lop vil balde alsus zergât.   . 1 1

3, 11-14   manec wîbes schoene an lobe ist breit:
ist dâ das herze konterfeit, '
die lobe ich als ich solde
daz safer in dem golde.   1 1 2

3, 15-19   ich enhân daz niht vür lihtiu dinc,
swer in den kranken messinc
verwürket edelen rubîn
und al die âventiure sîn: '
dem gelîche ich rehten wîbes muot.   . 2 2

3, 20-22   diu ir wîpheit rehte tuot,
dâ ensol ich varwe prüeven niht
noch herzen dach daz man   siht.   1 . 1

4, 2-8   nû lât mîn eines wesen drî
der ieslîcher sunder phlege
daz miner künste widerwege
(dar zuo gehôrte wilder vunt):
ob si iu gerne taeten kunt
daz ich iu eine künden wil,
si heten arbeite vil.   . 1 1

		M	O	T
4, 15	er _stahel_, swâ er ze strîte quam	1	.	1
4, 20-23	er wibes _ougen sueze_, ' und da bi wibes _herzen suht_, ' vor missewende ein wariu _vluht_, den ich hie zuo han erkorn.	3	.	3
. . . .	. . . .	. . . .		
Totals:	116 lines of text	15	18	33

Gahmuret's Departure from Home 4, 27 - 13, 2   M   O   T

7, 6-9	er hât wênec und ich genuoc: daz sol im teilen sô mîn hant, daz des mîn saelde niht sî _phant_ ' vor dem der gît unde nimt.	1	1	2
8, 22-24	ir wâret ritter unde _diep_. ir kundet dienen unde heln: wan kunde ouch ich nû minne steln!	1	.	1
8, 28-30	ouwê daz ich dich ie gesach, sît dû mit schimphlîchen siten mîn ganzez herze hâs _versniten_.	1	.	1
9, 23-26	mîn herze iedoch nâch hoehe strebet: ich enweiz war umbe ez alsus lebet, daz mir _swillet_ sus mîn winster brust.	1	.	1
10, 24-25	ich hân _mîns herzenkraft_ begraben, ' die _süeze mîner ougen_:	2	.	2
12, 4-10	dô hete der helt unverzaget emphangen durch liebe kraft und durch wîplîch geselleschaft kleinoetes tûsent marke wert. swâ noch ein jude phandes gert, er möhtez dâ vür emphâhen, ez endorfte im niht versmâhen.	.	1	1
. . . .	. . . .	. . . .		
Totals:	246 lines of text	6	2	8

Gahmuret in Service of the Baruch 13, 3 - 16, 1   M   O   T

13, 12-14	des massenîe er wolde sîn, niwan eines der die _hoesten hant_ trüege ûf erde über elliu lant:	1	.	1

		M	O	T
14, 20-22	noch grüener denne ein smârât was geprüevet sîn gereite gar und nâch dem achmardî var	.	1	1
14, 30 - 15, 5	sîne anker heten niht bekort ganzes landes noch landes ort dâ enwâren si ninder în geslagen. der herre muoste vürbaz tragen disen wâpenlîchen last in manegiu lant, der werde gast, nâch dem anker disiu mâl	.	1	1

....

| Totals: | 89 lines of text | 1 | 3 | 4 |

<u>Gahmuret Goes to Zazamanc</u> 16, 2 - 23, 21   M O T

16, 7-8	des twanc in Belacâne, diu <u>süeze valsches âne</u>	1	.	1
17, 24-25	liute finster sô diu naht wâren alle die von Zazamanc	.	1	1
20, 4-6	manege tunkele vrouwen sach er beidenthalben sîn, nâch rabens varwe was ir schîn.	.	1	1
23, 7	dô saz der minnen geltes <u>lôn</u>	1	.	1

....

| Totals: | 230 lines of text | 2 | 2 | 4 |

<u>Gahmuret Received at Belacane's Court</u> 23, 22-36, 2   M O T

23, 24-28	dô si gesach den Anschevîn (der was minneclîch gevar), daz er <u>entslôz</u> ir herze gar, ez waere ir liep oder leit: daz <u>beslôz</u> da vor ir wîpheit	1	.	1
24, 6-7	ist iht liehters denne der tac dem gelîchte niht diu künegin	.	1	1
24, 10-11	der touwegen rôsen ungelîch, nâch swarzer varwe was ir schîn	.	1	1
25, 29-30	ir <u>herzen regen</u> die güsse warp, sît an der tjost ir herre starp	1	.	1

		M	O	T
26, 11-13	sîn lîp was tugende ein bernde rîs. ' der helt was küene unde wîs, der triuwe ein reht beklibeniu vruht.	2	.	2
26, 15	der was noch kiuscher denne ein wîp.	.	1	1
26, 21	er was gein valscher vuore ein tôr	1	.	1
28, 8	ûf mîner triuwe jâmer blüet	1	.	1
28, 14-16	ir kiusche was ein reiner touf ' und ouch der regen der si begôz, der wâc der von ir ougen vloz	2	.	2
29, 14-16	doch was ir lîp sîn selbes lîp: ouch hete er ir den muot gegeben, sîn leben was der vrouwen leben.	1	.	1
32, 24-26	dô hete diu müede sunne ir liehten blic hin zir gelesen: des banekens muoste ein ende wesen	1	.	1
34, 16-17	des herze truoc ir minnen last, daz selbe ouch ir von im geschach	1	.	1
35, 23-25	er want sich dicke als ein wit, daz im kracheten diu lit: strît und minne was sîn ger.	.	1	1
35, 27 - 36, 1	sîn herze gap von stôzen schal, ' wande ez nâch ritterschefte swal. ' daz begunde dem recken sîne brust beide erstrecken, ' sô diu senewe tuot daz armbrust.	2	2	4
. . . .	. . . .			. . . .
Totals:	371 lines of text	13	6	19

Gahmuret Battles for Belacane 36, 3 - 43, 30

		M	O	T
39, 22-23	er bluome an mannes schoene, ' sîn varwe an schoene hielt den strît	2	.	2
39, 30 - 40, 2	iuwer wilde wirt vil zam (daz sage ich iu ûf die triuwe mîn), bestêt ir den Anschevîn,	.	1	1
40, 26-27	er was vor in ein netze: swaz drunder kom, daz was beslagen.	1	.	1

		M	O	T
41, 16-17	aldâ tet sîner krefte <u>mat</u> der helt von Anschouwe.	1	.	1
42, 10-14	daz er niht îsen als ein strûz und starke vlinse verslant, ' daz machte daz er ir niht envant. sîn zorn begunde limmen und als ein lewe brimmen.	.	2	2
43, 6-8	starp er âne toufen sît, sô erkenne sich über den degen balt der aller wunder hât gewalt.	.	1	1
. . . .	. . . .	. . . .		
Totals:	238 lines of text	4	4	8

Gahmuret as New Lord of Zazamanc 44, 1 - 53, 14		M	O	T
44, 20-23	ein declachen zobelîn und ein bette wol gehêret, dar an im wart gemêret ein heimlîchiu êre.	.	1	1
49, 22-26	mich vienc diu künegîn mit ir hant: dô werte ich mich mit minne. sus rieten mir die sinne. ' ' ich waene, dir hât din <u>süeziu wer</u> betwungen beidenthalp diu her. '	1	.	1
50, 6	din strûz stuont hôch sunder nest.	.	1	1
50, 14-16	hete er den prîs behalden sô an vrevelen helden sô dîn lîp, vür zucker gaezen in diu wîp.	.	1	1
. . . .	. . . .	. . . .		
Totals:	284 lines of text	1	3	4

Conclusion of the Adventures in Zazamanc 53, 15 - 58, 26		M	O	T
53, 15-18	swie verwüestet waere sîn lant, doch kunde Gahmuretes hant swenken solher gâbe solt als al die boume trüegen golt.	.	1	1
55, 22-23	ich bin dirre verte ein <u>diep</u>: die muoste ich dir durch jâmer steln.	1	.	1

		<u>M</u>	<u>O</u>	<u>T</u>
56, 1-4	erst erborn von Anschouwe. diu minne wirt sîn <u>vrouwe</u>: ' sô wirt aber er an strîte ein <u>schûr</u>, ' den vînden herter <u>nâchgebûr</u>.	3	.	3
57, 1-2	wem hât sîn manlîchiu zuht hie lâzen sîner minne <u>vruht</u>?	1	.	1
57, 9	der jâmer gap ir herzen <u>wîc</u>.	1	.	1
57, 10-14	ir vreude vant <u>den dürren zwîc</u>, ' als noch diu turteltûbe tuot. diu hete ie den selben muot: swenne ir an trûtschefte gebrast, ir triuwe kôs den dürren ast.	1	1	2
57, 23-25	der wart ein <u>waltswende</u>: die tjoste sîner hende manec sper zebrâchen	1	.	1
57, 27-28	als ein agelster wart gevar sîn hâr und ouch sîn vel vil gar.	.	1	1
. . . .	. . . .	. . . .		
Totals:	162 lines of text	8	3	11
<u>Book One Totals</u>:	1736 lines of text	50	41	91

BOOK II

<u>Gahmuret Goes to Kanvoleis</u> 58, 27 - 61, 28

		<u>M</u>	<u>O</u>	<u>T</u>
60, 5-6	sîn ouge ninder hûs dâ sach, schilde waeren sîn ander dach	.	1	1
60, 18-21	diz maere manegen valte hinderz ors ûf den sâmen. die solh gevelle nâmen, ir schanze wart gein vlust gesaget.	.	1	1
. . . .	. . . .	. . . .		
Totals:	92 lines of text	0	2	2

<u>Arrival at Herzeloide's Tournament</u> 61, 29 - 68, 16

		<u>M</u>	<u>O</u>	<u>T</u>
63, 16-17	sîn munt als ein rubîn schein ' von der roete als ob er brünne	.	2	2

	M	O	T
64, 4-8 — von dem liehten schîne, der von der künegin erschein, zucte im neben sich sîn bein: ûf rihte sich der degen wert als ein vederspil, daz gert.	.	1	1
64, 19-20 — dô vuor er springende als ein tier, ' er was der vreuden soldier.	1	1	2
65, 29 - 66, 2 — hie hât manegen Bertûn der künec Utepandragûn. ein maere in stichet als ein dorn, daz er sîn wîp hât verlorn	.	1	1
66, 23-25 — hie hât der künec von Patrigalt von spern einen ganzen walt. ' des vuore ist dâ engein gar ein wint	2	.	2
68, 7-13 — stêt dîn strûz noch sunder nest, dû solt dîn sarapandratest gein sînem halben grîfen tragen. ' mîn anker vaste wirt geslagen durch lenden in sîns poinders hurt. ' er müeze selbe suochen vurt hinterm ohrse ûf dem grieze.	1	2	3

Totals:	198 lines of text	4	7	11

Events During the Vesperie 68, 17 - 82, 20	M	O	T
(A) — Queen Amphlise's Message 76, 1 - 77, 28			
76, 13-14 — daz ist rêgîn de Franze, die rüeret dîner minnen lanze.	1	.	1
76, 26-27 — dîn minne ist slôz unde bant mîns herzen und des vreude.	1	.	1
(B) — Gahmuret Drops Out for Grief 80, 6 - 81, 4			
80, 6-8 — zegegen kom im gehurtet bî ein vürste von Anschouwe (diu riuwe was sîn vrouwe)	1	.	1
(C) — His Superiority Acknowledged 81, 5 - 82, 4			
81, 5-9 — swie Gahmuret waere och mit klage,			

		<u>M</u>	<u>O</u>	<u>T</u>
	doch hete er an dem halben tage gevrumt sô vil der sper enzwei, waere worden der turnei, sô waere verswendet der walt.	.	1	1
81, 20-22	den truoc er vür die vrouwen: er was von golde dennoch guot, er gleste als ein glüendec gluot.	.	1	1
81, 30 - 82, 2	ieslîcher neme mîns wunsches war, wan si sint mir alle sippe von dem Adâmes rippe.	.	1	1
(D)	The Fighting 68, 17-75, 30; 77, 29-80, 5; 82, 5-20			
71, 12-16	er schein als ob hie brünne bî der naht ein queckez viur. ' verblichen varwe was im tiur, sîn glast die blicke niht vermeit: ein boesez ouge sich dran <u>versneit</u>.	1	1	2
72, 8	dem anker volcte nâch der strûz.	.	1	1
72, 17-25	gelîcher baniere man gein im vuorte viere (küene rotten riten drunde, ir herre strîten kunde), an ieslîcher eins grîfen zagel. daz hinder teil ' was ouch ein <u>hagel</u> an ritterschaft, des wâren die. daz vorder teil des grîfen hie der künec von Gascône truoc	1	1	2
72, 29- 73, 1	er nam sich vor den andern ûz, dô er ûf dem helme ersach den strûz. · der anker kom doch vor an in.	.	1	1
73, 4-6	... dâ was grôz gedranc, hôhe vürhe sleht <u>getennet</u>, ' mit swerten vil <u>gekemmet</u>.	2	.	2
73, 7-8	dâ wart <u>verswendet der walt</u> und manec ritter abe gevalt.	1	.	1
73, 14-15	der minnen gernde Rîwalîn, von des sper <u>snîte</u> ein niuwe leis.	1	.	1

		M	O	T
75, 4-7	dâ liefen unde giengen vil manec werder man in îsenwât, den wart dâ gâlûnet ir brât mit treten und mit kiulen.	1	.	1
79, 20-22	dâ gienc ez ûz der kinde spil: si worhten mit ir 'henden daz den walt begunde swenden.	2	.	2
82, 16-20	nûst zît daz man si kêre von ein ander: niemen hie gesiht. si enwert der phandaere liehtes niht: ' wer solde ouch vinsterlingen spiln? es mac die müeden doch beviln.	1	1	2
. . . .	. . . .	. . . .		
Totals:	424 lines of text	13	8	21
Subtotals:	(A) Queen Amphlise's Message (58 lines) (B) Gahmuret...Grief (29 lines) (C) His Superiority (30 lines) (D) The Fighting (307 lines)	2 1 0 10	0 0 3 5	2 1 3 15

Results of the Vesperie 82, 21 - 90, 6		M	O	T
84, 13-15	vrou Herzeloide gap den schîn, waeren erloschen gar die kerzen sîn, dâ waere doch lieht von ir genuoc.	.	1	1
85, 21-23	dir enkünne an sô bewantem spiln gelîche niemen hie gezîln. des lise ich hie den wâren brief.	1	.	1
86, 7-9	dû enmaht mîn doch verkoufen niht, wande etswer wandel an mir siht. din munt ist lobes ze vil vernomen.	1	.	1
88, 1-6	diu liefen elliu driu vür in und sprâchen: 'herre, hâstû sin (dir zelt regîn de Franze der werden minne schanze), ' sô mahtû spiln sunder phant. din vreude ist kumbers ledec zehant. '	2	.	2
88, 13-16	dô begreif im diu gehiure sîne quaschiure mit ir linden handen wîz,			

		<u>M</u>	<u>O</u>	<u>T</u>
dar an <u>lac der gotes vliz</u>.		1	.	1

. . . .

Totals:	226 lines of text	5	1	6

<u>Gahmuret's Grief</u> 90, 7 - 93, 30   <u>M</u>   <u>O</u>   <u>T</u>

90, 8-11	dô wart getrüebet in der schal: den wirt sîn triuwe mente daz er sich wider sente, wan jâmer ist ein scharpher <u>gart</u>.	1	.	1
91, 4-6	nû waent manec ungewisser man daz mich ir swerze jagete dan: die sach ich <u>vür die sunnen</u> an.	1	.	1
91, 7-8	ir wîplîch prîs mir vüeget leit. sist ein <u>buckel</u> ob der werdekeit.	1	.	1
92, 9-14	dô er vernam des bruoder tôt, daz was sîn ander herzenôt. mit jâmer sprach er disiu wort: 'wie hât nû mînes ankers ort in riuwe ergriffen landes habe! ' der wâpen tet er sich do abe:	.	1	1
92, 17-21	'von Anschouwe Gâlôes (vürbaz darf neimen vrâgen des, ez enwart nie manlîcher zuht geborn), der wâren milde vruht uz <u>dînem herzen</u> blüete. '	1	.	1
93, 5-6	sîn kumber leider was ze grôz, ein <u>güsse</u> im von den ougen vlôz.	1	.	1

. . . .

Totals:	114 lines of text	5	1	6

<u>Herzeloide's Claim Contested and Accepted</u> 94, 1 - 101, 20   <u>M</u>   <u>O</u>   <u>T</u>

94, 17-20	oder sol mir gein iu schade sîn der Franzoiser künegîn, der boten sprâchen süeziu wort? si <u>spilten ir maere</u> unz an den ort. '	1	.	1
99, 11-16	kêrt ûf den schilt nâch sîner art. gehabet iuch an <u>der vreuden vart</u>: '			

		M	O	T
	ich sol mîns vater wâpen tragen.			
	sîn lant mîn anker hât beslagen.			
	der anker ist ein recken zil:			
	den trage und neme nû swer der wil.	1	1	2
99, 24-26	daz si durch den dienest mîn			
	belîben, unz ir mich gewert			
	des minnen werc zer minnen gert.	.	1	1
100, 8-13	juncvrouwen und diu künegîn			
	in vuorten dâ er vreude vant			
	und al sîn trûren gar verswant.	.	1	1
100, 16-18	diu munde wâren ungespart:			
	die begunden si mit küssen zern '			
	und den jâmer von den vreuden wern.	2	.	2
....	....		....	
Totals:	230 lines of text	4	3	7

Gahmuret Recalled to Serve the Baruch 101, 21 - 102, 22   None

32 lines of text

Herzeloide's Ordeal 102, 23 - 105, 7

		M	O	T
102, 26	diu was alsô diu sunne lieht	.	1	1
103, 18-19	dô brast ir vreuden klinge			
	mitten in dem hefte enzwei.	1	.	1
104, 13-16	und wie ein trache ir brüste süge			
	und daz der gâhes von ir vlüge,			
	sô daz si in nimmer mêr gesach.			
	daz herze er ir ûz dem lîbe brach.	1	.	1
....	....		....	
Totals:	75 lines of text	2	1	3

Gahmuret's Death Described 105, 8 - 109, 1

		M	O	T
105, 22-24	den man noch mâlet vür daz lamp			
	und ouch daz kriuze in sîne klân,			
	den erbarme daz dâ wart getan.	.	1	1
106, 8-9	mit tôde er mînem herren lôn			
	gap, daz er in nider stach	.	1	1
....	....		....	

THE IMAGES IN PARZIVAL

		M	O	T
Totals:	114 lines of text	0	2	2

Birth of Parzival 109, 2 - 114, 4		M	O	T
109, 10-11	wan diu truoc in ir libe der aller ritter bluome wirt	1	.	1
109, 24-27	ich was vil junger danne er und bin sin muoter und sin wip: ich trage alhie doch sinen lip und sines verhes sâmen,	1	.	1
110, 18-21	daz waere Gahmuretes ander tôt, ob ich mich selben slüege, die wile ich bi mir trüege daz ich von siner minne emphienc	1	.	1
110, 30 - 111, 2	'dû bist kaste eins kindes spise.' die hât ez vor im her gesant, sit ichz lebendec in dem libe vant.'	1	1	2
111, 3-5	diu vrouwe ir willen dar an sach, daz diu spise was ir herzen dach, diu milch in ir tütteltn:	1	.	1
112, 9-12	hiest der âventiure wurf gespilt' und ir bogen ist gezilt, wande er ist alrêst geborn, dem diz maere wart erkorn.	2	.	2
112, 16-17	nû wizzet wâ von iu si komen dises maeres sachewalde	1	.	1
112, 28-29	er wart mit swerten sit ein smit, vil viures er von helmen sluoc	1	.	1
113, 27-29	sich begôz des landes vrouwe mit ir herzen jâmers touwe: ir ougen regenden ûf den knaben.	2	.	2
114, 3-4	si vreute sich ir suns geburt: ir schimph ertranc in riuwen vurt.	1	.	1

Totals:	153 lines of text	12	1	13

Epilogue to the Gahmuret Books 114, 5 - 116, 4		M	O	T
114, 12-16	ich bin Wolfram von Eschenbach			

		M	O	T
	und kan ein teil mit sange			
	und bin ein habendiu zange			
	mînen zorn gein einem wîbe	1	.	1
114, 26-28	iedoch ensuln si sich vergâhen niht			
	mit hurte an mîn hâmît:			
	si vindent werlîchen strît.	1	.	1
115, 5-7	sîn lop hinket an dem spat, '			
	swer allen vrouwen sprichet mat			
	durch sîn eines vrouwen.	2	.	2
115, 19-20	vil hôhes topels er doch spilt			
	der an ritterschaft nâch minnen zilt.	1	.	1
115, 29-30	disiu âventiure			
	vert âne der buoche stiure.	1	.	1
116, 1-4	ê man si hete vür ein buoch,			
	ich waere ê nacket âne tuoch,			
	sô ich in dem bade saeze,			
	ob ich squesten niht vergaeze.	.	1	1
. . . .	. . . .	. . . .		
Totals:	60 lines of text	6	1	7
Book Two Totals: 1718 lines of text		51	27	78

BOOK III

Prologue 116, 5 - 14

		M	O	T
Totals:	10 lines of text	.	.	.

Herzeloide and Parzival in the Wilderness 116, 15 - 120, 21

		M	O	T
116, 28-29	vrou Herzeloide diu rîche			
	ir drîer lande wart ein gast	1	.	1
117, 3-5	ein nebel was ir diu sunne. '			
	si vlôch der werlde wunne,			
	ir was gelîch naht und der tac	1	1	2
117, 11-13	ir herzen jâmer was sô ganz,			
	si enkêrte sich an keinen kranz,			
	er waere rôt oder val.	.	1	1
117, 27-29	'nû habet iuch an der witze kraft			
	und helt in alle ritterschaft. '			
	der site vuor angestlîche vart.	1	.	1

		<u>M</u>	<u>O</u>	<u>T</u>
118, 9-10	sô weinde er unde roufte sich, an sîn hâr <u>kêrte er gerich</u>.	1	.	1
118, 16-17	diu süeze in sîn herze dranc: daz <u>erstracte</u> im sîniu brüstelîn.	1	.	1
119, 2-5	ir bûliute und ir enken die hiez si vaste gâhen, vogele würgen unde vâhen. die vogele wâren <u>baz geriten</u>.	1	.	1
119, 17-19	'ouwê muoter, waz ist got?' 'sun, ich sage dirz âne spot: er ist noch liehter denne der tac.'	.	1	1
119, 25-26	sô heizet einer der helle wirt: derst swarz, untriuwe in niht verbirt.	.	1	1
119, 29-30	sîn muoter underschiet im gar daz vinster und daz lieht gevar.	.	1	1
. . . .	. . . .	. . . .		
Totals:	116 lines of text	6	5	11

Parzival Meets <u>the Knights</u> 120, 11 - 129,4

		<u>M</u>	<u>O</u>	<u>T</u>
121, 13-17	aller manne schoene <u>ein bluomen kranz</u>, den vrâcte Karnahkarnanz: 'juncherre, sahet ir vür iuch varn zwêne ritter die sich niht bewarn kunnen an ritterlîcher zunft?	1	.	1
123, 12-13	von den helden er geschouwet wart: <u>dô lac diu gotes gunst an im</u>.	1	.	1
126, 9-10	'muoter, ich sach vier man noch liehter danne got getân '	.	1	1
128, 26-30	sus vuor die lônes bernden vart ' <u>ein wurzel der güete</u> ' und ein <u>stam der diemüete</u>. ouwê daz wir nû niht enhân ir sippe unz an den eilften spân!	2	1	3
. . . .	. . . .	. . . .		
Totals:	264 lines of text	4	2	6

61

Parzival and Jeschute 129, 5 - 132, 24		M	O	T
129, 7-8	er kom an einen bach geriten, den hete ein hane wol überschriten	.	1	1
130, 3-6	diu vrouwe was entslâfen, si truoc der minne wâfen, einen munt durchliuhtec rôt und gerndes ritters herzen nôt.	1	.	1
130, 8-9	der munt ir von ein ander lief: der truoc der minne hitze viur.	1	.	1
130, 10	sus lac des wunsches âventiur.	1	.	1
130, 21-23	si was geschicket und gesniten, an ir was künste niht vermiten: got selbe worhte ir süezen lîp.	.	1	1
131, 19-21	diu vrouwe was mit wîbes wer, ir was sîn kraft ein ganzez her: doch wart dâ ringens vil getân.	1	.	1
132, 1-3	er enruochte wâ diu wirtîn saz: einen guoten kroph er az, dar nâch er swaere trünke tranc.	1	.	1
Totals:	110 lines of text	5	2	7

Orilus and Jeschute 132, 15 - 137, 30		M	O	T
137, 1-4	iuwer zoum muoz sîn ein bestîn seil iuwer phert bejaget wol hungers teil, iuwer satel wol gezieret der wirt enschumphieret.	1	.	1
137, 15-19	koeme ich an in (des würde ich geil), der hie nam iuwer minne teil, ich bestüende in doch durch âventiur, ob sîn âtem gaebe viur als eines wilden trachen.	.	1	1
Totals:	156 lines of text	1	1	2

Parzival Meets Sigune 138, 1 - 142, 10		M	O	T
138, 13-14	ein vrouwe ûz rehtem jâmer schrei: ir was diu wâre vreude enzwei	1	.	1

		M	O	T
139, 15-18	hete er gelernt sîns vater site, die werdeclîche im wonten mite, diu buckel waere gehurtet baz, dâ diu herzoginne al eine saz	1	.	1
140, 4-5	si vrâcte in wie er hieze, und jach er trüege den gotes vlîz.	1	.	1
140, 18-20	grôz liebe ier solh herzen vurch mit dîner muoter triuwe: dîn vater liez ir riuwe.	1	.	1
. . . .	. . . .	. . . .		
Totals:	130 lines of text	4	0	4

Parzival and the Fisherman 142, 11 - 143, 20		M	O	T
142, 13-14	dô ersach der tumpheit genôz ein hûs ze guoter mâze grôz.	1	.	1
142, 23-24	der sprach: 'ich engaebe iu ein halbez brôt niht ze drîzec jâren.	.	1	1
. . . .	. . . .	. . . .		
Totals:	40 lines of text	1	1	2

At King Arthur's Court 143, 21 - 161, 8		M	O	T
(A)	Arrival and Reception 143, 21 - 150, 28			
143, 25-27	bitet hüeten sîn vor spotte. er enist gîge noch diu rotte:' si suln ein ander gampel nemen	2	.	2
143, 29 - 144, 2	anders iuwer vrouwe Enîte und ir muoter Karsnafîte werdent durch die mül gezucket und ir lop gebucket.	2	.	2
144, 3-4	sol ich den munt mit spotte zern, ich wil mînen vriunt mit spotte wern.	1	.	1
145, 17-18	sîn harnas was gar sô rôt, daz ez den ougen roete bôt.	.	1	1
145, 22	sîn schilt noch roeter danne ein viur	.	1	1
146, 9-10	dû bist der wâren minne blic, ' ir schumphentiure ' und ir sic:	3	.	3

		M	O	T
148, 23-25	diz was selpschouwet, geherret noch gevrouwet ' wart nie minneclîcher vruht.	2	.	2
148, 26-27	got was in einer süezen zuht, dô er Parzivâlen worhte.	.	1	1
149, 25-26	der wol geborne knappe hielt gagernde als ein trappe.	.	1	1
150, 9-10	ez ist Îthêr von Gaheviez der trûren mir durch vreude stiez.	1	.	1
150, 15-17	sol iemen bringen uns den koph. hie helt diu geisel, dort der toph: lâtz kint in umbe trîben	1	.	1
150, 21-22	ich ensorge umbe ir deweders leben: man sol hunde nâch ebers houbet geben.	.	1	1
(B)	Cunneware's Beating 150, 29 - 153, 20			
151, 27-30	ir rücke wart dehein eit gestabet, ' doch wart ein stap sô dran gehabet, unz daz sîn siusen gar verswanc, durch die wât und durch ir vel ez dranc.	.	2	2
152, 2-6	iuwerm werden prîse ist gegeben ein smaehiu letze: ich bin sîn vengec netze, ' ich sol in wider in iuch smiden daz irs emphindet ûf den liden.	2	.	2
153, 9-12	sîn brât wart gâlûnet, ' mit slegen vil gerûnet dem witzehaften tôren mit viusten in sîn ôren:	2	.	2
(C)	Parzival Fights Ither 153, 21- 159, 12			
155, 15-18	swelhiu sîner minne emphant, durch die vreude ir was gerant ' und ir schimph enschumphieret, gein der riuhe gekondewieret.	2	.	2
158, 13-16	als uns diu âventiure giht, von Kölne noch von Mâstrieht dehein schildaere entwürfe in baz, denne als er ûf dem orse saz.	.	1	1

		M	O	T
158, 27-30	mich müent ir jaemerlîchen wort, diu enrüerent mir dehein herzen ort: jâ muoz enmitten drinne sîn der vrouwen ungedienter pîn.	1	.	1
(D)	Grief over Ither 159, 13 - 161, 8			
160, 4-5	Artûses werdekeit enzwei sol brechen noch diz wunder	1	.	1
160, 14-15	er was vor wildem valsche zam: der was vil gar von im geschaben.	1	.	1
160, 16-20	nû muoz ich alze vruo begraben ein slôz ob dem prîse. ' sîn herze an zühten wîse, ob dem slôze ein hantveste, riet im benamen daz beste	2	.	2
160, 24-26	ein berndiu vruht al niuwe ist trûrens ûf diu wîp gesaet. ' ûz dîner wunden jâmer waet.	2	.	2
. . . .	. . . .	. . . .		
Totals:	528 lines of text	25	8	33
Subtotals:	(A) Arrival and Reception (218 lines)	12	5	17
	(B) Cunneware's Beating (82 lines)	4	2	6
	(C) Parzival Fights Ither (172 lines)	3	1	4
	(D) Grief over Ither (56 lines)	6	0	6

Parzival and Gurnemanz 161, 9 - 179, 6

		M	O	T
(A)	Reception as a Stranger 161, 9 - 170, 6			
161, 17-20	gewâpent reitz der tumbe man den tac sô verre, ez hete lân ein blôz wîser, solde erz hân geriten zwêne tage, ez waere vermiten.	.	1	1
162, 24-25	des site was vor valsche ein vluht, der emphienc den gast. daz was sîn reht:	1	.	1
164, 12-18	dieswâr sô werdeclîche vruht erkôs nie mîner ougen sehe. an im liget der saelden spehe mit reiner süezen hohen art. ' wiest der minnen blic alsus bewart? '			

		M	O	T
	mich jâmert immer daz ich vant			
	an der werlde vreude alsolh gewant.	4	.	4
165, 8-12	sîn underwant sich Gurnemanz.			
	solh was sîn underwinden,			
	daz ein vater sînen kinden,			
	der sich triuwe kunde nieten,			
	möhtez in niht baz erbieten.	.	1	1
165, 27-29	der gast sich dâ gelabete:			
	in den barn er sich sô habete,			
	daz er der spîse swande vil.	1	.	1
166, 16	sô werde vruht gebar nie wîp.	1	.	1
167, 8-9	jâ endorfte in niht ellenden			
	der dâ was witze ein weise.	1	.	1
167, 16-20	ez dorfte in dunken niht ze vruo,			
	wan von in schein der ander tac. '			
	der glast alsus en strîte lac,			
	sîn varwe laschte beidiu lieht:			
	des was sîn lîp versûmet niht.	2	.	2
168, 20	sîn munt dâ bî vor roete bran.	1	.	1
168, 26-27	mit triuwen lobeten si daz wîp,			
	diu gap der werlde alsolhe vruht.	1	.	1
(B)	Instructed by Gurnemanz 170, 7 - 175, 6			
170, 7-9	dô man den tisch hin dan genam,			
	dar nâch wart wilder muot vil zam.			
	der wirt sprach zem gaste sîn:	1	.	1
170, 17-20	verschamter lîp, waz touc der mêr?			
	der wont in der mûze rêr,			
	dâ im werdekeit entrîset			
	und in gein der helle wîset.	1	.	1
171, 3-4	swenne ir dem tuot kumbers buoz,			
	sô nâhet iu der gotes gruoz.	.	1	1
172, 15-23	gein werder minne valscher list			
	hât gein prîse kurze vrist.			
	dâ wirt der slîchaere klage			
	daz dürre holz in dem hage,			
	daz bristet unde krachet:			
	der wahtaere erwachet.			

		M	O	T
	ungeverte und hâmît, dar gedîhet manec strît: diz zelt gein der minne.	.	1	1
173, 1-5	man und wîp diu sint al ein als diu sunne diu hiute schein, und ouch der name der heizet tac. ' der enwederz sich gescheiden mac: si blüent ûz einem kerne gar.	1	1	2
173, 14-17	wie kômet ir zuo mir geriten! ich hân beschouwet manege want, dâ ich den schilt baz hangen vant denne er iu ze halse taete.	.	1	1
174, 7-9	unvuoge er im sus werte baz denne ein swankel gerte diu argen kinden brichet vel.	.	1	1
174, 29-30	des wirtes ritter niht gesaz, al vallende er den acker maz.	1	.	1
(C)	Hosted as Potential Son-in-Law 175, 7 - 177, 9			
175, 14-15	ob wir in bî witzen schouwen sô lischet im sîn jâmers nôt:	1	.	1
175, 26-28	dû solt dich küssen lâzen disen ritter, biut im êre: er vert mit saelden lêre.	1	.	1
176, 9-10	iedoch kuste er si an den munt, dem was wol viurs varwe kunt.	.	1	1
177, 5-7	in dûhte, wert gedinge daz waere ein hôhiu linge ze disem lîbe hie und dort.	1	.	1
(D)	Parzival's Departure 177, 10 - 179, 12			
177, 13-14	dô sprach der vürste ûz triuwe erkorn: 'ir sît mîn vierder sun verlorn.'	1	.	1
177, 18-24	der nû mîn herze envieriu mit sîner hende slüege und ieslîchez stücke trüege, daz diuhte mich ein grôz gewin, einz vür iuch (ir rîtet hin),			

		M	O	T
	diu driu vür mîniu werden kint			
	diu ellenthaft erstorben sint.	.	1	1
177, 25-26	sus lônt iedoch diu ritterschaft:			
	ir zagel ist jâmerstricke haft.	1	.	1
178, 4-5	des ist mir dürkel als ein zûn '			
	mîn herze von jâmers sniten.	1	1	2
179, 10-12	des vürsten jâmers drîe			
	was riuwec an daz quater komen,			
	die vierden vlust hete er genomen.	1	.	1
. . . .	. . . .	. . . .		
Totals:	544 lines of text	23	10	33
Subtotals:	(A) Reception as Stranger (268 lines)	12	2	14
	(B) Instructed by Gurnemanz (150 lines)	4	5	9
	(C) Hosted as Pot. Son-in-Law (63 lines)	3	1	4
	(D) Parzival's Departure (63 lines)	4	2	6
Book Three Totals: 1898 lines of text		69	29	98

BOOK IV

On the Way to Pelrapeire 179, 13 - 181, 10

		M	O	T
179, 18-26	im was diu wîte ze enge '			
	und ouch diu breite gar ze smal, '			
	elliu grüene in dûhte val, '			
	sîn rôt harnas in dûhte val, '			
	sîn herze diu ougen des betwanc,			
	sît er tumpheit âne wart.			
	dô enwolde in Gahmuretes art			
	denkens niht erlâzen			
	nâch der schoenen Liâzen	.	4	4
180, 9-14	genuoge hânt des einen site			
	und sprechent sus, swer irre rite			
	daz der den slegel vünde:			
	slegels urkünde			
	lac dâ âne mâze vil,			
	suln grôze ronen sîn slegels sil.	.	1	1

		M	O	T
180, 29 - 181, 2	daz wazzer vuor nâch bolze siten, die wol gevidert und gesniten sint, sô si armbrustes span mit senewen swanke trîbet dan.	.	1	1
181, 7-10	seht wie kint ûf schocken varn, die man schockes niht wil sparn, sus vuor diu brücke âne seil: ' diu was vor jugende niht sô geil.	.	2	2

Totals: 58 lines of text   0   8   8

Arrival and Reception at Pelrapeire 181, 11 - 186, 16   M   O   T

183, 16-19	dâ stuont ouch manec koufman mit hâschen und mit gabilôt, als in ir meisterschaft gebôt, die truogen alle slachen balc.	.	1	1
184, 1-3	ouch was diu jaemerlîche schar elliu nâch aschen var ' oder alsô valwer leim	.	2	2
184, 4-6	mîn herre der grâve von Wertheim waere ungerne soldier dâ gewesen: er möhte ir soldes niht genesen.	.	1	1
184, 9-11	si liezen zenstüren sîn ' und smalzten ouch deheinen wîn mit ir munde, sô si trunken.	.	2	2
184, 14-15	gerumphen als ein Ungers zager was in diu hût zuo den riben:	.	1	1
184, 18	in trouf vil wênec in die koln.	.	1	1
184, 22-26	sich vergôz dâ selten mit dem mete der zuber oder diu kanne. ' ein Trühendingaere phanne mit kraphen selten dâ erschrei: ' in was der selbe dôn enzwei.	2	1	3
184, 29 - 185, 5	wan dâ ich dicke bin erbeizet und dâ man mich herre heizet, dâ heime in mîn selbes hûs, dâ wirt gevreut vil selten mûs, wan diu müeste ir spîse steln. '			

		M	O	T
	die dörfte niemen vor mir heln: ich envinde ir offenliche nîht.	.	2	2
185, 10-12	nû sol diz maere wider komen, wie Pelrapeire stuont jâmers vol. dâ gap diu diet von vreuden zol.	1	.	1
185, 17-18	ir lîp ist nû benennet phant, si enloese drûz diu hoeste hant.	2	.	2
186, 1-5	er was in ungelîche var: dô er den râm von im sô gar getwuoc mit einem brunnen, dô hete er der sunnen verdecket vil nâch ir liehten glast.	.	1	1

| Totals: | 156 lines of text | 5 | 12 | 17 |

Meeting with Condwîrâmûrs 186, 17 - 190, 8

		M	O	T
186, 19-20	von der küneginne gienc ein liehter glast, ê si in emphienc.	1	.	1
187, 12-21	Condwîrâmûrs ir schîn doch schiet von disen strîten: Jeschûten, Ênîten und Cunnewâren de Lalant und swâ man lobes die besten vant, dâ man vrouwen schoene gewuoc, ir glastes schîn vaste under sluoc und beider Îsalden. jâ muoste prîses walden Condwîrâmûrs.	.	1	1
188, 1-5	der gast gedâhte, ich sage iu wie: 'Lîâze ist dort, Lîâze ist hie. mir wil got sorge mâzen: nû sihe ich Lîâzen, des werden Gurnemanzes kint.'	1	.	1
188, 6-13	Lîâzen schoene was ein wint gein der megede diu hie saz ' (an der got wunsches niht vergaz, diu was des landes vrouwe), als von dem süezen touwe diu rôse ûz ir belgelîn			

		M	**O**	**T**
	blecket niuwen werden schîn, der beidiu wîz ist unde rôt.	1	1	2
189, 15-17	vrouwe, ich reit bî disem tage von einem man, den ich in klage liez mit triuwen âne schranz.	1	.	1
189, 30 - 190, 1	wir haben manegen sûren tac mit nazzen ougen verklaget	1	.	1
Totals:	112 lines of text	5	2	7

Relief through Condwîrâmûrs' Cousins 190, 9 - 191, 16   **M** **O** **T**

191, 12-14	waeren die burgaere vederspil, si enwaeren überkrüphet niht, des noch ir tischgerihte giht.	.	1	1
Totals:	38 lines of text	0	1	1

Condwîrâmûrs Night-Visit and Plea 191, 17 - 196, 9   **M** **O** **T**

191, 27-29	kint im entschuohten, sân er slief, unz im der wâre jâmer rief und liehter ougen herzen regen.	1	.	1
192, 5-8	die twanc urliuges nôt und lieber helfaere tôt ir herze an solhez krachen, daz ir ougen muosten wachen.	1	.	1
192, 9-12	dô gienc diu küneginne, niht nâch solher minne diu solhen namen reizet der megede wîp heizet:	.	1	1
192, 14-17	an ir was werlîchiu wât, ein hemde wîz sîdîn: waz möhte kamphlîcher sîn dan gein dem man sus komende ein wîp?	2	.	2
192, 28-29	von kerzen lieht sô der tac was vor sîner slâfstat.	.	1	1
194, 5-8	es was dennoch sô spaete, daz ninder huon dâ kraete: ' hanboume stuonden dâ blôz,			

		M	O	T
	der zadel hüener von in schôz.	.	2	2
195, 4-6	er mannes schoene ein blüende rîs, er kunde valscheit mâzen, der bruoder Lîâzen.	1	.	1
195, 10-11	sîn hôher muot kom in ein tal: daz riet Lîâzen minne.	1	.	1
....	....	....		
Totals:	143 lines of text	6	4	10

Parzival Battles Kingrun 196, 9 - 199, 21   M O T

		M	O	T
197, 20-25	Parzivâl im brâhte gelt mit siner ellenthaften hant, daz Kingrûn seneschalt wânde vremder maere, wie ein pheteraere mit würfen an in seicte.	.	1	1
198, 19-22	mit swerten waere mîn lîp verzert kleine sô daz in sunnen vert, wande ich hân herzeleit getân dort inne manegem küenen man.	.	1	1
....	....	....		
Totals:	103 lines of text	0	2	2

Parzival Becomes Lord of Pelrapeire 199, 22 - 203, 11   M O T

		M	O	T
200, 20-21	si möhten vliegen sô diu loup: die magern und die sîhten	.	1	1
200, 24-27	der küneginne marschalc tet den schiffen solhen vride, daz er gebôt bî der wide daz sich ir deheiner ruorte.	1	.	1
201, 4	den burgaeren in die koln trouf	.	1	1
201, 13-14	er wolde niht ir laeren magen überkrüphe lâzen tragen.	1	.	1
201, 21 - 202, 1	er lac mit solhen vuogen, des nû niht wil genuogen manegiu wîp, swer in sô tuot. daz si durch arbeitlîchen muot ir zuht sus parrierent			

		M	O	T
	und sich dâ gegen zierent!			
	vor gesten sint si an kiuschen siten:			
	ir herzen wille hât versniten			
	swaz mac an den gebaerden sîn.			
	ir vriunt si heimlîchen pîn			
	vüegent mir ir zarte.	1	.	1
203, 6	si vlâhten arm unde bein.	1	.	1
....	....	....		
Totals:	110 lines of text	4	2	6

Preparation for Battle: Clamide and Parzival 203, 12 - 206, 4

		M	O	T
205, 3-4	man und mâge sult ir manen			
	und suoht die stat mit zwein vanen	1	.	1
205, 8	dieswâr wir tuon in schimphes buoz.	1	.	1
....	....	....		
Totals:	83 lines of text	2	0	2

Kingrun at Arthur's Court 206, 5 - 207, 3

		M	O	T
206, 29 -	'der kezzel ist uns undertân,			
207, 3	mir hie und dir ze Brandigân.			
	hilf mir durch dîne werdekeit			
	Cunnewâren hulde um kraphen breit.'	.	1	1
....	....	....		
Totals:	29 lines of text	0	1	1

Battle with clâmidê 207, 4 - 216, 4

		M	O	T
210, 4	dô wâpenden sich die kamphes smide.	1	.	1
211, 25-26	ir ieweder des geruochte,			
	daz erz viur im helme suochte.	1	.	1
211, 29	dô zerstuben in die schilde,			
212, 1	als der mit schimphe spilde			
	und vedern würfe in den wint	.	1	1
212, 4-10	dô wânde Clâmidê daz der vride			
	waere gebrochen ûz der stat:			
	sînen kamphgenôz er bat,			
	daz er sich selben êrte			
	und mangen würfe werte.			
	ez giengen ûf in slege grôz,			

73

		M	O	T
	die wâren wol <u>mangensteins genôz</u>.	1	.	1
213, 11-14	dîn lant ist erloeset. als der sîn schif eroeset (ez ist vil deste lîhter), mîn gewalt ist sîhter.	.	1	1
213, 15-16	reht manlîchiu wünne ist worden an mir <u>dünne</u>	1	.	1
213, 22-25	ich trage den <u>lebendegen tôt</u>, sît ich von ir gescheiden bin, ' diu mir herze unde sin ie mit ir gewalt <u>beslôz</u>	2	.	2
214, 24-25	sîns hers mich bevilde: ir kom ouch kûme <u>der sâme</u> wider.	1	.	1
215, 30 - 216, 1	die tôten mit den bâren vrumte er an ir <u>reste</u>.	1	.	1
. . . .	. . . .	. . . .		
Totals:	271 lines of text	8	2	10

Clâmidê at Arthur's Court 216, 5 - 222, 9

		M	O	T
216, 10-12	von Dîanazdrûn der plân muoste zeltstangen wonen mêr danne in Spehteshart sî ronen	.	1	1
217, 1-2	etslîcher hin zir spraeche, daz in ir minne <u>staeche</u>	1	.	1
217, 11-15	diu massenîe vor im az, manec werder man gein valsche laz und manec juncvrouwe stolz, daz niht wan tjoste was ir <u>bolz</u>: <u>ir vriunt si</u> gein dem vîent <u>schoz</u>.	1	.	1
219, 7-10	dô wurden an den stunden sîne hende also gewunden, daz si begunden krachen so die dürren spachen	.	1	1
219, 16-18	ich hân sô wirdec her verlorn, daz muoter nie gebôt ir brust dem der erkande hôher vlust.	.	1	1
219, 22-23	mirst vreude <u>gestîn</u>, hochmuot gast. ' Condwîrâmûrs <u>vrumt mich grâ</u>.	2	.	2

		M	O	T
219, 24 -	Pilâtus von Ponciâ			
220, 4	und der arme Jûdas,			
	der bî einem kusse was			
	an der triuwenlôsen vart '			
	dâ Jêsus verrâten wart,			
	swie daz ir schephaere raeche,			
	die nôt ich niht verspraeche,			
	daz Brôbarzaere vrouwen lîp			
	mit ir hulden waere mîn wîp,			
	sô daz ich si umbevienge,			
	swiez mir dar nâch ergienge.	1	1	2
221, 26-27	die Berteneise ir lobes rîs			
	waenent nû hôch gestôzen hân:	1	.	1
222, 5-6	man sach dâ viur ûz helmen waen			
	und swert in henden umbe draen.	1	.	1
Totals:	185 lines of text	7	4	11

Peace at Pelrapeire 222, 10 - 223, 14		M	O	T
222, 10-11	hie sule wir diz maere lân			
	und komens wider an die vart	1	.	1
Totals:	35 lines of text	1	0	1

Parzival Leaves to Seek Herzeloide 223, 15-30		M	O	T
16 lines of text		none		

Book Four Totals: 1338 lines of text		38	38	76

BOOK V

Parzival Aimlessly Wandering 224, 1-30		M	O	T
224, 22-25	uns tuot diu âventiure bekant,			
	daz er bî dem tage reit,			
	ein vogel hetes arbeit,			
	solde erz allez hân ervlogen.	.	1	1
Totals:	30 lines of text	0	1	1

Parzival Meets the Fisher-King 225, 1 - 226, 9   <u>M</u>   <u>O</u>   <u>T</u>

		M	O	T
225, 8-12	einen er in dem schiffe sach, der hete an im alsolh gewant, ob im dienden elliu lant, daz ez niht bezzer möhte sîn gefurriert.	.	1	1
Totals:	39 lines of text	0	1	1

Arrival at the Grail Castle 226, 10 - 229, 22   <u>M</u>   <u>O</u>   <u>T</u>

		M	O	T
226, 14-17	diu burc an veste niht betrogen: si stuont als si waere gedraet. ' ez envlüge oder hete der wint gewaet, mit sturme ir niht geschadet was.	.	2	2
226, 20-22	ob si suochten elliu her, si engaeben vür die selben nôt ze drîzec jâren niht ein brôt.	.	1	1
228, 4-5	alde und junge wânden daz von im ander tac erschine	.	1	1
229, 10-14	dô er sîn swert wol gemâl ninder bî im ligen vant, zer viuste twanc er sus die hant, daz daz bluot ûz den nageln schôz und im den ermel gar begôz.	.	1	1
229, 21-22	'dar gêt (ir sît im werder gast) und schütet ab iu zornes last.'	1	.	1
Totals:	103 lines of text	1	5	6

Dinner with the Grail Company 229, 23 - 242, 18   <u>M</u>   <u>O</u>   <u>T</u>

		M	O	T
(A)	General Narrative 229, 23 - 231, 14; 236, 23 - 240, 30; 242, 1-18			
230, 18-20	ez was worden wette zwischen im und der vreude: er lebete niht wan teude.	1	.	1
237, 7-8	der wirt dô selbe wazzer nam. der was an hôchmuote lam.	1	.	1
238, 18-24	es enwürde nie dehein bilde,			

		M	O	T
	beginnet manger sprechen: der wil sich übel rechen, wan der grâl was der saelden vruht, ' der werlde süeze alsolh genuht, er wac vil nâch gelîche als man saget von himelrîche.	1	1	2
239, 11-13	er dâhte: 'mir riet Gurnemanz mit grôzen triuwen âne schranz, ich solde vil gevrâgen niht.	1	.	1
240, 29-30	ich macz wol sprechen âne guft, er was noch wîzer dan der tuft.	.	1	1
242, 16-18	nû solde ich schrîen wâfen umbe ir scheiden daz si tuont: ez wirt grôz schade in beiden kunt.	1	.	1
(B)	The Grail Ceremony 231, 15 - 236, 22			
231, 15-18	dâ saz manec ritter kluoc, dâ man jâmer vür si truoc. ein knappe spranc zer tür dar în, der truoc eine glaevîn:	1	.	1
231, 15-18	dâ wart geweinet und geschrît ûf dem palase wît, daz volc von drîzec landen ' möhtez den ougen niht enblanden.	1	1	2
232, 5-8	wil iuch nu niht erlangen, so wirt hie zuo gevangen daz ich iuch bringe an die vart, wie da mit zuht gedienet wart.	1	.	1
233, 4	ir munt nâch viurs roete schein.	.	1	1
233, 28-29	viere die taveln legeten ûf helfenbein wîz als ein snê.	.	1	1
234, 3-4	an diesen ehte vrouwen was röcke grüener denne ein gras	.	1	1
234, 18-26	zwei mezzer snîdende als ein grât ' brâhten si durch wunder ûf zwein tweheln al besunder: daz was silber herte und wîz. dar an lac ein spaeher vlîz:			

		M	O	T
	im was solh scherphen niht vermiten,			
	ez hete stahel wol versniten.	.	2	2
235, 15-17	nâch den kom diu künegîn.			
	ir antlitze gap den schîn,			
	si wânden alle es wolde tagen.	.	1	1
235, 20-24	ûf einem grüenen achmardî			
	truoc si den wunsch von pardîs,			
	beide wurzeln unde rîs: '			
	daz was ein dinc, daz hiez der grâl,			
	erden wunsches überwal.	2	.	2
(C)	Wolfram's Apology for Delay 241, 1-30			
241, 4-30	diu werden iu von mir genant			
	her nâch sô des wirdet zît,			
	bescheidenlîchen âne strît			
	und âne allez vür zogen. '			
	ich sage die senewen âne bogen. '			
	diu senewe ist ein bîspel.			
	nû dunket iuch der boge snel:			
	doch ist sneller daz diu senewe jaget. '			
	ob ich iu rehte hân gesaget,			
	diu senewe gelîchet maeren sleht: '			
	diu dunkent ouch die liute reht.			
	swer iu saget von der krümbe,			
	der will iuch leiten ümbe.			
	swer den bogen gespannen siht,			
	der senewen er der slehte giht,			
	man welle si zer biuge erdenen			
	sô si den schuz muoz menen.			
	swer aber dem sîn maere schiuzet, '			
	des in durch nôt verdriuzet			
	(wan daz hât dâ ninder stat			
	und vil gerûmeclîchen phat '			
	zeinem ôren în, zem andern vür), '			
	mîn arbeit ich gar verlür,			
	ob den mîn maere drünge:			
	ich sagete oder sünge,			
	daz ez noch baz vernaeme ein boc '			
	oder ein ulmeger stoc.	5	4	9
Totals:	386 lines of text	15	13	28

THE IMAGES IN PARZIVAL

		M	O	T
Subtotals:	(A) General Narrative (198 lines)	5	2	7
	(B) Grail Ceremony (158 lines)	5	7	12
	(C) Wolfram's Apology (30 lines)	5	4	9

In Parzival's Bed-Chamber 242, 19 - 245, 16		M	O	T
(A)	Service to Him 242, 19 - 244, 30			
243, 1-3	dem bette armuot was tiur. als er glohte in einem viur, lac drûfe ein phellel lieht gemâl.	.	1	1
243, 9-11	vil kerzen und diu varwe sîn die gâben ze gegenstrîte schîn: ' waz möhte liehter sîn der tac?	.	2	2
243, 28 - 244, 3	Parzivâl der snelle man spranc underz declachen. si sageten: 'ir sult wachen durch uns noch eine wîle.' ein spil mit der île hete er unz an den ort gespilt.	1	.	1
244, 4-6	daz man gein liehter varwe zilt, daz begunde ir ougen süezen, ê si emphiengen sîn grüezen.	1	.	1
244, 19-22	er bat die vrouwen sitzen. si sprach: 'lât mich bî witzen. sô waeret ir dienstes ungewert, als mîn her vür iuch ist gegert.'	1	.	1
(B)	Parzival's Nightmare 245, 1-16			
245, 9-11	sus wart gesteppet im sîn troum, mit swertslegen umbe den soum dâ vor mit maneger tjoste rîch.	1	.	1
245, 12-16	von rabîne hurteclîch er leit in slâfe etslîch nôt. möhte er drîzecstunt sîn tôt, ' daz hete er wachende ê gedolt: ' sus teilde im ungemach den solt.	2	1	3
. . . .	. . . .	. . . .		
Totals:	88 lines of text	6	4	10

		M	O	T
Subtotals:	(A) The Service (72 lines)	3	3	6
	(B) The Nightmare (16 lines)	3	1	4

Abandoned at Munsalvaesche 245, 17 - 248, 16

		M	O	T
247, 26-28	'ir sult varn der sunnen haz' ' sprach der knappe, 'ir sît ein gans!. ' möhtet ir gerüeret hân den vlans.'	2	1	3
248, 3-5	swie vil er nâch geriefe, rehte als er gênde sliefe warp der knappe und sluoc die porten zuo.	.	1	1
248, 6-9	dô was sîn dan scheiden ze vruo an der vlustbaeren zît dem der nû zins von vreuden gît: ' diu ist an im verborgen.	2	.	2
248, 10-13	umbe den wurf der sorgen wart getopelt, dô er den grâl vant, mit sînen ougen âne hant und âne würfels ecke.	1	.	1
....	....	....		
Totals:	90 lines of text	5	2	7

Meets Sigune Second Time, Learns His Error 248, 17 - 256, 10

		M	O	T
249, 23-25	si was doch sîner muomen kint. al irdisch triuwe was ein wint, wan die man an ir lîbe sach.	1	.	1
252, 4-6	wol dich der saelden reise! wan swaz die lüfte hânt beslagen, dar obe muostû hoehe tragen	.	1	1
252, 14-17	dû endarft dich niht der sippe schamen, daz dîn muoter ist mîn muome. wîplîcher kiusche ein bluome ' ist si, geliutert âne tou.	1	1	2
253, 9-14	dô nazten diu ougen ir die wât. ouch was vroun Lûneten rât ninder dâ bî ir gewesen. diu riet ir vrouwen: 'lât genesen disen man, der den iuwern sluoc: er mac ergetzen iuch genuoc.'	.	1	1

		M	O	T
255, 13-16	gunêrter lîp, vervluochet man!			
	ir truoget den eiterwolves zan,			
	dâ diu galle in der triuwe			
	an iu bekleip sô niuwe.	1	.	1

....

Totals:	234 lines of text	3	3	6

Parzival Effects Reconciliation Between Orilus and Jeschute
256, 11 - 271, 23

		M	O	T
256, 17-19	ir phert gein kumber was verselt: '			
	man hete im wol durch hût gezelt			
	elliu sîniu rippe gar.	1	1	2
256, 27	ez was dürre als ein zunder.	.	1	1
257, 10-13	swâ daz mit zerren was gerüeret,			
	dâ sach er vil der stricke,			
	dar unde liehte blicke,			
	ir hût noch wîzer denne ein swane.	.	1	1
257, 18-20	swiez ir kom, ir munt was rôt:			
	der muoste alsolhe varwe tragen,			
	man hete viur wol drûz geslagen.	.	1	1
257, 26-32	durch iuwer zuht geloubet mir:			
	si truoc ungedienten haz,			
	wîplîcher güete si nie vergaz.			
	ich sagete iu vil armuot:			
	war zuo? diz ist als guot.			
	doch naeme ich solhen blôzen lîp			
	vür etslîch wol gekleidet wîp.	.	1	1
258, 24-29	al weinde diu vrouwe reit,			
	daz si begôz ir brüstelîn.			
	als si gedraet solden sîn,			
	diu stuoden blanc hôch sinewel:			
	jâ enwart nie draehsel sô snel,			
	der si gedraet hete baz.	.	1	1
259, 19-21	si sprach: 'es gert ein werder degen:			
	der hât sich strîtes sô bewegen,			
	iuwer sehse koemens in arbeit.	.	1	1
259, 23-25	ich was etswenne sîn wîp:			
	nû möhte min vertwâlet lîp			
	des heldes dierne niht gesîn.	.	1	1

		M	O	T
260, 8-11	wîplîcher kiusche lobes kranz truoc si mit armüete: si phlac der wâren güete sô daz der valsch an ir verswant.	1	.	1
262, 30	diu ors in sweize muosten baden	1	.	1
263, 2-5	die blicke von den swerten und viur daz von helmen spranc, und manec allenthafter swanc, die begunden verre glesten.	1	.	1
263, 14-19	prîs gediende Parzivâl, daz er sich alsus wern kan wol hundert trachen und eines man. ' ein trache wart versêret, sîne wunden gemêret, der ûf Orilus helme lac.	.	2	2
263, 24-25	vroun Jeschûten wart der gruoz mit swertes schimphe aldâ bejaget.	1	.	1
265, 14-15	als eine garben heberîn vaste er in under die arme swanc,	.	1	1
265, 20-21	'dû garnes daz sich hât versent disiu vrouwe von dînem zorne.'	1	.	1
265, 27-29	Parzivâl der werde degen dructe in an sich, daz bluotes regen spranc durch die barbiere.	1	.	1
267, 25-29	dar zuo wil ich schouwen in dînen hulden dise vrouwen mit suone âne vâre oder dû muost eine bâre tôt hinnen rîten.	1	.	1
268, 1	merke diu wort und wis der werke ein wer	1	.	1
269, 2-3	er nam daz heilectuom, drûf er swuor. sus stabete er selbe sînen eit.	1	.	1
269, 15-17	dirre worte si mit werken phant mîn gelücke vor der hoesten hant (ich hânz dâ vür, die treget got)	1	.	1
270, 14-21	ich hân doch selten vrouwen wâpenröcke an gesehen tragen,			

	$\underline{M}$	$\underline{O}$	$\underline{T}$

die waeren in strîte alsus zeslagen:
von ir krîe wart ouch nie turnei
gesameliert noch sper enzwei
gestochen, swâ daz solde sîn.
der guote knappe und Lembekîn
die tjost zesamene trüegen baz. . 1 1

. . . .

Totals: 463 lines of text   11 12 23

The Reconciliation 271, 24 - 273, 30 $\underline{M}$ $\underline{O}$ $\underline{T}$

271, 28-30   daz volc was al gelîche geil
              daz suone was worden schîn
              gein der saeldebernden herzogîn   1   .   1

272, 14-18   grôz liebe ist vreude und jâmers zil. '
              swer von der liebe ir maere
              treget ûf den seigaere,
              ob erz immer wolde wegen,
              ez enkan niht ander schanze phlegen.   2   .   2

. . . .

Totals: 67 lines of text   3   0   3

Orilus and Jeschute at Arthur's Court 274, 1 - 279, 30 $\underline{M}$ $\underline{O}$ $\underline{T}$

275, 26-30   ir wâret mir beide ie bereit
              ze dieneste als ich iuch gebat:
              mir waere ûf den triuwen mat,
              solde ich gein iu kriegen
              un mîn selber zuht betriegen.   1   .   1

278, 12-18   über eines brunnen ursprinc
              stuont ir poulûn ûf dem plân,
              als ez obene ein trache in sînen klân
              hete sganzen aphels halben teil. '
              den trachen zugen vier wintseil,
              rehte als er lebendec dâ vlüge
              undz poulûn gein den lüften züge.   .   2   2

279, 3-5   Keie durch daz sîn dienest liez:
              unsaelde in svürsten swester hiez
              ze sêre âlûnen mit einem stabe.   1   .   1

. . . .

Totals: 180 lines of text   2   2   4

	M	O	T
Book Five Totals: 1680 lines of text	46	43	89

BOOK VI

Arthur Seeking the Red Knight 280, 1 - 281, 9   M   O   T

281, 2-5	welt ir danne vür ein ander schehen alsô vreche rüden, den meisters hant abe stroufet ir bant, dar zuo trage ich niht willen.	.	1	1
....	....	....		
Totals:	39 lines of text	0	1	1

Parzival Entranced by the Drops of Blood 281, 10 - 305, 6   M   O   T

(A)	Source of the Trance 281, 10 - 283, 23			
281, 14-22	ez enwas iedoch niht snêwes zît, ist ez als ichz vernomen hân. Artûs der meienbaere man, swaz man ie von dem gesprach, zeinen phingesten daz geschach oder in des meien bluomenzît. waz man im süezes luftes gît! diz maere ist hie vaste undersniten: ez parrieret sich mit snêwes siten.	1	.	1
282, 20-22	ûz ir wunden ûf den snê vielen drî bluotes zeher rôt, die Parzivâle vuocten nôt.	1	.	1
282, 24-27	dô er die bluotes zeher sach ûf dem snê (der was al wîz), ' dô dâhte er: 'wer hât sînen vlîz gewant an dise varwe klâr?	1	.	1
283, 20-23	dirre varwe truoc gelîchen lîp von Pelrapeire diu künegin. diu zucte im wizzenlîchen sin: sus hielt er als er sliefe.	.	1	1
(B)	Discovery by Cunneware's Page 283, 24 - 284, 29			
284, 20-22	alsus rief der garzûn: 'tavelrunder ist geschant: iust durch die snüere alhie gerant.'	1	.	1

(C)	Segramors Begs Consent to Fight 284, 30 - 286, 23	M	O	T
285, 6-10	ninder ist sô breit der Rîn, saehe er strîten an dem andern stade, dâ würde wênec nâch dem bade getast: ez waere warm oder kalt, ' er viele sus dran, der degen balt.	1	1	2
(D)	Segramors Fights Parzival 286, 24 - 290, 2			
286, 30 - 287, 3	man möhte in wol geworfen hân zem vasân inz dornach: swem sîn ze suochen waere gâch, der vünde in bî den schellen.	.	1	1
287, 5-6	sus vuor der unbescheiden helt zuo dem der minne was verselt.	1	.	1
288, 13-14	dô er der zeher niht mêr sach, vrou Witze im aber sinnes jach.	1	.	1
288, 27-30	Parzivâl reit âne vrâgen dâ diu bluotes zeher lagen. dâ er die mit den ougen vant, vrou Minne in stricte an ir bant:	2	.	2
289, 16-17	der minne er muoste ir siges jehen, diu Salomônen ouch betwanc.	.	1	1
289, 20-26	swer in hazte oder der in wol emphienc, den was er al gelîche holt: sus teilde er bâgens grôzen solt. ' er sprach: 'ir habet des vreischet vil, ritterschaft ist topelspil ' und daz ein man von tjoste viel. ez sinket halt ein mers kiel.	2	1	3
(E)	Keie Fights Parzival 290, 3-30; 293, 19 - 294, 20; 295, 1 - 296, 12			
290, 18	ûf unsern prîs sîn ellen zert	1	.	1
290, 24-25	dô wolde er swenden den walt mit tjost ûf disen komenden gast	1	.	1
290, 28-30	ez ist sünde, swer im mêr nû tuot: ouch hats diu minne kranken prîs. diu stiez ûf in ir krefte rîs.	1	.	1

		M	O	T

293, 24-27	swâ twingende vrouwen sint, die suln im heiles wünschen nuo, wande in brâhte ein wîp dar zuo, daz minne witze von im spielt.	1	.	1
294, 2-5	welt ir mir volgen, sôst mîn rât und dunket mich iuwer bestez heil, nemt iuch selben an ein brackenseil und lât iuch vür in ziehen.	1	.	1
294, 10-20	... Keie sînen schaft ûf zôch und vrumte im einen swanc ans houbet, daz der helm erklanc. dô sprach er: 'dû muost wachen. âne lînlachen wirt dir dîn slâfen hie benant. ' ez zilt al anders hie mîn hant: ûf den snê dû wirst geleget. der den sac von der mül treget, wolde man in sô bliuwen, in möhte lazheit riuwen.'	.	2	2
295, 1-7	Keie hurte vaste an in und dranc imz ors alumbe hin, unz daz der Wâleis übersach sîn süeze sûrez ungemach, ' sîns wîbes gelîchen schîn, von Pelrapeire der künegîn, ich meine den geparrierten snê.	2	.	2
295, 13-15	Keie sîne tjoste brâhte als im der ougen mez gedâhte, durch Parzivâles schilt ein venster wît.	1	.	1
296, 1-4	Parzivâl der valscheitswant, ' sin triuwe in lêrte daz er vant snêwec bluotes zeher drî, die in vor witzen machten vrî.	2	.	2
296, 5-8	sin pensiuren umbe den grâl und der künegîn gelîchiu mâl, iewederz was ein strengiu nôt. an im wac vür der minnen lôt,	1	.	1
(F)	Wolfram's Complaint to Vrou Minne 291, 1 - 293, 18; 294, 21-30			

		<u>M</u>	<u>O</u>	<u>T</u>
291, 15-18	vrou Minne, ir habet ein êre und wênec deheine mêre: vrou Liebe iu gît geselleschaft, anders waere vil <u>dürkel</u> iuwer kraft.	1	.	1
292, 1-4	vrou Minne, sît ir habet gewalt, daz ir die jugent sus machet alt, der man doch zelt vil kurziu jâr, iuwer werc sint <u>hâlscharlîcher vâr</u>.	1	.	1
292, 9-11	ir habet mir mangel vor gezilt und <u>mîner ougen ecke alsô verspilt</u>, daz ich iu niht getrûwen mac.	1	.	1
292, 16-17	iuwer druc hât sô strengen <u>ort</u>, ' ir ladet ûf herze swaeren <u>soum</u>.	2	.	2
292, 18-25	her Heinrîch von Veldeke sînen boum mit kunst gein iuwerm arte maz: ' hete er uns dô bescheiden baz wie man iuch sül behalden! er hat her dan <u>gespalden</u> wie man iuch sol erwerben. ' von tumpheit muoz verderben maneges tôren <u>hôher vunt</u>.	2	1	3
292, 28	ir sît <u>slôz</u> ob dem sinne.	1	.	1
293, 12-15	Kardeiz fîz Tampenteire, ir bruoder, nâmet ir ouch sîn leben. sol man iu solhe <u>zinse</u> geben, wol mich daz ich von iu niht hân	1	.	1
294, 21-24	vrou Minne, hie seht ir zuo: ich waene manz iu ze laster tuo, wan ein gebûr spraeche san: 'mînem herren sî diz getan. '	.	1	1
(G)	Wolfram in Defense of Keie 296, 13 - 297, 29			
297, 8-12	ze scherme dem herren sîn partierre unde valsche diet, von den werden er die schiet: er was ir vuore ein strenger <u>hagel</u>, ' noch scherpher dan der bîen ir zagel,	1	1	2
297, 16-18	von Düringen vürste Herman, etslîch dîn ingesinde ich maz,			

		M	O	T
	daz ûzgesinde hieze baz	.	1	1

(H)   Gawan Fetches Parzival 297, 30 - 305, 6

298, 12-14	Keie der zornes rîche sprach: 'herre, erbarmet iuch mîn lîp? sus solden klagen aldiu wîp.	.	1	1
298, 25-27	ir sît mir râche ze wol geborn: hetet aber ir einen vinger dort verlorn, dâ wâcte ich gegen mîn houbet.	.	1	1
299, 3-6	ouch enist hie minder <u>vrouwen hâr</u> weder sô mürwe noch sô klâr, ez enwaere doch ein veste bant ze wern strîtes iuwer hant.	1	.	1
299, 7-12	swelh man tuot solhe diemuot schîn, der êret ouch diu muoter sîn: vaterhalben solde er ellen hân. kêrt muoterhalp, her Gâwân, sô werdet ir swertes blicke bleich und manlîcher herte weich.	.	1	1
299, 13-15	sus was der wol gelobete man <u>gerant zer blôzen sîten an</u> mit rede: er kunde ir gelden niht	1	.	1
300, 1-2	er kêrte ûz dâ er den Wâleis vant. des witze was der minnen <u>phant</u>	1	.	1
301, 5-6	des künec Gahmuretes kint, dreun und vlêhen was im <u>ein wint</u>.	1	.	1
302, 1-5	dô diu veile wart der <u>zeher</u> dach, ' sô daz ir Parzivâl niht sach, <u>im gap her wider witze sîn</u> von Pelrapeire diu künegîn: ' diu <u>behielt iedoch sîn herze dort</u>.	3	.	3
302, 14-15	... <u>ougen nebel</u> hât dich bî liehter sunnen hier mir benomen, jâ enweiz ich wie.	1	.	1
303, 20-24	sîne swester hete der künec Lôt, diu mich <u>zer werlde brâhte</u>. ' swes got an mir gedâhte, ' daz biutet dienest <u>sîner hant</u>.			

		M	O	T
	der künec Artus ist er genant.	2	1	3
304, 16-18	ein werdiu maget mir lachen bôt, die blou der seneschalt durch mich, daz von ir reis der walt.	1	.	1
. . . .	. . . .	. . . .		
Totals:	717 lines of text	43	15	58
Subtotals:	(A) Source of the Trance (74 lines)	3	1	4
	(B) Discovery by the Page (36 lines)	1	0	1
	(C) Segramors Begs to Fight (54 lines)	1	1	2
	(D) Segramors Fights (99 lines)	6	3	9
	(E) Keie Fights (102 lines)	11	2	13
	(F) Complaint to Vrou Minne (88 lines)	9	2	11
	(G) In Defense of Keie (47 lines)	1	2	3
	(H) Gawan Fetches Parzival (217 lines)	11	4	15

Parzival Received by Arthur's Court 305, 7 - 312, 1

		M	O	T
305, 21-23	sus sach si komen Parzivâl. der was gevar durch îsers mâl als touwege rôsen waeren dar gevlogen.	.	1	1
305, 30 - 306, 3	ich hete lachen gar vermiten, unz iuch mîn herze erkande, dô mich an vreuden phande Keie, der mich dô sô sluoc.	1	.	1
306, 26-27	swer in sach, der jach vür wâr, er waere geblüemet vür alle man.	1	.	1
307, 27-29	Keie hât verphendet.' sîn dreun ist nû gelendet. ich vürhte wênec sînen swanc	2	.	2
308, 1-3	dô truoc der junge Parzivâl âne vlügel engels mâl, ' sus geblüet ûf der erden.	1	1	2
311, 10-12	an disem ringe niemen saz, der muoter brust ie gesouc, des werdekeit sô lützel trouc	.	1	1
311, 16-17	sô hât sich manec vrouwe ersehen in trüeber glase dan waere sîn munt.	.	1	1
311, 19-25	an dem kinne und an den wangen sîn varwe zeiner zangen			

		M	O	T
	waere guot: si möhte staete haben, '			
	diu den zwîvel wol hin dan kan schaben.			
	ich meine wîp die wenkent			
	und ir vriuntschaft überdenkent.			
	sîn glast was wîbes staete ein <u>bant</u>:	2	.	2
....	....	....		
Totals:	205 lines of text	7	4	11

<u>Cundrie</u> 312, 2 - 319, 19

(A)	Her Arrival 312, 2 - 314, 10			
312, 7-10	einen mûl hôch als ein kastelân, '			
	val und dennoch sus getân,			
	nassnitec und verbrant,			
	als ungerschiu marc erkant.	.	2	2
312, 28-30	<u>in dem munde niht diu lame</u>			
	(wan der geredete ir genuoc),			
	vil hôher vreude si <u>nider sluoc</u>.	2	.	2
313, 4-6	ein brûtlachen von Gent,			
	noch blâwer denne ein lasûr, '			
	hete an geleget <u>der vreuden schûr</u>.	1	1	2
313, 14-15	ir maere was ein <u>brücke</u>:			
	über vreude ez jâmer truoc.	1	.	1
313, 17-20	über den huot ein zoph ir swanc			
	unz ûf den mûl: der was sô lanc,			
	swarz, herte und niht ze klâr,			
	linde als eins swînes rückehâr.	.	1	1
313, 21-23	si was genaset als ein hunt, '			
	zwêne ebers zene ir vür den munt			
	giengen wol spannen lanc	.	2	2
313, 29	Cundrîe truoc ôren als ein ber:	.	1	1
314, 5-6	gevar als eines affen hût			
	truoc hende diz gaebe trût.	.	1	1
314, 7-9	die nagele wâren niht ze lieht,			
	wan mir diu âventiure giht,			
	si stüenden als eins lewen klân.	.	1	1
(B)	The Denunciation 314, 11 - 318, 10			

		M	O	T
314, 26-30	die besten über elliu lant saezen hie mit werdekeit, wan daz ein galle ir prîs versneit: tavelrunder ist entnihtet, der valsch hât dran gephlihtet.	1	.	1
315, 3-6	dîn stîgender prîs nû sinket, ' dîn snelliu wirde hinket, ' dîn hôhez lop sich neiget, ' dîn prîs hât valsch erzeiget.	3	.	3
315, 7-9	tavelrunder prîses kraft hât erlemt ein geselleschaft, die drüber gap her Parzivâl.	1	.	1
316, 4-6	daz iu der munt noch werde wan, ich meine der zungen drinne, als iuz herze ist rehter sinne!	.	1	1
316, 7-8	gein der helle ir sît benant ze himele vor der hoesten hant:	1	.	1
316, 11-15	ir heiles ban, ' ir saelden vluoch, ' des ganzen prîses reht unruoch, ir sît manlîcher êren schiech und an der werdekeit sô siech, nehein arzet mac iuch des ernern.	3	.	3
316, 20	ir vederangel, ' ir nâtern zan	2	.	2
316, 24	ir sît der hellehirten' spil	2	.	2
316, 28	ir vreuden letze, ' ir trûrens wer	2	.	2
317, 26-27	grôz herze und kleine gallen, dar obe was sîn brust ein dach.	1	.	1
317, 28-30	er was riuse ' und vengec vach:' sîn manlîchez ellen kunde den prîs wol gestellen.	3	.	3
318, 5-6	Cundrîe was selbe sorgens phant	1	.	1
(C)	Her Plea for the Captive Queens 318, 11-30			
318, 20-21	al âventiure ist ein wint, wan die man da bezaln mac	1	.	1
(D)	Court's Grief for Parzival 319, 1-19			

		M	O	T
319, 6-10	und dennoch mêr im was bereit schame ob allen sînen siten: den rehten valsch hete er vermiten, wan schame gît prîs ze lône und ist doch der sêle krône.	1	.	1
319, 16-17	herzen jâmer ougen saf gap maneger werden vrouwen	1	.	1
319, 19	Cundrîe was ir trûrens wer	1	.	1
....	....	....		
Totals:	228 lines of text	28	10	38
Subtotals:	(A) Cundrie's Arrival (69 lines)	4	9	13
	(B) The Denunciation (120 lines)	20	1	21
	(C) Plea for the Captives (20 lines)	1	0	1
	(D) Court's Grief for Parzival (19 lines)	3	0	3

Kingrimursel Challenges Gawan 319, 20 - 326, 14		M	O	T
320, 1-4	sîn muot stuont hôch, doch jâmers vol. die beide schanze ich nennen sol: hôchvart riet sîn manheit, jâmer lêrte in herzenleit.	1	.	1
320, 11-12	der vreuden ellende truoc daz swert in sîner hende	1	.	1
321, 2-4	ach ich arm man und ouwî, daz er mîn herze iu sus versneit! ' mîn jâmer ist von im ze breit.	2	.	2
321, 8-12	unprîs sîn hete aldâ gewalt, dô in sîn gir dar zuo vertruoc, im gruoze er minen herren sluoc. ein kus, den jûdas teilde, ' im solhen willen veilde	1	1	2
326, 5-8	Artûses her was an dem tage komen vreude unde klage: ein solh geparriertez leben was den helden dâ gegeben.	1	.	1
....	....	....		
Totals:	205 lines	6	1	7

		M	O	T
Reactions to Cundrie's News 326, 15 - 334, 30				
(A)	Betrothal of Clamide and Cunneware 326, 15 327, 30	.	.	.
(B)	News of Feirefiz 328, 1-30			
328, 16-17	erst aller mannes varwe ein gast: wîz und swarz ist er erkant.	1	.	1
328, 27-29	sô milder lîp gesouc nie brust, ' sîn site ist valscheite vlust, Feirefîz Anschevîn	1	1	2
(C)	Attempts to Comfort Parzival 329, 1 - 330, 30			
329, 4-9	nû liget diu hoeste stiure an iu, des al getouftiu diet mit prîse sich von laster schiet, sol guot gebaerde iuch helfen iht, und daz man iu wit wârheit giht liehter varwe und manlîcher site.	1	.	1
330, 17-24	ir gâbet mir alle geselleschaft, die wîle ich stuont in prîses kraft: der sît nû ledec, unz ich bezal dâ von mîn grüeniu vreude ist val. ' mîn sol grôz jâmer alsô phlegen, daz herze gebe den ougen regen, sît ich ûf Munsalvaesche liez daz mich von wâren vreuden stiez	2	.	2
(D)	Parzival Leaves to Seek Grail 331, 1 - 333, 30			
332, 17-18	ir scheiden gap in trûren ze strengen nâchgebûren.	1	.	1
332, 29-30	swenne ir sît trûrens niht erwert, iuwer sorge mîne vreude zert.	1	.	1
(E)	Knights to Seek Schastel Marveile 334, 1-30	.	.	.
. . . .	. . . .	. . . .		
Totals:	256 lines of text	7	1	8
Subtotals:	(A) Betrothal, Clamide, Cunneware (46 lines)	0	0	0
	(B) News of Feirefiz (30 lines)	2	1	3
	(C) Attempts to Comfort Parzival	3	0	3

	M	O	T
(D) Parzival Leaves for Grail (90 lines)	2	0	2
(E) Knights off to Schastel Marveile (30 lines)	0	0	0

Departures of Gawan, Clamide, Cunneware, Orilus, and Jeschute   M   O   T
335, 1 - 336, 30

335, 8-9	der werdekeit ein <u>weise</u> wart nû diu tavelrunder.	1	.	1
. . . .	. . . .	. . . .		

Epilog to Books I - VI: Wolfram's Kind Feelings Toward Women   M   O   T
337, 1-30

337, 11-12	sît gap vroun Herzeloiden troum siufzebaeren <u>herzeroum</u>.	1	.	1
337, 19-20	wie wart vrou Cunnewâre <u>gâlûnet</u> mit ir hâre!	1	.	1
337, 23-30	ze machen neme diz maere ein man, der âventiure prüeven kan und rîme künne sprechen, beidiu samenen und zebrechen. ich taetez iu gerne vürbaz kunt, woldez gebieten mir ein munt, den doch ander vüeze tragent dan die mir ze stegereifen wagent.	.	1	1
. . . .	. . . .	. . . .		
Totals:	30 lines of text	2	1	3

Book Six Totals: 1740 lines of text   94   33   127

BOOK VII

Introduction to the Gawan Episodes 338, 1-30   M   O   T

338, 11-21	nû waere der liute volge guot, swer dicke lop mit wârheit tuot: wan, swaz er sprichet oder sprach, diu rede <u>belîbet âne dach</u>. ' wer sol sinnes wort behalden, es enwellen die wîsen walden? valsch lügelîch ein maere, daz, waene ich, baz noch waere âne wirt ûf einem snê,			

		M	O	T
	sô daz dem munde würde wê, derz ûz vür wârheit breitet:	1	1	2
338, 29-30	er mîdetz ê, han er sich schemen: den site sol er ze vogete nemen.	1	.	1
. . . .	. . . .	. . . .		
Totals:	30 lines of text	2	1	3

The Great, Unknown Army 339, 1 - 342, 8

		M	O	T
339, 5-7	sîn herze was ze velde ein burc, gein scharphen striten wol sô kurc, in strîtes gedrenge man in sach.	1	.	1
340, 14-15	dô erbeizte er zuo der erden, rehte als er habete einen stal.	.	1	1
341, 20-22	etslîchiu den zwelften gürtel truoc ze phande nâch ir minne. ez wâren niht küneginne.	.	1	1
341, 28-30	etslîcher zaeme baz an der wide, den er daz her dâ mêrte und werdez volc unêrte.	1	.	1
. . . .	. . . .	. . . .		
Totals:	98 lines of text	2	2	4

The Squire's Explanation 342, 9 - 349, 27

		M	O	T
(A)	Identifying the Army 342, 9 - 344, 10			
343, 23-26	dâ vert ein unbescheiden lîp, dem minne nie gebôt dehein wîp: er treget der unvuoge kranz unde heizet Meljacanz.	1	.	1
344, 5-7	waz hilft sîn manlîcher site? ein swînmuoter, liefe ir mite ir verheln, diu werte ouch sie.	.	1	1
(B)	The Quarrel of Meljanz and Obie 344, 11 - 348, 14			
344, 24-26	unerloeset phandes stuont sîn ellenthaftez leben: daz muoste sich dem tôde ergeben.	1	.	1
345, 5-7	den bat er ziehen sînen sun.			

		M	O	T
	er sprach: 'dû maht an im nû tuon dîner triuwe hantveste!	1	.	1
346, 15-17	ir sît mir liep (wer lougent des?) als Annôren Gâlôes, diu sît den tôt durch in erkôs	.	1	1
347, 14	hie belîbet vil der sper enzwei.	.	1	1
347, 19-24	gein dirre ungeschihte bôt sîn gerihte und anders wandels genuoc Lippaôt, der unschulde truoc. ez waere krump oder sleht, er gerte sîner genôze reht,	1	.	1
347, 28-30	genaedeclîcher hulde er vaste sînen herren bat. dem tet der zorn ûf vreuden mat.	1	.	1
(C)	Concluding Details on the Army 348, 15 - 349, 27			
349, 7-10	Bêârosche ist sô ze wer, ob wir heten zweinzec her, ieslîchez groezer dan wir hân, wir müesten si unzevüeret lân.	.	1	1
. . . .	. . . .	. . . .		
Totals:	229 lines of text	5	4	9
Subtotals:	(A) Identifying the Army (62 lines) (B) Quarrel of Meljanz and Obie (124 lines) (C) Concluding Details of Army	1 4 0	1 2 1	2 6 1

Gawan to Bearosche: Disputed by Obie and Obilot 349, 28 - 354, 3		M	O	T
350, 3	sôst al mîn prîs verloschen gar.	1	.	1
350, 10-12	sîn nôt sich in ein ander klamph: gein sîner kamphes verte was ze belîben alze herte.	1	.	1
350, 19-21	ouch gleste gein im schône aller ander bürge ein krône mit türnen wol gezieret.	1	.	1
350, 30 - 351, 1	der zwîvel was sins herzen hovel, dâ durch in starkiu angest sneit.	1	.	1

		M	O	T
353, 7	ob im saz wîbe hers ein vluot.	1	.	1
. . . .	. . . .	. . . .		
Totals:	126 lines of text	5	0	5

Battle Preparations 354, 4 - 356, 25		M	O	T
356, 13-15	wir solden wol gedingen dort in ir snüeren ringen, wan Poidiconjunzes kraft:	.	1	1
356, 21-23	dâst ouch sîn sun Meljacanz. hete den erzogen Gurnemanz, sô waere sîn prîs gehoehet gar	.	1	1
. . . .	. . . .	. . . .		
Totals:	82 lines of text	0	2	2

The Vesperie 356, 26 - 260, 5		M	O	T
357, 12-14	die ûz dem her dar komen sint, die begunden dâ vil werde tât: die burgaere phanden si ûf der sât.	1	.	1
358, 9-14	ich gibe im noch gein ellen trôst, daz er dîns spottes wirt erlôst. er sol dienest gein mir kêren und ich wil im vreude mêren. sît dû gihs er sî ein koufman, er sol mins lônes market hân.	1	.	1
359, 16-19	'herre, iuwer neve was dâ vor, der künec, und al sîn her von Lîz: solde iuwer her an slâfes vlîz die wîle sich hân gekêret?'	1	.	1
. . . .	. . . .	. . . .		
Totals:	100 lines of text	3	0	3

Gawan's Involvement 360, 6 - 372, 12		M	O	T
(A)	Obie's Hostility 360, 6 - 361, 18; 362, 20 - 363, 19			
360, 25-28	er sprach: 'vart hin, ir ribalt! mûlslege al ungezalt sult ir hie vil emphâhen, welt ir mir vürbaz nâhen.'	1	.	1

		<u>M</u>	<u>O</u>	<u>T</u>
(B)	Scherules' Courtesy 361, 19 - 362, 19; 363, 20 - 364, 30			
361, 20-21	der selten ellens ie vergaz, an dem er vant <u>krancheite vlust</u>	1	.	1
362, 9-12	Scherules der lobes gehêrte sprach als in sîn triuwe lêrte: 'sît ez sich hât an mich gezoget, ich bin vor vlust nû iuwer <u>voget</u>,	1	.	1
363, 26-29	er engewan nie münzîsen, ' welt ir der rehten maere losen. sîn lîp getruoc nie wehselphosen. ' seht sîne gebaere und hoeret sîniu wort	.	2	2
364, 4-9	swer im dar über tuot gewalt, waerez mîn vater oder mîn kint, alle die gein im in zorne sint, mîne mâge oder mîn bruoder, die müesten diu strîtes <u>ruoder</u> <u>gein mir ziehen</u>: ich wil in wern	1	.	1
364, 12-17	ûz schiltes ammet in einen sac wolde ich mich ê ziehen, ' sô verre ûz arte vliehen dâ mich niemen erkande, ê daz ir iuwer schande, herre, an im begienget.	.	2	2
(C)	Wolfram's Discourse on Obie and Love 365, 1 - 366, 2			
365, 4-7	daz herze ist rehter minne <u>ein phant</u>, alsô versetzet und verselt, dehein munt ez nimmer gar volzelt, waz minne wunders vüegen kan.	1	.	1
365, 20-23	si kom dicke ûz vrouwenlîchen siten: sus <u>vlaht ir kiusche sich in zorn</u>. ' ez was ir beider ougen <u>dorn</u>, swâ si den werden man gesach:	2	.	2
(D)	Lippaot Asks Gawan's Help 366,3 - 368, 9			
366, 26-28	nû muoz ichz durch daz mîden, herre, unz ein mîn kamph ergêt, dâ mîn triuwe sô hôhe <u>phandes stêt</u>	1	.	1

		M	O	T
367, 24-28	swer sol mit sîner tohter weln, swie ir verboten sî daz swert, ir wer ist anders alsô wert: si erwirbet im kiuscheclîche einen sun vil ellens rîche	1	.	1
(E)	Obilot Wins Gawan's Help 368, 10 - 372, 12			
369, 9-10	wan mir mîn meisterîn verjach, diu rede waere des sinnes dach.	1	.	1
369, 12-20	daz lêrt mich endehafter pîn. den nenne ich iu, geruochet irs: habet ir mich ihtes deste wirs, ich var doch ûf der mâze phat, ' wande ich dâ ziu mîn selber bat. ir sît mit der wârheit ich. swie die namen teilen sich, mîns lîbes namen sult ir hân: nû sît maget unde man.	2	.	2
370, 18-21	nû dâhte er des, wie Parzival wîben baz getrûte dan gote: sîn bevelhen was dirre megede ein bote Gâwân in daz herze sîn.	1	.	1
370, 24-30	er begunde ir vürbaz mêre sagen: 'in iuwer hende sî mîn swert. ob iemen tjoste gein mir gert, den poinder müezt ir rîten, ir sult dâ vür mich strîten. man mac mich dâ in strîte sehen: der muoz mînhalp von iu geschehen.'	1	.	1
371, 2-3	ich bin iuwer scherm und iuwer schilt ' und iuwer herze ' und iuwer trôst.	2	.	2
371, 5-8	ich bin vür ungevelle iuwer geleite und iuwer geselle, ' vür ungelückes schûr ' ein dach ' bin ich iu senfteclîch gemach.	4	.	4
371, 13-14	ich bin wirt und wirtîn und wil in strîte bî iu sîn.	1	.	1
372, 5-8	dô sprach er: 'sult ir werden alt, trüege dan niht wan sper der walt			

		M	O	T
als erz am andern holze hât,'				
daz würde iu zwein ein ringiu sât.'		1	1	2
....	....	....		
Totals:	367 lines of text	21	5	26

Subtotals:		M	O	T
	(A) Obie's Hostility (73 lines)	1	0	1
	(B) Scherule's Courtesy (72 lines)	3	4	7
	(C) Discourse on Obie and Love (32 lines)	3	0	3
	(D) Lippaôt Asks for Help (67 lines)	1	0	1
	(E) Obilôt Wins Gawan's Help	13	1	14

Obilôt's Token for Gawan 372, 13 - 375, 30

		M	O	T
373, 3-4	ô wol der vruht diu an dir lac!			
	dîn geburt was der saelden tac.	1	.	1
374, 24	sîn blic ist rehte ein meien glast.	1	.	1
....	....	....		
Totals:	108 lines of text	2	0	2

Battle Preparations During the Night 376, 1 - 378, 4

		M	O	T
376, 4-5	waere sûzern hers niht solhiu vluot,			
	sô heten die innern strîtes vil.	1	.	1
377, 30 -	ein Regenspurger zindâl			
378, 4	dâ waere ze swachem werde:			
	vor Bêârosche ûf der erde			
	man sach dâ wâpenröcke vil			
	hôher an der koste zil.	.	1	1
....	....	....		
Totals:	64 lines of text	1	1	2

The Battle at Bearosche 378, 5 - 387, 30

		M	O	T
(A)	General Survey 378, 5 - 379, 30			
378, 5-9	diu naht tet nâch ir alden site,			
	an dem orte ein tac ir zogete mite: '			
	den kôs man niht bî lerchen sanc.	1	1	2
378, 10-11	man hôrte diu sper dâ krachen			
	rehte als ez waere ein wolken rîz.	.	1	1
378, 15-17	dâ erhal manec rîchiu tjoste guot,			
	als der würfe in grôze gluot			

		M	O	T
	ganze kastâne.	.	1	1
379, 4-8	wan Poidiconjunz was hêr: der reit dar zuo mit solher kraft, waere Swarzwalt ieslîch stûde ein schaft, man dorfte dâ niht mêr waldes sehen, swer sîne schar wolde spehen.	.	1	1
379, 11-12	pusûner gâben dôzes klac, alsô der doner der ie phlac vil angestlîcher vorhte.	.	1	1
379, 16-20	wart inder dâ kein stuphenhalm getretet, des enmohte ich niht: Erffurter wîngarte giht von tretene noch der selben nôt. manec orses vuoz die slâge bôt.	.	1	1
379, 23	dâ wurden tjoste <u>gewetzet</u>.	1	.	1
(B)	Gawan 380, 1 - 383, 22			
380, 1-3	dô ersach mîn her Gâwân daz <u>gevlohten</u> was der plân, die vriunt in der vînde schar	1	.	1
383, 12	dô <u>liefen über</u> diu ougen sîn.	1	.	1
(C)	The Red Knight 383, 23 - 384, 14			
384, 7-13	sîn tjoste wâren mit hurte hel, wande er den künec Schirniel und sînen bruoder dâ vienc. dennoch dâ mêr von im gergienc: sicherheit er niht erliez den herzogen Marangliez. die wâren des ortes herte.	1	.	1
(D)	Gawan Captures Meljanz 384, 15 - 385, 30			
385, 16-19	dâ waere zwein gebûren gedroschen mêr dan genuoc: ieweder des andern garbe truoc, stückeht die wurden hin geslagen.	.	1	1
(E)	Lippaôt 386, 1-21	.	.	.

		M	O	T
(F)	Gawan Unhorses Meljacanz 386, 22 - 387, 30			
386, 30 - 387, 5	dô kom ouch mîn her Gâwân: des kom Meljacanz in nôt, daz im der werde Lanzelôt nie sô vaste zuo getrat, dô er von der swertbrücke phat kom und dâ nâch mit im streit.	.	1	1
387, 21-26	Meljacanz wart getret, durch sîn kursît gewet manec ors daz sît nie gruose enbeiz:' ez reis ûf in der bluotec sweiz. dâ ergienc der orse schelmetac, dar nâch den gîren ir bejac.	1	1	2
. . . .	. . . .	. . . .		
Totals:	296 lines of text	6	9	15
Subtotals:	(A) General Survey (56 lines)	2	6	8
	(B) Gawan (112 lines)	2	0	2
	(C) Red Knight (22 lines)	1	0	1
	(D) Gawan Captures Meljanz (46 lines)	0	1	1
	(E) Lippaot (21 lines)	0	0	0
	(F) Gawan Unhorses Meljacanz (39 lines)	1	2	3
The Red Knight's Dispensations 388, 1 - 390, 11		M	O	T
389, 29-30	dâ holtez des rôten ritters hant: des wart verdürkelt etslîch rant.	1	.	1
. . . .	. . . .	. . . .		
Totals:	71 lines of text	1	0	1
The Conflict at Bearosche Resolved 390, 12 - 397, 30		M	O	T
394, 12-13	der sprach: 'Obilôt wirt kranz aller wîplîchen güete.'	1	.	1
395, 22-23	er dructe daz kint wol gevar als eine tocken an sîne brust:	.	1	1
395, 28-30	aller mîner vreuden wer sitzet an dem arme mîn: ir gevangen sult ir sîn.	1	.	1
397, 30	Gâwân gein kummer was verselt.	1	.	1
. . . .	. . . .	. . . .		

		$\underline{M}$	$\underline{O}$	$\underline{T}$
Totals:	229 lines of text	3	1	4

Book Seven Totals: 1800 lines of text   51   25   76

BOOK VIII

Gawan Arrives at Schanpfanzun 398, 1 - 399, 24 $\underline{M}$ $\underline{O}$ $\underline{T}$

		M	O	T
398, 1-6	Swer was ze Bêârosche komen, doch hete Gâwân dâ genomen den prîs ze beider sît al ein, wan daz dâ vor ein ritter schein, bî rôtem wâpen unerkant, des prîs man in die hoehe bant.	1	.	1
398, 18-21	nû wart der walt gemenget, hie ein schache, dort ein velt, etslîchez sô breit daz ein gezelt vil kûme drûfe stüende.	.	1	1
399, 11-14	disiu burc was gehêret sô, daz Ênêas Kartâgô nie sô herrenlîche vant, ' dâ vroun Dîdôn tôt was minnen phant.	1	1	2
399, 15-19	waz si palase phlaege und wie vil dâ türne laege? ir hete Acratôn genuoc, diu âne Babilône ie truoc an dem griffe die groesten wîte	.	1	1

....

Totals:	54 lines of text	2	3	5

Vergulaht Hunting; His Invitation 399, 25 - 404, 16 $\underline{M}$ $\underline{O}$ $\underline{T}$

		M	O	T
400, 4-6	ein râvît von Spâne hôch reit der künec Vergulaht. sîn blic was tac wol bî der naht:	1	.	1
400, 10-12	in dûhte er saehe den meien in rehter zît von bluomen gar, swer nam des küneges varwe war.	.	1	1
400, 13-15	Gâwânen des bedûhte, dô der künec sô gein im lûhte, ' ez waere der ander Parzivâl,	1	1	2

		M	O	T
401, 6-19	âvoi nû wart dâ niht vermiten,			
	er enwürde baz emphangen			
	dan ze Karidôl waere ergangen			
	Ereckes emphâhen,			
	dô er begunde nâhen			
	Artûs nâch sînem strîte			
	und dô vrou Ênite			
	sîner vreude was ein kondewier...	.	1	1
403, 29 -	sô daz ir site und ir sin			
404, 2	was gelîch der marcgrâvin,			
	diu dicke von dem Heitstein			
	über al die marke schein.	.	1	1
404, 13-15	ich enruoche um die ungetriuwen.			
	mit dürkelen triuwen			
	hânt si alle ir saelekeit verlorn:	1	.	1
....	....	.....	....	....
Totals:	142 lines of text	3	4	7

Gawan with Antikonie 404, 17 - 413, 30

		M	O	T
(A)	The Attempted Seduction 404, 17 - 407, 9			
404, 24-25	sol wîplîch êre sîn gewin,			
	des koufes hete si vil gephlegen	1	.	1
405, 5-7	si enspraeche: 'herre, gêt nâher mir.			
	mîner zühte meister daz sît ir:			
	nû gebietet unde lêret.	1	.	1
406, 3-8	ich erbiutez iu durch mins bruoder bete,			
	daz ez Amplîse Gahmurete			
	mînem oeheim nie baz erbôt, '			
	âne bî ligen (mîn triuwe ein lôt			
	an dem orte vürbaz waege,			
	der uns wegens ze rehte phlaege)	1	1	2
406, 28 -	Gâwân des gedâhte,			
407, 1	dô si alle von im kômen ûz,			
	daz dicke den grôzen strûz			
	vaehet ein vil kranker ar.	.	1	1
(B)	Under Attack 407, 10 - 411, 3			
408, 14-15	sîn arge nâchgebûre			
	entwichen im dicke mit ir schar.	1	.	1

		<u>M</u>	<u>O</u>	<u>T</u>
409, 5-9	diu küneginne rîche streit dâ ritterlîche: bî Gâwâne si werltche schein, daz diu koufwîp ze Tolenstein an der vasnaht nie baz gestriten	.	1	1
409, 25-29	baz geschicket an spizze hasen, ich waene den gesâht ir nie, dan si was dort unde hie, zwischen der hüffe und ir brust.	.	1	1
410, 2-4	ir engesâht nie âmeizen, diu bezzers gelenkes phlac, dan si was dâ der gürtel lac.	.	1	1
410, 8-9	sîn benandez <u>gîsel</u> was der tôt und anders dehein gedinge.	1	.	1
410, 29-30	Gâwân muoste bîten unz der künec gewâpent wart: <u>er huop sich selbe an strîtes vart.</u>	1	.	1
(C)	Rescue by Kingrimursel 411, 4 - 412, 2			
(D)	Vergulaht Persuaded to Truce 412, 3 - 413, 30			
412, 18-20	werltlîch prîs iu sînen haz teilt, erslahet ir iuwern gast: ir ladet ûf iuch <u>der schanden last.</u>	1	.	1
413, 14-16	ez hete ein ander man getân, wande der stolze Ehkunat eine lanzen durch in <u>lêrte phat.</u>	1	.	1
. . . .	. . . .	. . . .		
Totals:	284 lines of text	8	5	13
Subtotals:	(A) The Attempted Seduction (83 lines)	3	2	5
	(B) Under Attack (114 lines)	3	3	6
	(C) Rescue by Kingrimursel (29 lines)	.	.	.
	(D) Vergulaht Persuaded to Truce (57 lines)	2	0	2

<u>Arguments About the Right and Wrong</u> 414, 1 - 418, 25		<u>M</u>	<u>O</u>	<u>T</u>
(A)	Antikonie 414, 1 -, 415, 8			
414, 4-5	gunêrt sî <u>diu strîtes vart,</u> die ze Schampfanzûn tet Vergulaht	1	.	1

		M	O	T
414, 18-23	dô was ich âne wer ein maget, wan daz ich truoc doch einen schilt, ûf den ist werdekeit gezilt. ' des wâpen sol ich nennen, ob ir ruochet diu bekennen: guot gebaerde und kiuscher site.	2	.	2
(B)	Kingrimursel 415, 9 - 416, 16			
415, 25-30	daz sippe reicht abe iu an mich. waere daz ein kebeslîcher slich mînhalp, swâ uns diu wirt gezilt, ir hetet iuch gahes an mir bevilt, wande ich bin ein ritter doch	1	.	1
416, 1-4	ouch sol mîn prîs erwerben daz ichs âne müeze ersterben: des ich vil wol getrûwe gote. des sî mîn saelde gein im bote.	1	.	1
416, 13-16	mir vrumt sîn angestlîcher strît vil engez lop. mîn laster wît daz sol mir vreude swenden und mich ûf êren phenden.	1	.	1
(C)	Liddamus 416, 17 - 417, 10	.	.	.
(D)	Kingrimursel's Reply 417, 11 - 418, 25			
417, 28-30	dâ taetet ir wîbes widerwanc. swelh künec sich lât an iuwern rât, vil twerhes dem diu krône stât.	1	.	1
418, 18-20	der sorgen zeinem kranze trage ich unz ûf daz tegedinc, daz ich gein iu kume in den rinc	1	.	1
Totals:	145 lines of text	8	0	8
Subtotals:	(A) Antikonie (38 lines) (B) Kingrimursel (38 lines) (C) Liddamus (24 lines) (D) Kingrimursel's Reply (45 lines)	3 3 0 2	0 0 0 0	3 3 0 2

		M	O	T
Liddamus' Discourse on Fighting 418, 26 - 422, 1				
419, 11-13	sus sprach der rîche Liddamus:			

		M	O	T
	'welt irz sîn der Turnus,			
	sô lât mich sîn her Tranzes	.	1	1
419, 22-24	swaz ir und ieslîch Bertûn			
	mir dâ ze schaden meget getuon,			
	ich engevloehe nimmer vor iu huon.	.	1	1
420, 22-24	waz Wolfhartes solde ich sîn? '			
	mirst in den strît <u>der wec vergrabet</u>, '			
	gein vehtene <u>diu gir verhabet</u>.	2	1	3
420, 26-30	ich taete ê als Rûmolt,			
	der dem künec Gunther riet,			
	dô er von Wormze gein den Hiunen schiet:			
	er bat in lange sniten baen			
	und in sînem kezzel umme draen.	.	1	1
421, 13-18	'des volge ich, ' sprach Liddamus,			
	'wan swaz sîn oeheim Artus			
	hât und die von Indîâ,			
	der mirz hie gaebe als siz hant dâ,			
	der mirz ledeclîche braehte,			
	ich liezez ê daz ich vaehte.	.	1	1
421, 20-21	Segramors enbin ich niht,			
	den man durch vehten binden muoz	.	1	1
. . . .	. . . .	. . . .		
Totals:	96 lines of text	2	6	8

The Evening Truce 422, 2 - 426, 9

		M	O	T
(A)	Ordered by Vergulaht 422, 2 - 19			
422, 14-18	'nû nim den gesellen dîn			
	und ouch den lantgrâven ze dir			
	(die mir guotes günnen, die gên mit mir)			
	und rât mirz waegest waz ich tuo. '			
	si sprach: 'dâ lege dîn triuwe zuo, ' (2)	.	1	1
(B)	In Antikonie's Chambers 422, 20 - 424, 6			
422, 20-22	diu künegîn genomen hât			
	ir vetern sun und ir gast:			
	<u>daz dritte was der sorgen last</u>.	1	.	1
423, 13-15	sus wâren die zwêne dâ inne			
	bî der küneginne,			
	unz daz der tac <u>liez sînen strît</u>.	1	.	1

107

		M	O	T
423, 29 - 424, 5	swaz man dâ kniender schenken sach, ir deheinem diu hosennestel brach: ' ez wâren megede als von der zît, den man diu besten jâr noch gît. ich bin des unervaeret, heten si <u>geschaeret</u> als ein valke sîn gevider: (3)			
		1	1	2

(C)   Vergulaht's Council 424, 7 - 426, 9

		M	O	T
424, 27-30	dâ râtet umme: des ist nôt. <u>mîn bester schilt</u> was vür den tôt daz ich dar um bôt mîne hant, als iu mit rede ist hie bekant:	1	.	1
425, 19-21	swes iuch dort twanc der eine man, des sî hie phant her Gâwân: der <u>vederslaget ûf iuwern kloben.</u>	1	.	1
426, 3-6	swaz erden hât umslagen zmer, dâ engelac nie hûs sô wol ze wer als Munsalvaesche: swâ diu stêt, von strîte <u>rûher wec</u> dar gêt.	1	.	1

. . . .

		M	O	T
Totals:	128 lines of text	6	2	8
Subtotals:	(A) Ordered by Vergulaht (18 lines)	0	1	1
	(B) In Antikonie's Chambers (47 lines)	3	1	4
	(C) Vergulaht's Council (63 lines)	3	0	3

<u>Morning of Judgment</u> 426, 10 - 432, 30   M   O   T

(A)   Antikonie Escorts Gawan to the King 426, 10 - 427, 30

		M	O	T
426, 29	<u>ir munt den bluomen nam ir prîs:</u>	1	.	1
427, 2-4	swem si güetlîche ir küssen bôt, des <u>muoste swenden sich der walt</u>	1	.	1
427, 9-11	wan si lebete in solhen siten, daz ninder was <u>underriten</u> ir prîs mit valschen worten.	1	.	1
427, 13-18	ieslîch munt ir wunschte dô daz ir prîs bestüende alsô bewart vor valscher trüeben jehe, (.) lûter virrec als ein valkensehe. ( ) '			

		M	O	T
	was balsemmaezec staete an ir, (.)			
	daz riet ir werdeclîchiu gir. (4)	1	1	2
(B)	Vergulaht's Offer: Gawan to Seek Grail 428, 1-29	.	.	.
(C)	Gawan and His Company Reunited 428, 30 - 430, 20			
429, 24-26	sîn munt, sîn ougen und sîn nase			
	was rehte der minne kerne:			
	al diu werlt sach in gerne.	1	.	1
(D)	Gawan Leaves on the Grail Quest 430, 21 - 432, 30			
431, 14	iuwer prîs vür alle prîse wiget:	1	.	1
432, 4-5	der wart an vreuden ungesunt,			
	daz er sô gâhes von ir reit.	1	.	1
. . . .	. . . .	. . . .		
Totals:	201 lines of text	7	1	8
Subtotals:	(A) Antikonie Escorts Gawan (51 lines)	4	1	5
	(B) Vergulaht's Offer (29 lines)	0	0	0
	(C) Gawan and Company Reunited (51 lines)	1	0	1
	(D) Gawan Leaves on Grail Quest	2	0	2
Book Eight Totals: 1050 lines of text		36	21	57

BOOK IX

Transition from Gawan to Parzival Again 433, 1 - 435, 1		M	O	T
(A)	Vrou Âventiure 433, 1 - 434, 10			
433, 19-21	oder ob sîn ganziu werdekeit			
	sî beidiu lanc unde breit,			
	oder ist si kurz oder smal?	1	.	1
434, 8-9	habet er sich an die wîte			
	oder hât er sider sich verlegen?	.	1	1
(B)	Parzival's Interim Wanderings 434, 11 - 435, 1			
434, 14-19	ez waere lantman oder mâc,			
	der tjoste poinder gein im maz,			
	daz der deheiner nie gesaz.			
	sus kan sîn wâge seigen,			

		M	O	T
	sîn selbes prîs ûf steigen und die anderen lêren sîgen.	1	.	1
434, 20-24	in manegen herten wîgen hât er sich schumfentiure erwert, den lîp gein strît alsô gezert, ' swer prîs zim wolde borgen, der müestez tuon mit sorgen.	2	.	2
Totals:	61 lines of text	4	1	5
Subtotals:	(A) Vrou Aventiure (40 lines) (B) Interim Wanderings (21 lines)	1 3	1 0	2 3

Sigune in the Hermit Cell (3rd Meeting) 435, 2 - 442, 25

		M	O	T
435, 16-18	wîplîcher sorgen urhap ûz ir herzen blüete alniuwe und doch durch alde triuwe.	1	.	1
435, 23-25	Sigûne doschesse hôrte selten messe: ir leben was doch ein venje gar.	1	.	1
436, 4-10	ob si worden waere sîn wîp, da hete sich vrou Lûnete gesûmet an sô gaeher bete als si riet ir selber vrouwen: ' man mac doch dicke schouwen vroun Lûneten rîten zuo etslîchem râte gar ze vruo.	1	1	2
436, 20-22	behelt si dennoch êre, si entreget deheinen sô liehten kranz, gêt si durch vreude an den tanz.	.	1	1
438, 6-8	daz steinlîn was ein grânât, des blic gap ûz der vinster schîn als ein ander gensterlîn.	.	1	1
440, 3	der rehten minne ich bin sîn wer	1	.	1
440, 13-14	der rehten ê diz vingerlîn vür got sol mîn geleite sîn.	1	.	1
440, 15-16	daz ist ob mîner triuwe ein slôz, ' von dem herzen mîner ougen vlôz.	2	.	2

THE IMAGES IN PARZIVAL

		M	O	T
441, 8-9	ûf erde nie sô schoener lîp wart geborn von menneschlîcher vruht.	1	.	1
441, 26-27	nû muoz dîn vreude sîn verzaget und al dîn hôher muot erlemt.	1	.	1
441, 28-30	dîn herze sorge hât gezemt, ' diu dir vil wilde waere, hetes gevrâget dû der maere.	2	.	2
. . . .	. . . .	. . . .		
Totals:	234 lines of text	11	3	14

Seeking Cundrie, Fights Grail Knight 442, 26 - 445, 30

		M	O	T
444, 4-6	er dâhte: 'ich waere unernert, rite ich über dises mannes sât: wie würde dan sîns zornes rât?	.	1	1
444, 8-10	mir engeswîchen hende, ieweder arm, ich gibe vür mîne reise ein phant, daz ninder bindet mich sîn hant.	.	1	1
444, 21-26	er traf in dâ man haeht den schilt, sô man ritterschefte spilt, daz von Munsalvaesche der templeis von dem orse in eine halden reis sô verre hin abe (diu was sô tief), daz dâ sîn leger wênec slief	.	1	1
444, 30 - 455, 3	Parzival eins zêders ast begreif mit sînen handen. nû jehts im niht ze schanden, daz er sich âne schergen hienc.	.	1	1
445, 10-12	wolde er teilen den gewin den er erwarp an Parzivâl, sô half im baz dâ heime der grâl.	.	1	1
. . . .	. . . .	. . . .		
Totals:	95 lines of text	0	5	5

The Good Friday Pilgrims 446, 1 - 451, 2

		M	O	T
448, 13-16	herre, phleget ir toufes, sô jâmer iuch des koufes: er hât sîn werdeclîchez leben mit tôde vür unser schult gegeben.	1	.	1

111

		M	O	T
449, 2-5	sîne gîserten arme, swie ritterlîch die sîn gestalt, uns dunkt doch des, si haben kalt: er ervrüre, waeren sîn eines drî.	.	1	1
. . . .	. . . .	. . . .		
Totals:	152 lines of text	1	1	2

Horse Takes Parzival to Trevrizent 451, 3 - 452, 30		M	O	T
451, 3	hin ritet Herzeloide <u>vruht</u>.	1	.	1
. . . .	. . . .	. . . .		
Totals:	58 lines of text	1	0	1

Wolfram Tells of Discovery of Grail Story 453, 1 - 455, 24		M	O	T
453, 28-29	. . . unz unser <u>schilt</u> der touf wart vürz helleviur.	1	.	1
454, 4-8	wie mac der tiuvel solhen spot gevüegen an sô wîser diet, daz si niht scheidet oder schiet dâ von der treget <u>die hoesten hant</u> und dem elliu wunder sint bekant?	1	.	1
454, 27-30	sît muoz sîn phlegen <u>getouftiu vruht</u> mit alsô kiuschlîcher zuht: diu mennescheit ist immer wert, der zuo dem grâle wirt gegert.	1	.	1
. . . .	. . . .	. . . .		
Totals:	84 lines of text	3	0	3

Parzival's Reception by Trevrizent 455, 25 - 460, 27		M	O	T
457, 2-3	dô sprach aber der guote man: 'ich bin râtes iuwer <u>wer</u>.	1	.	1
457, 16-18	nie kiuscher <u>vruht</u> von lîbe wart geborn dan sîn selbes kint, diu iu dâ widergangen sint.	1	.	1
457, 30 - 458, 2	ich hân ouch menneschlîchen list: hetet irz niht vür einen ruom, sô trüege ich vluht noch <u>magetuom</u>.	1	.	1
458, 6-9	ich was ein ritter, als ir sît, der ouch nâch hôher minne ranc.			

		M	O	T
	etswenne ich sündebaeren gedanc			
	gein der kiusche parrierte.	1	.	1
459, 1-4	Parzivâl stuont ûf dem snê.			
	ez taete einem kranken manne wê,			
	ob er harnas trüege			
	dâ der vrost sus an in slüege.	1	.	1

. . . .

Totals:	153 lines of text	5	0	5

Trevrizent Instructs About God 460, 28 - 467, 18   M   O   T

461, 1-2	. . . 'mirst vreude ein troum: '			
	ich trage der riuwe swaeren soum.'	2	.	2
461, 9-26	ouch trage ich hazzes vil gein gote,			
	wande er ist mîner sorgen tote: '			
	die hât er alz hôhe erhaben.			
	min vreude ist lebendec begraben. '			
	kunde gotes kraft mit helfe sîn,			
	waz ankers waere diu vreude mîn? '			
	diu sinket durch der riuwe grunt. '			
	ist mîn manlîch herze wunt '			
	(oder mac ez dâ von wesen ganz,			
	daz diu riuwe ir scharphen kranz '			
	mir setzet ûf werdekeit,			
	die schiltes ammet mir erstreit			
	gein werlîchen handen?),			
	des gihe ich dem ze schanden,			
	der aller helfe hât gewalt,			
	ist sîn helfe helfe balt,			
	daz er mir denne hilfet niht,			
	sô vil man im der helfe giht.	6	.	6
462, 11-17	doch ich ein leie waere,			
	der wâren buoche maere			
	kunde ich lesen unde schrîben,			
	wie der mensche sol belîben			
	mit dienste gein des helfe grôz,			
	den der staeten helfe nie verdrôz			
	vür der sêle senken.	1	.	1
463, 10-14	Astirot und Belcimôn,			
	Bêlet und Radamant			
	und ander die ich dâ hân erkant,			

<u>M</u> <u>O</u> <u>T</u>

diu liehte himelesche schar
wart durch nît nâch <u>helle var</u>.   1 . 1

463, 23-26   von in zwein kom gebürte <u>vruht</u>: '
einem riet sîn ungenuht
daz er durch gîteclîchen ruom
<u>sîner anen nam den magetuom</u>.   2 . 2

464, 11-19   <u>diu erde Adâmes muoter was</u>: '
von erden vruht Adâm genaz.
dannoch <u>was diu erde ein maget</u>:
noch hân ich iu niht gesaget
wer ir den magetuom benam.
Kâíns vater was Adam,
er sluoc Abêlen um krankez guot:
dô ûf die reinen erden zbluot
viel, <u>ir magetuom was vervarn</u>.   3 . 3

464, 28-30   got selbe antlitze hât genomen
nâch <u>der êrsten megede'vruht</u>:
daz was sîner hôhen art ein zuht.   2 . 2

465, 1-6   von Adâmes künne
huop sich riuwe und wünne,
sît er uns sippe lougent niht,
den ieslîch engel ob im siht,
und daz diu sippe ist <u>sünden wagen</u>,
sô daz wir sünde müezen tragen.   1 . 1

465, 21-27   der pareliure Plâtô
sprach bî sînen zîten dô
und Sibilíie diu profêtisse,
<u>sunder vâlierens misse</u>
si sageten dâ vor manec jâr,
uns solde komen al vür wâr
vür die hoesten schulde phant.   1 . 1

465, 28-30   zer helle uns nam <u>diu hoeste hant</u>
mit der gotlîchen minne:
die unkiuschen liez er dinne.   1 . 1

466, 1-4   von dem wâren minnaere
sagent disiu süezen maere.
der ist <u>ein durchliuhtec lieht</u>
und wenket sîner minne niht.   1 . 1

466, 8-9   aller werlde ist <u>geveilet</u>
beidiu sin minne und ouch sîn haz.   1 . 1

	M	O	T

466, 13-28   swer aber wandelt sünden schulde,
der dient nâch werder hulde.
die treget der durch gedanke vert. '
gedanc sich sunnen blickes wert: '
gedanc ist âne slôz gespart, '
vor aller krêatiure bewart.
gedanc ist vinster âne schîn: '
diu gotheit dan lûter sîn,
si glestet durch der vinster want '
und hât den helden sprunc gerant, '
der endiuzet noch enklinget. '
sô er von dem herzen springet, '
ez ist dehein gedanc sô snel,
ê er von dem herzen vür daz vel
kom, 'er ensî versuochet:
des kiuschen got geruochet.

	7	2	9

Totals: 201 lines of text

	29	2	31

Trevrizent Instructs About the Grail 467, 19 - 474, 22

	M	O	T

467, 28-29   ûf erde nie schoener lîp
gesouc an deheiner muoter brust.

	.	1	1

474, 7-8   diu wâpen gap in Anfortas,
dô er der vreuden herre was

	1	.	1

Totals: 214 lines of text

	1	1	2

Revelation of Parzival's Identity and Kinship Guilt 474, 23 - 477, 30

	M	O	T

475, 5-6   genam ich ie den rêroup,
sô was ich an den witzen toup:

	1	.	1

476, 1-2   missewende was sîn riuwe.
er balsem ob der triuwe,

	1	.	1

476, 15-18   was saget ir nû?' sprach Parzivâl.
'waere ich dan herre über den grâl,
der möhte mich ergetzen niht
des maeres mir iuwer munt vergiht.

	.	1	1

477, 2-3   mîn swester Schoisiâne ein kint
gebar: der vrühte lac si tôt.

	1	.	1

477, 11-12   ir wîplîch herze was sô guot,

115

		M	O	T
	ein arke vür unkiusche vluot.	1	.	1
. . . .	. . . .	. . . .		
Totals:	98 lines of text	4	1	5

The Story of Anfortas 478, 1 - 484, 30

		M	O	T
478, 8-10	dô mîn bruoder gein den jâren kom vür der gransprunge zît, mit solher jugent hât minne ir strît:	1	1	2
479, 3-6	eins tages der künec al eine reit (daz was gar den sînen leit) ûz durch âventiure durch vreude an minnen stiure	1	.	1
482, 5-10	des nâme wir uns muoze und gewunnen zrîs ze buoze, ob daz sper ungehiure in dem helleschen viure waere gelüppet oder geloetet, daz uns an vreuden toetet.	1	.	1
482, 12-14	ein vogel heizt pelicânus: swenne der vruht gewinnet, alze sêre er die minnet.	1	.	1
484, 6-7	von der hoesten hende dâ mite ist Anfortas genesen	1	.	1
484, 20	swachiu wünne ist mîner jâre wer.	1	.	1
. . . .	. . . .	. . . .		
Totals:	210 lines of text	6	1	7

Trevrizent's Hospitality 485, 1 - 487, 30

		M	O	T
485, 7	mîn küche riuchet selten	.	1	1
486, 4	ir munt wart selten lachens lût.	.	1	1
486, 11-12	dâ enwas gesoten noch gebrâten ' und ir küchen unberâten.	.	2	2
487, 1-4	swaz dâ was spîse vür getragen, beliben si dâ nâch ungetwagen, daz enschadete in an den ougen niht, als man vischegen handen giht.	.	1	1
487, 5-10	ich wil vür mich geheizen,			

		M	O	T
	man möhte mit mir beizen, waere ich vür vederspil erkant, ich swünge al gernde von der hant, bî solhen kröphelînen taete ich vliegen schînen.	.	1	1
487, 20-22	von der hoesten hende emphiengen si um ir kummer solt: got was und wart in beiden holt.	1	.	1
....	....	....		
Totals:	90 lines of text	1	6	7

Parzival's Confession 488, 1-20

		M	O	T
Totals:	20 lines of text	.	.	.

Trevrizent's Response 488, 21 - 489, 21

		M	O	T
489, 5-19	diu mennescheit hât wilden art. etswâ wil jugent an witze vart: ' wil dennez alter tumpheit üeben und lûter site trüeben, ' dâ von wirt daz wîze sal ' und diu grüene tugent val, ' dâ von beklîben möhte daz der werdekeite töhte. ' möhte ich dirz wol begrüenen und dîn herze alsô erküenen daz dû den prîs bejagetes und an got niht verzagetes, sô gestüende noch dîn linge an sô werdeclîchem dinge, daz wol ergetzet hieze.	6	0	6
489, 21	ich bin von gote dîn râtes wer.			
....	....	....		
Totals:	31 lines of text	7	0	7

Remaining Grail Phenomena Clarified 489, 22 - 495, 12

		M	O	T
490, 11-12	sô tuot im grôzer vrost sô wê, sîn vleisch wirt kelter dan der snê.	.	1	1
490, 16-17	den vrost ez ûz dem lîbe treget, al um daz sper glasvar als îs.	.	1	1

		M	O	T
493, 10-14	si emphiengen jâmers soldiment: ' daz sper in vreude entvuorte, daz ir herzen verh sus ruorte. ' dô machte ir jâmers triuwe des toufes lêre al niuwe.	3	.	3
495, 1-5	sus gît man von dem grâle dan offenlîch megede, verholne diu man durch vruht ze dienste wider dar, ob ir kint des grâles schar mit dienste suln mêren.	1	.	1

Totals: 171 lines of text   4   2   6

Trevrizent's Youth, Gahmuret, Ither 495, 13 - 499, 12   M   O   T

| 498, 9-11 | mîne kefsen, die dû saehe ê, (diust noch grüener dan der klê) hiez ich würken ûz einem steine | . | 1 | 1 |

Totals: 120 lines of text   0   1   1

The Confession Completed, Repentance Begun 499, 13 - 501, 18   M   O   T

| 499, 26-30 | nû volge mîner raete, nim buoze vür missewende und sorge et um dîn ende, daz dir dîn arbeit hie erhol daz dort diu sêle ruowe dol. | 1 | . | 1 |
| 501, 7-8 | wênec wart in bette und kulter brâht: si giengen et ligen ûf ein baht. | . | 1 | 1 |

Totals: 66 lines of text   1   1   2

Titurel 501, 19 - 502, 3   M   O   T

Totals: 15 lines of text   .   .   .

Final Instruction and Parting 502, 4-30   M   O   T

| 502, 7-8 | wîp und phaffen sint erkant, die tragent unwerlîche hant: | 1 | . | 1 |
| 502, 15-19 | sîn munt die marter sprichet, | | | |

		M	O	T
	diu unser vlust zebrichet. ' ouch grîfet sîn gewîhtiu hant an daz hoeheste phant daz ie vür schult gesetzet wart:	1	.	1
502, 25-26	er sprach: 'gip mir dîn sünde her (vor gote ich bin dîn wandels wer)	1	.	1
. . . .	. . . .	. . . .		
Totals:	27 lines of text	3	0	3

Book Nine Totals: 2100 lines of text   81   25 106

BOOK X

Introduction 503, 1-4   M   O   T

Totals: 4 lines of text   .   .   .

Summary of Gawan's Release from Conflict with Vergulaht   M   O   T
503, 4 - 504, 6

Totals: 32 lines of text   .   .   .

Gawan Meets Lady with Wounded Knight 504, 7 - 507, 30   M   O   T

504, 24-30	sol dâ ein tjost ergên ze vuoz, obz halt vrou Kamille waere, diu mit ritterlîchem maere vor Laurente prîs erstreit, waere si gesunt als si dort reit, ez würde iedoch versuocht an sie, ob si mir striten büte alhie.	.	1	1
505, 4-8	der tjoste venster was gesniten ' mit der glaevîne wît. alsus mâlet si der strît: wer gültes den schiltaeren, ob ir varwe alsus waeren?	2	.	2
505, 10	ouch saz ein vrouwe an vreuden lam	1	.	1
507, 17-20	'des entuo niht' sprach der wunde man. 'der wârheit ich dir jehen kan: dar engêt niht kinde reise, ez mac wol heizen vreise. '	1	.	1

		M	O	T
507, 25-26	er vant al bluotec ir slâ, als ein hirz waere erschozzen dâ:	.	1	1
. . . .	. . . .	. . . .		
Totals:	114 lines of text	4	2	6

Gawan Meets Orgeluse de Logrois 508, 1 - 512, 25

		M	O	T
508, 2-4	nâch trendeln mâze was ir berc: swâ si verre sach der tumme, er wânde si liefe alumme.	.	1	1
508, 21-23	aller wîbes varwe ein bêâ flûrs. ' âne Condwîrâmûrs wart nie geborn so schoener lîp:	1	.	1
508, 27-30	ouch saget uns diu âventiur von ir, si waere ein reizel minnen gir, ' ougen süeze âne smerzen ' und ein spansenewe sherzen.	3	.	3
509, 17-21	waere mîn lop gemeine, daz hieze ein wirde kleine, dem wisen und dem tummen, dem slehten und dem krummen: wâ rihte ez sich danne vür?	1	.	1
509, 27-28	'ir sît mînem herzen bî.' 'verre ûzerhalp, niht drinne.'	1	1	2
510, 1-6	wie habet ir minne an mich erholt? maneger sîniu ougen bolt, er möhte si ûf einer slingen ze senfterm wurfe bringen, ob er sehen niht vermîdet, daz im sîn herze snîdet.	2	.	2
510, 15-19	dô sprach er: 'vrouwe, ir saget mir wâr. mîn ougen sint des herzen vâr: ' die hânt an iuwerm lîbe ersehen, daz ich mit wârheit des muoz jehen daz ich iuwer gevangen bin.	2	.	2
510, 21-23	swies iuch habe verdrozzen, ir habet mich în geslozzen: nû lieset oder bindet.	1	.	1
. . . .	. . . .	. . . .		

		M	O	T
Totals:	145 lines of text	11	2	13

He Recovers Orgeluse's Horse, Wins Grudging Acceptance		M	O	T
512, 26 - 517, 10				
514, 15-20	des hant daz mer gesalzen hât, ' der gebe iu vür kummer rât. hüetet daz iuch iht gehoene mîner vrouwen schoene, wan diu ist bî der süeze al sûr, rehte als ein sunnenblicker schûr.	.	2	2
514, 27-28	sîns herzen voget er dâ vant: diu was vrouwe über daz lant.	1	.	1
515, 4-6	kamphbaeriu lide treget ein wîp die man vindet so: diu waere vil lîhte eins schimphes vrô.	1	.	1
515, 13	si sprach: 'weset willekomen, ir gans.'	1	.	1
515, 24-26	'welt ir, ich hebe iuch ûf diz phert.' si sprach:'des hân ich niht gegert. iuwer unversichert hant mac grifen wol an smaeher phant.'	1	.	1
Totals:	135 lines of text	4	2	6

Encounter with Malcreatiure 517, 11 - 521, 18		M	O	T
(A)	Description 517, 11-30			
517, 22-23	im stuont ouch ietweder zan als einem eber wilde	.	1	1
517, 25-27	im was daz hâr ouch niht sô lanc als ez Cundrîen ûf den mûl dort swanc: ' kurz, scharph als igels hût ez was.	.	2	2
(B)	Explanation of Cundrie and Malcreatiure 518, 1 - 520,2			
518, 11-14	dô sîniu kint der jâre kraft gewunnen, daz si berhaft wurden menneschlîcher vruht, er widerriet in ungenuht, swa siner tohter keiniu truoc	1	.	1
518, 18-20	vil würze er si mîden hiez, die menschen vruht verkêrten und sîn geslehte unêrten	1	.	1

		M	O	T
(C)	Quarrel with Malcreatiure 520, 3 - 521, 18			
520, 24-26	sît aber ir ein sarjant, sô werdet ir gâlûnt mit staben, daz irs gerne wandel möhtet haben.	1	.	1
521, 12-14	sîn igelmaezec hâr sich rach: daz versneit Gâwân sô die hant, diu wart von bluote al rôt erkant.	1	.	1
. . . .	. . . .		. . . .	
Totals:	128 lines of text	4	3	7
Subtotals:	(A) Description of Malcreatiure (20 lines)	0	3	3
	(B) Explanation of him and Cundrie (62 lines)	2	0	2
	(C) Quarrel with Malcreatiure (46 lines)	2	0	2

Wounded Knight Warns Gawan Against Orgeluse and Steals his Horse	M	O	T
521, 19 - 524, 8			

523, 16-21	ez enwont ûf erde nihtes niht under krône und alle die krône tragent und die vreudehaften prîs bejagent, der gein iu teilte ir gewin, sô raetet mir mîns herzen sin daz ichz in lâzen solde.	1	.	1
. . . .	. . . .		. . . .	
Totals:	80 lines of text	1	0	1

Story of Urjans and Gawan 524, 9 - 529, 16	M	O	T
Totals:	158 lines of text	.	.	.

Gawan and Malcreatiure's Nag 529, 17 - 531, 30	M	O	T
531, 19-23	. . . ir scharphiu saliure ' in dûhte sô gehiure, daz er enruochte waz si sprach, wan immer swenne er an si sach, sô was sîn phant ze riuwe quît.	2	.	2
531, 24-25	si was im rehte ein meien zît, ' vor allem blicke ein flôrî,	2	.	2
. . . .	. . . .		. . . .	
Totals:	74 lines of text	4	0	4

Amor and Cupido: Discourse on Minne 532, 1 - 534, 8		M	O	T
532, 23-24	er ist doch âne schande, liget er in minnen bande.	1	.	1
533, 1-5	lât nâher gên, her minne druc. ir tuot der vreude alsolhen zuc, daz sich dürkelt vreuden stat ' und bant sich der riuwen phat. ' sus breitet sich der riuwen slâ:	3	.	3
533, 25-30	swâ liep gein liebe erhüebe lûter âne trüebe, ' der enwederz des verdrüzze daz minne ir herze slüzze mit minne von der wanc ie vlôch, diu minne ist ob den andern hôch.	2	.	2
Totals:	68 lines of text	6	0	6

Gawan and Orgeluse Arrive Outside Schastel Marveil 534,9 - 543, 29		M	O	T
Totals:	61 lines of text	.	.	.

Gawan Fights Lischois Gwelljus 536, 10 - 543, 29		M	O	T
537, 18-20	die wurden alsô hin gesniten, ir beleip in lützel vor der hant, wan der schilt ist immer strîtes phant.	1	.	1
537, 21	man sach dâ blicke und helmes viur.	1	.	1
537, 27-29	es waeren müede zwêne smide, ob si halt heten starker lide, von alsô manegem grôzen slage.	.	1	1
539, 15-18	swâ vreischet man oder wîp daz überkomen ist mîn lîp, des prîs sô hôhe ê swebete enbor, sô stêt mir baz ein sterben vor	1	.	1
541, 27-28	helme und ir swert liten nôt: diu wâren ir schilte vür den tôt.	1	.	1
542, 11-13	man sach dâ viurs blicke und diu swert ûf werfen dicke ûz ellenthaften henden.	1	.	1
Totals:	230 lines of text	5	1	6

<u>Ferryman Claims Gringuljete, Receives Lischois Instead</u> <u>M</u> <u>O</u> <u>T</u>
543, 30 - 547, 2

		M	O	T
545, 26-27	woldet ir gemaches grîfen zuo, sô ritet ir sanfter einen stap.	.	1	1
546, 2-3	<u>einer mûlinne voln</u> <u>möhtet ir noch ê gewinnen.</u>	1	.	1
546, 17-20	vür wâr sîn prîs was ie sô hel, vünf hundert ors starc und snel ungerne ich vür in naeme, wande ez mir niht gezaeme.	.	1	1
. . . .	. . . .	. . . .		
Totals:	93 lines of text	1	2	3

<u>Ferryman's Hospitality to Gawan</u> 547, 3 - 552, 30 <u>M</u> <u>O</u> <u>T</u>

		M	O	T
547, 19-24	ouwê <u>vindenlîchiu vlust</u>, ' <u>dû senkes mir die einen brust</u>, ' diu ê <u>der hoehe gerte</u>' dô mich got vreuden werte, dâ lac ein herze unden: ich waene <u>dast verswunden.</u>	4	0	4
548, 22-23	der verje Gâwânen bat: '<u>sît selbe wirt in mînem hûs.</u>'	1	.	1
550, 21-22	tohter, leiste al sîne ger: des bin ich mit der volge <u>wer</u>	1	.	1
552, 1-4	kunde Gâwân guoten willen zern, des möhte er sich dâ wol nern: ' nie muoter gunde ir kinde baz dan im der wirt des brôt er az.	.	2	2
552, 9-12	einez was ein phlûmît, des zieche ein grüener samît, des niht von der hôhen art: ez was ein samît <u>bastart.</u>	1	.	1
. . . .	. . . .	. . . .		
Totals:	178 lines of text	7	2	9

<u>Book Ten Totals:</u> 1500 lines of text 47 14 61

THE IMAGES IN PARZIVAL

BOOK XI

Gawan Inquires About Ladies of Schastel Marveil 553, 1 - 562, 17   <u>M</u>   <u>O</u>   <u>T</u>

(A)	Early Morning Curiosity 553, 1-20	.	.	.
(B)	Ferryman's Daughter 553, 21 - 555, 30	.	.	.
(C)	Ferryman Plipalinot 556, 1 - 562, 17			

557, 11-14   ist iu âventiure bekant,
swaz ie gestreit iuwer hant,
daz was noch gar ein kindes spil:
nû naehent iu riuwebaeriu zil.   1   .   1

557, 25-29   aller kummer ist ein niht, '
wan dem ze lîdene geschiht
disiu âventiure:
diust scharph und ungehiure
vür wâr und âne liegen.   2   .   2

559, 27-30   hetet ir selbe vragens niht erdâht,
nimmer waert irs innen brâht
von mir, waz hie maeres ist,
mit vorhten scharph ein strenger list.   1   .   1

560, 15-16   er sprach: 'traget mir mîn harnas her.'
der bete was der wirt sîn wer.   1   .   1

561, 23-27   daz bette und die stollen sîn,
von Marroch der mahmumelîn,
des krône und al sîn rîcheit,
waere daz dar gein geleit,
dâ mite ez waere vergolden niht.   .   1   1

. . . .

Totals:	287 lines of text	5	1	6
Subtotals:	(A) Early Curiosity (20 lines)	.	.	.
	(B) Ferryman's Daughter (70 lines)	.	.	.
	(C) Ferryman Plipalinot (197 lines)	5	1	6

The Merchant at the Castle Gate 562, 18 - 564, 22   <u>M</u>   <u>O</u>   <u>T</u>

563, 4-11   derz mit gelte widerwaege,
der bâruc von Baldac
vergülte niht daz drinne lac, '
alsô taete der katolicô
von Ranculat: dô Kriechen sô

		M	O	T
	stuont daz man hort dar inne vant,			
	dâ vergültez niht des keisers hant			
	mit jener zweier stiure.	.	2	2
....	....	....		
Totals:	65 lines of text	0	2	2

Gawan Enters the Castle 564, 23 - 566, 10   M O T

		M	O	T
564, 30 -	vür allen sturm niht ein ber'			
565, 4	gaebe si ze drîzec jâren, '	2	.	2
565, 3-4	mitten drûf ein anger:			
	daz Lechvelt ist langer.	.	1	1
565, 6-12	uns tuot diu âventiure kunt,			
	dô Gâwân den palas sach,			
	dem was alumme sîn dach			
	rehte als phâwîn gevider gar,			
	lieht gemâl und sô gevar,			
	weder regen noch der snê			
	entet des daches blicke wê.	.	2	2
....	....	....		
Totals:	48 lines of text	2	3	5

In the Chamber of the Lit Marveile 566, 11 - 573, 24   M O T

		M	O	T
(A)	The Bed 566, 11 - 568, 14			
566, 11-13	er gienc zer kemenâten în			
	(der was ir estrîches schîn			
	lûter, haele als ein glas),	.	1	1
566, 16-18	vier schîben liefen drunder			
	von rubînen lieht sinewel,			
	daz der wint wart nie sô snel:	.	1	1
567, 16-19	der vier wende deheine ez liez,			
	mit hurte an ieslîche ez swanc,			
	daz al diu burc dâ von erklanc.			
	sus reit er manegen poinder grôz.	1	.	1
567, 20-25	swaz der doner ie gedôz '			
	und al die pusûnaere,			
	ob der êrste waere			
	bî dem jungesten dinne			
	und bliesen nâch gewinne,			
	ez endorfte niht mêr dâ krachen.	.	2	2

		M	O	T
568, 1-8	er lac und liez es walden			
	den der helfe hât behalden			
	und den der helfe nie verdrôz, '			
	swer in sînem kummer grôz			
	helfe an in versuochen kan.			
	der wîse herzehafte man,			
	swâ dem kummer wirt bekant,			
	der rüefet an die hoesten hant	1	1	2
(B)	The Stones and Arrows 568, 15 - 569, 23			
569, 15-17	es möhte jugent werden grâ,			
	des gemaches alsô dâ			
	Gâwân an dem bette vant.	1	.	1
(C)	The Churl 569, 24 - 570, 30			
570, 5-7	einen kolben er in der hende truoc,			
	des kiule groezer dan ein kruoc			
	was.	.	1	1
570, 18-19	ich vüege aber wol daz iu geschiht			
	dâ von ir den lîp ze phande gebet.	1	.	1
(D)	The Lion 571, 1 - 573, 24			
571, 1-3	dô hôrte er ein gebrumme,			
	als der wol zweinzec trummen			
	slüege hie ze tanze.	.	1	1
573, 14-19	sîn wanküssen ungelîch			
	was dem daz Gimêle,			
	von Monte Ribêle			
	diu süeze und diu wîse,			
	legete Kahenîse,			
	dar ûfe er sînen prîs verslief.	.	1	1
. . . .	. . . .	. . . .		
Totals:	224 lines of text	4	8	12
Subtotals:	(A) The Bed (64 lines)	2	5	7
	(B) The Stones and Arrows (39 lines)	1	0	1
	(C) The Churl (37 lines)	1	1	2
	(D) The Lion (84 lines)	0	2	2

Nursed by the Ladies Under Arnive 573, 25 - 582, 30   M   O   T

| 573, 25-27 | verholne ez wart beschouwet,
daz mit bluote was betouwet
der kemenâten estrîch. | 1 | . | 1 |

| 577, 15-17 | wan einiu sol gewinnen
an vier küneginnen
daz botenbrôt, ir lebet noch. | 1 | . | 1 |

| 578, 27-30 | swelh sîn wunde stüende ze verhe,
daz waere diu vreuden twerhe: '
dâ mite waeren ouch wir erslagen
und müesten lebendec sterben tragen. | 2 | . | 2 |

| 582, 2-5 | er was et in der alden sene
nâch Orgelûsen der klâren,
wande im in sînen jâren
kein wîp sô nâhe nie gegienc | 1 | . | 1 |

. . . .

Totals: 276 lines of text   5   0   5

Book Eleven Totals: 900 lines of text   16 14 30

BOOK XII

Introduction: Gawan Oppressed by Love 583, 1 - 585, 4   M   O   T

| 583, 8-11 | swaz der werde Lanzelôt
ûf der swertbrücke erleit
und sît mit Meljakanze streit, '
daz was gein dirre nôt ein niht | 1 | 1 | 2 |

| 583, 20-23 | trüege dise phîle ein mûl,
er waere ze vil geladen dâ mite,
die Gâwân durch ellens site
gein sînem verhe snurren liez, | . | 1 | 1 |

| 584, 2-4 | solden dise kumber sîn al ein, '
Gâwâns kumber slüege vür,
waege iemen ungemaches kür | 1 | 1 | 2 |

| 584, 12-19 | wie kom, daz sich dâ verbarc
sô grôz wîp in sô kleiner stat?
si kom einen engen phat
in Gâwânes herze, '
daz aller sîn smerze | | | |

		M	O	T
	von disem kumber gar verswant.			
	ez was iedoch ein kurziu want,			
	dâ sô lanc wîp inne saz,	2	.	2
. . . .	. . . .	. . . .		
Totals:	64 lines of text	4	3	7

Vrou Minne: Discourse 585, 5 - 587, 14

		M	O	T
585, 20-25	îthêr von Gaheviez			
	iuwer insigel truoc:			
	swâ man vor wîben sîn gewuoc,			
	des wolde sich ir keiniu schamen,			
	swâ man nande sinen namen,			
	ob si der minne ir krefte jach.	1	.	1
586, 5-9	sîns vater lant von kinde er vlôch:			
	diu selbe künegîn in zôch,			
	ze Bertâne er was ein gast.			
	Flôrîe in luot mit minnen last,			
	daz si in verjagete vür daz lant.	1	.	1
587, 10-14	ez solden minnaere klagen,			
	waz dem von Norwaege was,			
	dô er der âventiur genas,			
	daz in bestuont der minnen schûr			
	âne helfe gar ze sûr.	1	.	1
. . . .	. . . .	. . . .		
Totals:	70 lines of text	3	0	3

Gawan Suffering for Orgeluse 587, 15 - 588, 30

		M	O	T
Totals:	46 lines of text	.	.	.

In the Tower of the Magic Pillar 589, 1 - 594, 13

		M	O	T
(A)	The Pillar and Windows 589, 1 - 590, 16; 591, 27 - 592, 20			
589, 7-9	si was lieht unde starc,			
	dô grôz, vroun Kamillen sarc			
	waere drûfe wol gestanden.	.	1	1
589, 12-13	werc, daz hie stuont enbor,			
	sinewel als ein gezelt ez was.	.	1	1
590, 7-11	in dûhte, daz im al diu lant			

		M	O	T
	in der grôzen siule waeren bekant			
	und daz diu lant alumbe giengen			
	und daz mit hurte emphiengen			
	die grôzen berge ein ander.	1	.	1
(B)	The Four Captive Queens 590, 17 - 591, 26			
591, 16-17	dirre megede blic ein nebeltac			
	was bî Orgelûsen gar.	1	.	1
591, 24-26	die truogen sô liehten süezen schîn			
	des lîhte ein herze waere versniten,			
	daz ê niht kumbers hete erliten.	1	.	1
(C)	Orgeluse Bringing the Turkoite 592, 21 - 594, 13			
593, 14-18	ist diu nieswurz in der nasen			
	draete unde strenge, '			
	durch sîn herze enge			
	kom alsus diu herzogîn,			
	durch sîniu ougen obene în.	1	1	2
594, 6-7	er hât mit spern prîs bejaget,			
	es waeren gehêret driu lant.	.	1	1
Totals:	163 lines of text	4	4	8
Subtotals:	(A) The Pillar and Windows (70 lines)	1	2	3
	(B) The Four Queens (40 lines)	2	0	2
	(C) Orgeluse and Turkoite (53 lines)	1	2	3

The Turkoite 594, 14 - 599, 13		M	O	T
(A)	Gawan Prepares to Fight 594, 14 - 597, 13			
(B)	The Fight 597, 14 - 598, 15			
598, 2-3	man wart wol innen schiere,			
	wer dâ gevelles was sîn wer.	1	.	1
598, 2-3	der werdekeit ein bluome ie was, '			
	unz er verdacte alsus daz gras			
	mit valle von der tjoste,			
	sîner zimierde koste			
	im touwe mit den bluomen striten.	2	.	2
(C)	Orgeluse Taunts Gawan 598, 16 - 599, 13			

		M	O	T
599, 3-4	iu mac durch rüemen wesen liep der schilt dürkel als ein sip,	.	1	1
599, 8-9	lât iu den vinger ziehen: rîtet wider ûf zen vrouwen.	1	.	1
Totals:	150 lines of text	4	1	5
Subtotals:	(A) Gawan Prepares to Fight (90 lines) (B) The Fight (32 lines) (C) Orgeluse Taunts Gawan	0 3 1	0 0 1	0 3 2

Final Test: the Chasm Leap and the Wreath 599, 14 - 604, 6

		M	O	T
600, 8-10	diu künegîn Arnîve sprach: 'unser trôst hât im erkorn sîner ougen senfte, ' sherzen dorn.	2	.	2
601, 1-3	swaz dâ stuonden bluomen lieht, die wâren gein dirre varwe ein niht, die Orgelûse brâhte.	1	.	1
601, 14-16	Gâwân der degen balt sprach: 'vrouwe, wâ briche ich den kranz, des mîn dürkel vreude werde ganz?	1	.	1
603, 26-27	der boum was alsô bewart, waeren Gâwâns zwêne, die müesten ir leben um den kranz hân gegeben.	.	1	1
604, 1-3	daz wazzer hiez Sabîns. Gâwân holde unsenften zins, dô er undz ors drîn bleste.	1	.	1
Totals:	143 lines of text	5	1	6

Gramoflanz and Gawan 604, 7 - 611, 6

		M	O	T
605, 10-11	von samît grüene als ein gras der künec einen mantel vuorte	.	1	1
609, 9-11	kunde si tohter und swester sîn, sô waere si ir beider vogetîn, daz ir verbaeret disen haz.	1	.	1
Totals:	210 lines of text	1	1	2

Gawan Wins Orgeluse 611, 7 - 615, 20		M	O	T

612, 4-6	ich bin doch wol so wîse: ob der schilt sîn reht sol hân, an dem hât ir missetân.	1	.	1
612, 23-25	'herre, als ich iu not gesage, waz ich der im herzen trage, so gebet ir jamers mir gewin.'	1	.	1
613, 9-19	er was ein quecbrunne der tugent, ' mit alsô berhafter jugent ' bewart vor valscher phlihte. ûz der vinster gein dem liehte hete er sich enblecket, ' sînen prîs sô hôch gestecket, daz in niemen kunde erreichen, ' den valscheit möhte erweichen.' sîn prîs hôch wahsen kunde, daz die andern wâren drunde, ûz sînes herzen kernen.	6	0	6
613, 20-21	wie loufet ob al den sternen der snelle Saturnus?	.	1	1
613, 22-26	der triuwe ein monîzirus, sît ich die wârheit sprechen kan, sus was mîn erwünschet man. daz tier die megede solden klagen: ez wirt durch reinekeit erslagen.	1	.	1
613, 27	ich was sîn herze, ' er was mîn lîp.	2	.	2
614, 12-14	dem golde ich iuch gelîche, daz man liutert in der gluot: als ist geliutert iuwer muot.	.	1	1
. . . .	. . . .	. . . .		
Totals:	134 lines of text	11	2	13

Orgeluse and Anfortas 615, 21 - 617, 3		M	O	T

615, 27 - 616, 2	si sprach: 'herre, ich muoz iu klagen von dem, der mir hât erslagen den werden Zidegasten. des muoz mir jâmer tasten inz herze, dâ diu vreude lac, dô ich Zidegastes minne phlac.	1	.	1

		M	O	T
616, 4-10	ich enhabe doch sît geworben			
	des küneges schaden mit koste			
	und manege scharphe tjoste			
	gein sînem verhe gevrumt.			
	waz ob mir an iu helfe kumt,			
	diu mich richet und ergetzet,			
	daz mir jâmerz herze wetzet?	1	.	1
616, 27-29	nu jeht, wie solde ich armez wip,			
	sit ich han getriuwen lip,			
	alsolher not bi sinne sin?	1	.	1
....	....	....		
Totals:	43 lines of text	3	0	3

Orgeluse and Klingsor 617, 4 - 618, 14

		M	O	T
Totals:	41 lines of text	.	.	.

Orgeluse and Parzival 618, 15 - 619, 24

Totals:	40 lines of text	.	.	.

Triumphant Return to Schastel Marveile 619, 25 - 624, 30

622, 26-27	sîn riuwe begunde hinken			
	und wart sîn hôchgemüete snel.	1	.	1
....	....	....		
Totals:	156 lines of text	1	0	1

Messenger Sent to Arthur re Duel with Gramoflanz 625, 1 - 626, 30

		M	O	T
Totals:	60 lines of text	.	.	.

Book Twelve Totals: 1320 lines of text

	36	12	48

BOOK XIII

Arnive Plots to Learn Gawan's Secret 627, 1-18

		M	O	T
Totals:	18 lines of text	.	.	.

Festive Preparations, Lischois and Turkoite Freed 627, 19 - 631, 5

	M	O	T

		M	O	T
628, 8-10	er hete ouch bezzern slâfes muot denne snahtes, dô diu herzogin an ungemache im gap gewin	.	1	1
628, 12-13	doch hete er in slâfe strît gestriten mit der minne	1	.	1
629, 20-23	in Sekundillen lande stêt ein stat, heizet Tasmê: diust groezer danne Nînivê ' oder danne diu wîte Akratôn.	.	2	2
Totals:	107 lines of text	1	3	4

Gawan and Itonje Speak of Gramoflanz 631, 6 - 636, 14		M	O	T
632, 27-29	si sprach: 'daz hât der künec Gramoflanz, der der werdekeite kranz treget, als im diu volge giht.'	1	.	1
633, 24-26	si begunde al rôt verwen sich: als ê was gevar ir munt, ' wart al dem antlitze kunt.	1	1	2
634, 1-4	dô sprach si: 'herre, ich sihe nû wol, ob ich sô vor iu sprechen sol, daz ir von im rîtet, nâch dem mîn herze strîtet.	1	.	1
634, 17-19	Orgelûsen ich geküsset han, diu sînen tôt sus werben kan. daz was ein kus, den Jûdas truoc,	.	1	1
635, 1-4	'herre, ir bâtet mich alsus, daz ich emphâhen müeste ir kus, doch unverkorn, an mînen munt: des ist mîn herze ungesunt.'	1	.	1
635, 13-15	dô sprach er: 'vrouwe, nû lêrt mich wie. er hât iuch dort, ir habet in hie und sit doch underscheiden.	1	.	1
Totals:	159 lines of text	5	2	7

The Banquet and Dance 636, 15 - 641, 30		M	O	T
638, 1-8	nû begunde ouch strûchen der tac,			

134

		M	O	T
	daz sîn schîn vil nâch gelac '			
	und daz man durch diu wolken sach,			
	des man der naht ze boten jach,			
	manegen stern, der balde gienc, '			
	wande er der naht herberge vienc. '			
	nâch der naht baniere			
	kom si selbe schiere.	3	.	3
638, 15-19	dar zuo diu âventiure giht,			
	diu herzoginne waere sô lieht,			
	waere der kerzen keiniu brâht,			
	dâ waere doch ninder bî ir naht: '			
	(ir blic wol selbe kunde tagen)	1	1	2
639, 15-20	manec vrouwe wol gevar			
	giengen vür in tanzen dar.			
	sus wart ir tanz gezieret,			
	wol underparrieret			
	die ritter' underz vrouwen her. '			
	gein der riuwe kômen si ze wer.	3	.	3
640, 8-10	ir komens was er zuo zim vrô:			
	sîn riuwe smal und sîn vreude breit			
	wart dô. sis swant im al sîn leit.	1	.	1
641, 5-7	des vreude sich an sorgen rach,			
	swer dâ nâch werder minne sprach,			
	ob er vant süeziu gegenwort.	1	.	1
....	....	......		
Totals:	166 lines of text	9	1	10

Gawan's Night with Orgeluse 642, 1 - 644, 11		M	O	T
643, 1-2	kunnen si zwei nû minne steln,			
	daz mac ich unsanfte heln.	1	.	1
643, 8	zuht sî des slôz ob minne site.	1	.	1
643, 22 -	ob si im trüegen guote gunst,			
644, 6	mit temperîe ûz würze kraft,			
	âne wîplîch geselleschaft			
	sô müeste er sîne scharphe nôt '			
	hân brâht unz an den sûren tôt.			
	ich wil iuz maere machen kurz.			
	er vant die rehten hirzwurz,			
	diu im half, daz er genas,			

135

<table>
<tr><td></td><td>M</td><td>O</td><td>T</td></tr>
</table>

so daz im arges niht enwas:
diu wurz was bî dem blanken brûn. '
muoterhap der Bertûn,
Gâwân fil li roi Lôt,
süezer senfte vür sûre nôt
er mit werder helfe phlac
helfeclîche unz an den tac.

		M	O	T
so daz ... an den tac.		4	.	4
Totals:	71 lines of text	6	0	6

Gawan's Messenger 644, 12 - 655, 1 M O T

(A)   Ginover's Counsel 644, 12 - 647, 26

		M	O	T
644, 16-19	der künec Artûs was aldâ und des wîp, diu künegîn, und maneger vrouwen liehter schîn und der werden massenîe ein vluot.	1	.	1
644, 25-27	der knappe vür si kniete. der bôt ir vreuden miete: einen brief si nam ûz sîner hant,	1	.	1
645, 23-26	ich tuon im werden dienest dar mit wünneclîcher vrouwen schar, die vür wâr bî mîner zît an prîse vor ûz hânt den strît.	1	.	1
646, 1-3	daz Gâwân von Artûse reit, sît hât sorge unde leit mit krache ' ûf mich geleget ir vlîz.	2	.	2
647, 13-16	disen brief gip im in die hant, dar an er schiere hât erkant diniu maere und dîns herren ger. des ist er mit der volge wer.	1	.	1

(B)   Reception at the Court 647, 27 - 652, 14

		M	O	T
649, 27-30	iuwer trôst im zucket vreude enbor:' unz ûzerhalp der riuwe tor von sînem herzen kumber jaget, daz ir an im iht sît verzaget.	2	.	2
651, 7-14	Keie sprach in sînem zorn: 'wart aber ie sô werder man geborn, getorst ich des gelouben hân,			

		M	O	T
	sô von Norwaege Gâwân, ziu dar nâher! holt in dâ! sôst er lîhte anderswâ. wil er wenken als ein eichorn, ir muget in schiere hân verlorn.	.	1	1
(C)	Returning to Gawan 652, 15 - 655, 1			
654, 10-14	ob ritters prîs gewan ie kraft, ich meine an werdekeite, die lenge und ouch die breite treget iuwer prîs die krone ob andern prîsen schône.	1	.	1
654, 25	Gâwân ûz sorgen in vreude trat.	1	.	1
. . . .	. . . .		. . . .	
Totals:	320 lines of text	10	1	11
Subtotals:	(A) Ginover's Counsel (105 lines)	6	0	6
	(B) Reception at Court (138 lines)	2	1	3
	(C) Returning to Gawan (77 lines)	2	0	2

Gawan Learns About Klingsor from Arnive 655, 2 - 661, 5

		M	O	T
655, 19-21	getruoc mîn herze ie mannes sin, den hete diu edel herzogin mit ir gewalt beslozzen.	1	.	1
655, 24-26	minne und wunden waere ich tôt, wan daz iuwer helfeclîcher trôst mich ûz banden hât erlôst.	1	.	1
656, 20-21	er trat in prîse sô hôhen phat, an prîse was er unbetrogen.	1	.	1
656, 27-29	Îblis hiez sîn wîp. diu truoc den minneclîchsten lîp, der ie von brüste wart genomen.	.	1	1
659, 19-22	ellende vrumt mirz herze kalt. ' der die sterne hat gezalt, ' der müeze iuch helfe lêren und uns gein vreuden kêren.	1	1	2
659, 23 - 660, 2	ein muoter ir vruht gebirt, ' diu vruht sîner muoter muoter wirt: ' von dem wazzer kumt daz îs,			

			M	O	T
	daz laet denne niht deheinen wîs, daz wazzer enkome ouch wider von im. ' swenne ich gedanke an mich nim, daz ich ûz vreuden bin erborn, wirt vreude noch an mir erkorn, dâ gît ein vruht die andern vruht. diz sult ir vüegen, habet ir zuht.		1	2	3
660, 3-7	ez ist lanc, daz mir vreude entviel. von segel balde gêt der kiel: der man ist sneller, der drûfe gêt. ob ir diz bîspel verstêt, iuwer prîs wirt hôch und snel.		.	1	1
660, 23-28	nû sol ein ieslîch saelec wîp, ob si wil tragen werden lîp, erbietenz guoten liuten wol: si kumt vil lîhte in kumbers dol, daz ir ein swacher garzûn enger vreude gaebe wîten rum.		1	.	1
. . . .	. . . .		. . . .	. . . .	
Totals:	184 lines of text		6	5	11

Arthur's Court Arrives 661, 6 - 666, 1

			M	O	T
661, 16-19	swer samenunge warten sol, den lêrt sûmen den gedanc: er vürht, sîn helfe werde kranc. Artûs Gâwâne den zwîvel brach.		1	.	1
661, 21-26	Gâwân sich hal des tougen, daz sîniu liehten ougen weinen muosten lernen. zeiner zisternen wâren si beidiu dô enwiht, wan si habeten swazzers niht.		.	1	1
662, 7	gein der riuwe sult ir sîn ze wer.		1	.	1
664, 18-23	Artûs schaden vil gewan, ' ê daz er koeme vür Lôgrois. des wart etslîch Bertenois ze rehter tjost abe gevalt. Artûs her ouch wider galt market, den man in dâ bôt.		2	.	2

		M	O	T
664, 25-27	man sach die strîtmüeden komen von den sô dicke ist vernomen, daz si ir kotzen gerne werten.	.	1	1
665, 13-17	dâ wurden unverdrozzen die poinder sô geslozzen, des möhte swenden sich der walt. ' manec tjoste ungezalt rêrten trunzûne.	2	.	2
665, 23-24	man hardierte si den tac unz dar diu vluot des hers lac.	1	.	1
. . . .	. . . .	. . . .		
Totals:	146 lines of text	7	2	9

Gawan Prepares for Their Meeting 666, 2 - 670, 19

		M	O	T
666, 8-10	des milden Gâwânes hant begunde in sô mit willen geben, als er niht langer wolde leben.	.	1	1
. . . .	. . . .	. . . .		
Totals:	138 lines of text	0	1	1

The Reunion with Arthur 670, 20 - 672, 21

		M	O	T
Totals:	62 lines of text	.	.	.

Arthur and Orgeluse 672, 22 - 674, 21

		M	O	T
672, 28 - 673, 1	mirst gesaget, ir habet gesuochet sie: swaz ir des habet genozzen, daz zeiget unverdrozzen. ir möhtet zeiner witewen wol tuon.	1	.	1
674, 3-8	in des helfe ir sît geriten, ob der hât mit mir gestriten, dâ wart ich âne wer bekant und zer blôzen sîten an gerant. ob der noch strîtes gein mir gert, der wirt wol gendet âne swert.	1	.	1
. . . .	. . . .	. . . .		
Totals:	60 lines of text	2	0	2

Final Preparations for the Duel 674, 22 - 678, 17

(A)   Keie as an Example of a Poor Friend 675, 4 - 676, 2

		M	O	T
675, 17-20	der getriuwe ist vriundes êren vrô, der ungetriuwe wâfenô rüefet, swenne ein liep geschiht sinem vriunde und er daz siht.	1	.	1
(B)	Other Details 674, 22 - 675, 3; 676, 3 - 678, 17	.	.	.
....	....	....		
Totals:	116 lines of text	1	0	1
Subtotals:	(A) Keie as a Poor Friend (29 lines)	1	0	1
	(B) Duel Preparations (87 lines)	0	0	0

Parzival Re-enters the Narrative 678, 18-30 — M O T

		M	O	T
678, 18-30	er sach einen ritter halden bî dem wazzer Sabîns. den wir wol möhten heizen vlins der manlichen krefte, ' er schûr der ritterschefte, ' sîn herze valsch nie underswanc. ' er was des lîbes wol sô kranc swaz man heizet unprîs daz entruoc er nie deheinen wîs halbes vingers lanc noch spanne.' von dem selben werden manne muget ir wol ê hân vernomen: an den rehten stam diz maere ist komen.	5	.	5
....	....	....		
Totals:	13 lines of text	5	0	5

Book Thirteen Totals: 1560 lines of text — 52 14 66

BOOK XIV

Gawan and the Strange Knight Fight 679, 1 - 681, 1 — M O T

679, 7	der was in strîte eins mannes her.	1	.	1
679, 10-11	noch roeter denne ein rubîn was sîn kursît und sîn orses kleit.	.	1	1
680, 2-3	ûz der tjoste geslehte wâren si beide samt erborn.	1	.	1

		M	O	T
680, 7-9	gein ein ander stuont ir triuwe, der enweder alt noch niuwe dürkel scharten nie emphienc.	1	.	1
680, 16-17	von swem der prîs dâ wirt genomen, des vreude ist dar um sorgen phant.	1	.	1
680, 25-27	schildes schirben und daz grüene gras ein gelîchiu temperîe was, sît si begunden strîten.	1	.	1
. . . .	. . . .	. . . .
Totals:	61 lines of text	5	1	6

Gramoflanz's Entourage 681, 2 - 683, 10		M	O	T
Totals:	69 lines of text	.	.	.

Arthur's Messengers with Gramoflanz 683, 11 - 688, 3		M	O	T
683, 25-26	gein dem, der hôchverte hort truoc, si sprâchen disiu wort:	1	.	1
687, 18-20	ir triuwe er sô bekande, swâ im kumbers waere bevilt, dâ was ir minne vür ein schilt.	1	.	1
. . . .	. . . .	. . . .
Totals:	143 lines of text	2	0	2

Belated Recognition of Gawan and Parzival 688, 4 - 690, 15		M	O	T
688, 17-20	wan daz in klagende nanden kunt, diu in bekanden, der ê des was sîn strîtes wer, verbar dô gein im strîtes ger.	1	.	1
688, 29 - 689, 2	hie trat mîn ungelücke vür und schiet mich von der saelden kür. sus sint diu alden wâpen mîn ê dicke und aber worden schîn.	1	.	1
689, 25 690, 2	Gâwân sprach: 'dô was ez reht. hiest krumbiu tumpheit worden sleht.' hie hânt zwei herzen einvalt mit hazze erzeiget ir gewalt: dîn hant uns beide überstreit. nû lâ dirz durch uns beide sîn leit:			

		M	O	T
	dû hâs dir selben ane gesiget, ob dîn herze triuwen phliget.	2	.	2
....	....	....		
Totals:	72 lines of text	4	0	4

Duel Set for Gawan and Gramoflanz 690, 16 - 692, 30

		M	O	T
690, 16-20	ûz beiden hern geselleschaft mit rotte kom in hie und dort. ieweder her an sînen ort, dâ ir zil wâren gestôzen mit gespiegelten ronen grôzen.	1	.	1
692, 3-5	diu sach Gâwânen kreftelôs, den si vür al die werlt erkôs zir besten vreude krône.	1	.	1
692, 12-13	bî allen mannen, daz ist wâr, iuwer varwe ein manlîch spiegel was.	1	.	1
....	....	....		
Totals:	75 lines of text	3	0	3

Parzival's Offer to Fight in Gawan's Place Refused 693, 1-20

		M	O	T
693, 13-18	der wirt ûz Rosche Sabîns sprach: 'herre, er gît mir morgen zins:' der stêt ze gelde vür mînen kranz, des sîn prîs wirt hôch und ganz oder daz er jaget mich an die stat, aldâ ich trite ûf lasters phat.	2	.	2
....	....	....		
Totals:	20 lines of text	2	0	2

Vrou Bene Scolds Gramoflanz Because of Itonje's Relationship to Gawan 693, 21 - 694, 19

		M	O	T
693, 21-24	dô sprach Bênen süezer munt zem künege: 'ir ungetriuwer hunt!' iuwer herze in sîner hende liget, dar iuwer herze hazzes phliget:	2	.	2
694, 9-15	dô Bêne daz gehôrte mit waerlîchem worte, daz ir herre ir vrouwen bruoder was, der dâ solde strîten ûf dem gras,			

		M	O	T
	dô zugen jâmers ruoder ' in ir herzen wol <u>ein vuoder</u> <u>der herzenlîchen riuwe</u>	2	.	2
. . . .	. . . .	. . . .		
Totals:	29 lines of text	4	0	4

<u>Joy and Trouble Intermingled: Parzival, Itonje</u> 694, 20 - 698, 14		M	O	T
(A)	Parzival as Gawan's Guest 694, 20 - 696, 20; 697, 9-27	.	.	.
(B)	Itonje's Plight 696, 21 - 697, 8; 697, 28 - 698, 14			
697, 1-8	si sprach: 'ich mac wol weinen und immer klage erscheinen, wan sweder iuwer dâ beliget, nâch dem mîn vrouwe jâmers phliget. <u>diu ist ze beider sît erslagen.</u>' mîne vrouwen und mich muoz ich wol klagen. waz hilft, daz ir ir bruoder sît? <u>mit ir herzen welt ir vehten strît.</u>	2	.	2
. . . .	. . . .	. . . .		
Totals:	115 lines of text	2	0	2
Subtotals:	(A) Parzival as Gawan's Guest (80 lines) (B) Itonje's Plight (35 lines)	0 2	0 0	0 2

<u>Parzival's honor Restored at the Round Table</u> 698, 15 - 700, 24		M	O	T
698, 25-28	Artûs bôt im êre und dancte im des sêre, daz sîn hôhiu werdekeit <u>waere sô lanc und ouch sô breit.</u>	1	.	1
699, 1-5	der Wâleis zArtûse sprach: 'herre, dô ich iuch jungest sach, <u>dô wart ûf die êre mir gerant:</u> ' von prîse ich gap <u>sô hôhiu phant,</u> daz ich von prîse nâch was komen.	2	.	2
. . . .	. . . .	. . . .		
Totals:	70 lines of text	3	0	3

<u>Second Offer to Fight for Gawan Refused</u> 700, 25 - 702, 10		M	O	T
Totals:	46 lines of text	.	.	.

Parzival Fights Gramoflanz Without Consent 702, 11 - 709, 12		M	O	T
703, 26-28	der helt reit al eine dan gein den ronen spiegelîn, aldâ der kamph solde sîn.	1	.	1
705, 15-17	daz her zogete ûz über al, dâ si mit swerten hôrten schal und viur ûz helmen swingen	1	.	1
705, 19-23	der künec Gramoflanz phlac site, im versmâhte sêre, daz er strite mit einem man. dô dûhte in nuo, daz hie sehse griffen strîtes zuo: ez was doch Parzivâl al ein.	.	1	1
706, 13-14	sus emphienc der künec Gramoflanz sûren zins vür sînen kranz.	1	.	1
708, 10	dû sliche von uns als ein diep:	.	1	1
....	....	....		
Totals:	212 lines of text	3	2	5

Arthur Helps Itonje and Gramoflanz 709, 13 - 728, 19		M	O	T
710, 15	dô brast ir jâmer durch die scheme.	1	.	1
710, 28-30	'sol mir nû mîns bruoder hant mîns herzen verh versnîden daz möhte er gerne mîden.'	1	.	1
715, 5-10	unser minne gebent geselleschaft. daz ist wurzel mîner vreude kraft: ' dîn trôst vür ander trôste wiget, sît dîn herze gein mir triuwen phliget. dû bist slôz ob mîner triuwe. ' und ein vlust mîns herzen riuwe.	4	.	4
715, 16-20	als pôlus artanticus gein dem tremuntâne stêt, der neweder von der stete gêt, unser minne sol in triuwen stên und niht von ein ander gên.	.	1	1
718, 29-30	Itonjê hât Gramoflanz verleschet nâch ir liehten glanz.	1	.	1
719, 9-12	hie gît diu minne im einen schilt, des sînen kamphgenôz bevilt:			

		M	O	T
	ich meine gein minne hôhen muot,			
	der bî den vînden schaden tuot.	1	.	1
724, 19-21	im sagete, wer sîn vriundîn was,			
	ein brief, den er ze velde las:			
	ich meine, daz er ir bruoder sach,	1	.	1
728, 11-16	dô muoste der künec Gramoflanz			
	verkiesen um sînen kranz			
	und swaz er hazzes phlaege			
	gein Lôt von Norwaege,			
	der zegienc als in der sunnen snê			
	durch die klâren Itonjê	.	1	1
. . . .	. . . .	. . . .
Totals:	577 lines of text	9	2	11

Peace Established Among All 728, 20 - 729, 26   M   O   T

| Totals: | 37 lines of text | . | . | . |

Marriage Festivities All Around 729, 27 - 731, 30

| Totals: | 64 lines of text | . | . | . |

Parzival Slips Away 732, 1 - 733, 30   M   O   T

732, 10-14	daz vür wâr nie ander wîp			
	wart gewaldec sîner minne,			
	niwan diu küneginne			
	Kondwîrâmûrs,			
	diu geflôrierte bêâ flûrs.	1	.	1
. . . .	. . . .	. . . .
Totals:	60 lines of text	1	0	1

Book Fourteen Totals: 1650 lines of text   38   5   43

BOOK XV

Introduction: Wolfram Promises to Reveal the End 734, 1 - 735, 4   M   O   T

734, 1-9	Vil liute des hât verdrozzen,
	den diz maere was vor beslozzen: '
	genuoge kundenz nie erwarn
	(nû wil ich daz niht langer sparn,
	ich tuonz iu kunt mit rehter sage,

		M	O	T
	wande ich in dem munde trage			
	daz slôz dirre âventiure),	2	.	2
734, 18-19	swaz sin hant ie gestreit,			
	daz was mit kinden her getân.	1	.	1
734, 27 - 735, 1	daz müeze im vestenunge geben, daz er behalde nû sîn leben, sît ez sich hat an den gezoget, in bestêt ob allem strîte ein voget ûf sîner unverzageten reise.	1	.	1
. . . .	. . . .	. . . .		
Totals:	34 lines of text	4	0	4

Parzival Encounters Feirefiz; They Fight 735, 5 - 744, 24

		M	O	T
735, 15-22	swaz diende Artûses hant ze Bertâne und in Engellant, daz vergülde niht die steine, die mit edelem arte reine lâgen ûf des heldes wâpenroc. ' der was tiure âne al getroc: rubîne, kalzidône wâren dâ ze swachem lône.	.	2	2
737, 19-21	hie wellent ein ander varen, die mit kiusche lemmer waren ' und lewen an der vrecheit.	2	.	2
738, 9-10	die lûtern truopheite vrî, ieweder des andern herze truoc: ir vremde was heimlîch genuoc.	1	.	1
738, 19-22	den lewen sîn muoter tôt gebirt: von sîns vater galme er lebendec wirt. dise zwêne wâren ûz krache erborn, von maneger tjost nâch prîse erkorn:	1	.	1
739, 16-18	ezidemôn dem tiere wart etslîch wunde geslagen, ez mohte der helm dar under klagen.	1	.	1
740, 9-12	gein prîse truoc er willen durch die künegîn Sekindillen. diu daz lant ze Tribalibôt im gap, diu was sîn schilt in nôt.	1	.	1

		M	O	T
740, 26-30	man mac wol jehen, sus striten sie, der si beide nennen wil ze zwein. <u>si wâren doch beide niht wan ein:</u> mîn bruoder und ich daz ist ein lîp, als ist guot man und des guot wîp.	1	.	1
741, 23-25	durch minne heten si gegeben mit kamphe ûf urteil beide ir leben: <u>ieweders hant was sicherbote.</u>	1	.	1
742, 8-10	er was <u>schumphentiure ein gast</u>, daz er si nie gedolde, doch si maneger zim erholde.	1	.	1
742, 12-13	<u>viurs blicke ûz helmen sprungen</u>, ' von ir swerten <u>gienc der sûre wint</u>.	2	.	2
742, 18-22	sus begunden siz ouch meinen, waeren si ein ander baz bekant: <u>si ensazten niht sô hôhiu phant.</u> ir strît galt niht mêre wan vreude, saelde und êre.	1	.	1
743, 24-28	er dâhte (des was im niht ze vruo) an sîn wîp, die küneginne, und an ir werden minne, die er mit <u>swertes schimphe erranc</u>, ' dâ <u>viur von slegen ûz helmen spranc</u>,	2	.	2
744, 10-13	von Gaheviez daz starke swert mit slage ûf sheidens helme brast, sô daz der küene rîche gast <u>mit strûche venje suochte.</u>	1	.	1
744, 22-24	zurteile stêz in beiden vor <u>der hoesten hende</u>, daz diu ir sterben wende!	1	.	1
Totals:	290 lines of text	16	2	18

They Discover Their Relationship 744, 25 - 749, 30   M O T

| 747, 23-28 | tuo mir sîn antlitze erkant,
wie dir sîn varwe sî genant. '
dô sprach Herzeloiden kint:
'als ein geschriben permint
swarz und blanc her und dâ, |

		M	O	T
	sus nande mir in Ekubâ.'	.	1	1
748, 6-7	der heiden schiere wart erkant, wande er truoc agelstern mâl.	.	1	1
748, 30 - 749, 1	minnen slüzzel kurteis, ô wol diu wîp, diu dich suln sehen!	1	.	1
749, 16-17	Jûpiter hât sinen vliz, werder helt, geleget an dich.	1	.	1
Totals:	156 lines of text	2	2	4

The Brothers Speak of Gahmuret 750, 1 - 752, 30

		M	O	T
752, 8-17	beidiu mîn vater und ouch dû und ich, wir wâren gar al ein, ' doch ez an drîen stücken schein. swâ man siht den wîsen man, der enzelt deheine sippe dan, zwischen vater und des kinden, wil er die wârheit vinden. mit dir selben hâstû hie gestriten. ' gein mir selben ich kom ûf strît geriten, mich selben hete ich gerne erslagen.	2	.	2
Totals:	90 lines of text	2	0	2

Feirefiz Invites Parzival to View His Army 753, 1-24

		M	O	T
Totals:	24 lines of text	.	.	.

Parzival Invites Feirefiz to See Arthur's Court 753, 25 - 754, 28

		M	O	T
754, 5-7	dô der heiden hôrte nennen wîp (diu wâren et sin selbes lîp), er sprach: 'dâ vüere mich hin mit dir.'	1	.	1
Totals:	31 lines of text	1	0	1

Events At Court in Parzival's Absence 754, 29 - 755, 29

		M	O	T
755, 20-21	'swaz ie mit swerten waere geschehen, daz ist gein disem strîte ein niht.'	1	.	1

THE IMAGES IN PARZIVAL

		M	O	T
Totals:	31 lines of text	1	0	1

Parzival and Feirefiz as Gawan's Guests 755, 30 - 766, 18   M   O   T

		M	O	T
756, 30 - 757, 1	dar unde ein wâpenroc erschein, rûch gebildet, snêvar.	.	1	1
758, 11-12	'bin ich dîn mâc, daz ist ouch er: des sî Gahmuret din wer.'	1	.	1
759, 8-10	sprach Parzivâl. 'mîns bruoder hant twanc mich wer in grôzer nôt. wer ist ein segen vür den tôt.	1	.	1
760, 27-29	der rinc begreif sô wît ein velt, dâ waeren gestanden sehs gezelt âne gedrenge der snüere.	.	1	1
761, 24-30	sîniu wâpenlîchiu kleit niemen vergelden möhte. deheiner hant daz töhte: Löver, Bertâne, Engellant, von Pârîs unz an Wîzsant, der dâ gein legete al die terre, ez waere dem gelde verre.	.	1	1
766, 12-15	giht man vreude iht urbor, den zins muoz wâriu minne geben.' sus sach ich ie die werden leben: dâ saz dienest und lôn.	2	.	2
Totals:	319 lines of text	4	3	7

Arthur and Feirefiz Get Acquainted 766, 19 - 769, 28   M   O   T

		M	O	T
768, 1-4	ich vüere sô kreftegez her, Troiaere lantwer und jene, die si besâzen, müesten rûmen mir die strâzen.	.	1	1
769, 9-11	ich meine die herzoginne, diu hie sitzet, nâch ir minne ist waldes vil verswendet.	1	.	1
Totals:	100 lines of text	1	1	2

THE IMAGES IN PARZIVAL

	M	O	T
Listing of Knights by Feirefiz, Parzival, Arthur 769, 29 - 772, 30			

Totals: 92 lines of text   .   .   .

Arthur's Court Marvels at Feirefiz 773, 1 - 774, 12

Totals: 42 lines of text   .   .   .

Round Table Festival in Honor of Feirefiz 774, 13 - 778, 12

Totals: 120 lines of text   .   .   .

Cundrie Arrives, Proclaims Parzival Lord of the Grail 778, 13 - 782, 30	M	O	T

778, 17-20	ir kleider wâren tiure und wol gesniten, kostebaere nâch Franzoiser siten, ir kappe ein rîcher samît noch swerzer denne ein gênît:	.	1	1
780, 19-22	ir ougen stuonden dennoch sus, gel als ein topâzjus, ' ir zene lanc, ir munt gap schîn als ein vîol weitîn.	.	2	2
781, 14-15	dû krône menschen heiles, daz epitafium ist gelesen:	1	.	1
782, 14-16	die sint des firmamentes zoum, die enthalden sîne snelheit, ir kriec gein sînem loufte ie streit.	1	.	1
782, 17	sorge ist dînhalp nû weise.	1	.	1

Totals: 138 lines of text   3   3   6

Parzival's Joy, Preparations to Go with Cundrie 738, 1 - 786, 30	M	O	T

783, 2-3	durch liebe ûz sinen ougen vlôz wazzer, sherzen ursprinc.	1	.	1

Totals: 120 lines of text   1   0   1

Book Fifteen Totals: 1590 lines of text   35 11 46

BOOK XVI

Anfortas Pleading for Death 787, 1 - 789, 3		M	O	T
787, 26-29	ich hân tal unde berc mit manerger tjost überzilt und mit dem swerte alsô gespilt, daz es die vinde an mir verdroz	1	.	1
....	....	....		
Totals:	63 lines of text	1	0	1

Time of Greatest Pain Arrives 789, 4 - 792, 9		M	O	T
789, 21-23	swenne im diu scharphe ' sûre nôt daz strenge ungemach gebôt, sô wart der luft gesüezet.	2	.	2
792, 6-7	dâ mite si muosten vristen Anfortasen, der ir herze truoc	1	.	1
....	....	....		
Totals:	96 lines of text	3	0	3

Cundrie, Parzival, Feirefiz Arrive 792, 10 - 794, 26		M	O	T
792, 28- 793, 1	'unser sorge ein ende hât: mit sgrâles insigel hie kumt uns, des wir dâ gerten ie, sît uns der jâmerstric beslôz.	1	.	1
....	....	....		
Totals:	77 lines of text	1	0	1

Parzival Releases Anfortas 794, 27 - 796, 27		M	O	T
796, 7-15	Parzivâles schoene was nû ein wint ' und Absalôn Dâvîdes kint, ' von Ascalûn Vergulaht und al, den schoene was geslaht, und des man Gahmurete jach, dô man in în zogen sach ze Kanvoleiz sô wünneclîch, ir deheines schoene was der gelîch die Anfortas ûz siecheit truoc.	1	1	2
....	....	....		
Totals:	61 lines of text	1	1	2

151

Parzival Rides to Meet Condwiramurs 796, 28 - 799, 13		M	O	T
798, 2-5	'groezer wunder selten ie geschach, sît ir ab got erzürnet hât, daz sîn endelôsiu trînitât iuwers willen werschaft worden ist.	1	.	1
Totals:	76 lines of text	1	0	1

Reunion with Condwiramurs 799, 14 - 802, 10		M	O	T
801, 6-7	si sprach: 'mir hât gelücke dich gesendet, herzen vreude mîn.'	1	.	1
802, 1-5	gezucte im ie bluot und snê geselleschaft an witzen ê (ûf der selben ouwe erz ligen vant), vür solhen kumber gap nû phant Kondwîrâmûrs; diu hetez dâ.	1	.	1
Totals:	87 lines of text	2	0	2

Kardeiz Made King of Parzival's Lands 802, 11 - 803, 30		M	O	T
Totals:	50 lines of text	.	.	.

Parzival and Condwiramurs Bury Sigune 804, 1 - 805, 17		M	O	T
804, 14-16	. . . 'dâ wont ein maget al klagende ûf vriundes sarke. diust rehter güete ein arke.	1	.	1
804, 28-29	Schîanatulander schein unervûlet schône balsemvar	.	1	1
805, 14-15	ez ist niht krump alsô der boge, diz maere ist wâr unde sleht.	.	1	1
Totals:	47 lines of text	1	2	3

Condwiramurs Received at Munsalvaesch 805, 18 - 807, 10		M	O	T
805, 20-21	vil kerzen man dô enzunde, rehte ob brünne gar der walt.	.	1	1
806, 18-22	dâ stuont ouch swankel als ein rîs, der schoene und güete niht gebrach			

		M	O	T
	und der man im ze tohter jach,			
	von Rîle Jernîse:			
	diu maget hiez Amflîse.	.	1	1
806, 23-26	von Tenabroc, ist mir gesaget,			
	stuont dâ Klârischanze ein süeziu maget,			
	liehter varwe gar unverkrenket,			
	als ein âmeize gelenket.	.	1	1
....	....	....		
Totals:	53 lines of text	0	3	3

Grail Ceremony and Banquet 807, 11 - 810, 2		M	O	T
809, 13-14	ir herzen was vil kiusche bî,			
	ir vel des blickes flôrî	1	.	1
....	....	....		
Totals: 82 lines of text		1	0	1

Feirefiz Smitten by Love of Repanse 810, 3 - 813, 8		M	O	T
810, 14	ir blic mir inz herze gêt.	1	.	1
811, 1-5	Kondwîrâmûrs diu lieht erkant			
	vil nâch nû ebenhiuze vant			
	an der klâren megede velles blic.			
	dô slôz sich in ir minnen stric			
	Feirefîz der rîche gast.	1	.	1
....	....	....		
Totals:	96 lines of text	2	0	2

Need for Baptism Explained to Feirefiz 813, 9 - 815, 30		M	O	T
813, 17-22	der sprach: 'ist ez ein heidenesch man,			
	dô darf er des niht willen hân,			
	daz sîn ougen âne stoufes kraft			
	bejagen die geselleschaft,			
	daz si den grâl beschouwen:			
	dâst hâmît vür gehouwen.	1	.	1
813, 29-30	si wurben, daz er naeme den touf			
	und endelôsen gewinnes kouf.	1	.	1
814, 4-5	'ez was ie jenen her ein wint,			
	swaz mich strît oder minne twanc.'	1	.	1
815, 26-29	Feirefîz Anschevîn			

	M	O	T
sach si von im kêren.			
daz begunde im trûren mêren:			
<u>sîns herzen slôz</u> truoc dan den grâl.	1	.	1
....	....		
Totals: 82 lines of text	4	0	4

<u>Feirefiz's Baptism and Marriage to Repanse</u> 816, 1 - 818, 23

	M	O	T
817, 14-16 des drîvalt ist gemeine			
und <u>al gelîche gurbort</u>,			
got ist mensche und sîns vater wort.	1	.	1
....	....		
Totals: 83 lines of text	1	0	1

<u>Everyone's New Role Defined</u> 818, 24 - 820, 30

	M	O	T
Totals: 67 lines of text	.	.	.

<u>Feirefiz and Repanse Leave for India</u> 821, 1 - 823, 10

	M	O	T
Totals: 70 lines of text	.	.	.

<u>Conclusion: Summary of Lohengrin's Fate</u> 823, 11 - 826, 30

	M	O	T
823, 28-29 diu zageheit <u>sich an im barc</u>,			
dô er sich ritterschaft versan.	1	.	1
....	....		
Totals: 110 lines of text	1	0	1

<u>Epilog</u> 827, 1-30

	M	O	T
Totals: 30 lines of text	.	.	.

<u>Book Sixteen Totals</u>: 1230 lines of text   19   6   25

Table II: Thematic Passages in Sequence

Passage Topic	Lines	Images	Image/Line	Metaphors	Metaphor/Line	Metaphors %
Book I						
Prologue	116	33	1/ 3.5	15	1/ 7.7	45.4
Gahmuret's Departure	246	8	1/ 30.8	6	1/ 41	75
In Service of the Baruch	89	4	1/ 22.3	1	1/ 89	25
Goes to Zazamanc	230	4	1/ 57.5	2	1/ 115	50
Received by Belacane	371	19	1/ 19.5	13	1/ 28.5	68.4
Battles for Belacane	238	8	1/ 29.8	4	1/ 59.5	50
Lord of Zazamanc	284	4	1/ 71	1	1/ 284	25
Conclusion at Zazamanc	162	11	1/ 14.7	8	1/ 20.3	72.5
Book II						
Gahmuret to Kanvoleis	92	2	1/ 46	0	0/ 92	–
Arrives at Herzeloide's Tournam.	198	11	1/ 18	4	1/ 49.5	36.4
Events of Vesperie	424	21	1/ 20.2	13	1/ 32.6	61.9
(A. Queen Amphlise's Mess.)	(58)	(2)	(1/ 29)	(2)	(1/ 29)	(100)
(B. Gahmuret Drops Out)	(29)	(1)	(1/ 29)	(1)	(1/ 29)	(100)
(C. His Superiority)	(30)	(3)	(1/ 10)	(0)	(0/ 30)	–
(D. Fighting Described)	(307)	(15)	(1/ 20.5)	(10)	(1/ 30.7)	(66.6)
Results of the Vesperie	226	6	1/ 37.7	5	1/ 45.2	83.3
Gahmuret's Grief	114	6	1/ 19	5	1/ 22.8	83.3
Herzeloide's Claim	230	7	1/ 32.9	4	1/ 56	57.1
Recalled by the Baruch	32	0	0/ 32	0	0/ 32	–
Herzeloide's Dream Ordeal	75	3	1/ 25	2	1/ 37.5	66.6
Gahmuret's Death Described	114	2	1/ 57	0	0/ 57	–
Birth of Parzival	153	13	1/ 11.8	12	1/ 12.8	92.3
Epilogue to Books I - II	60	7	1/ 8.6	6	1/ 10	85.7

Passage Topic	Lines	Images	Image/Line	Metaphors	Metaphor/Line	Metaphors %
Book III						
Prologue	10	0	0/ 10	0	0/ 10	–
Herzeloide in Wilderness	116	11	1/ 10.6	6	1/ 19.3	55.5
Parzival Meets Knights	264	6	1/ 44	4	1/ 66	66.6
Parzival and Jeschute	110	7	1/ 15.7	5	1/ 22	71.4
Orilus and Jeschute	156	2	1/ 78	1	1/ 156	50
Parzival Meets Sigune	130	4	1/ 32.5	4	1/ 32.5	100
Parzival and Fisherman	40	2	1/ 20	1	1/ 40	50
At Arthur's Court	528	33	1/ 16	25	1/ 21.1	75.7
(A. Reception)	(218)	(17)	(1/ 12.8)	(12)	(1/ 18.2)	(70.5)
(B. Cunneware's Beating)	(82)	(6)	(1/ 13.6)	(4)	(1/ 20.5)	(66.6)
(C. Fights Ither)	(172)	(4)	(1/ 43)	(3)	(1/ 57.3)	(75)
(D. Grief over Ither)	(56)	(6)	(1/ 9.3)	(6)	(1/ 9.3)	(100)
Parzival and Gurnemanz	544	33	1/ 16.5	23	1/ 23.7	69.6
(A. Received as Stranger)	(268)	(14)	(1/ 19.1)	(12)	(1/ 22.3)	(85.7)
(B. Instructed by Gurnemanz)	(150)	(9)	(1/ 16.7)	(4)	(1/ 37.5)	(44.4)
(C. Hosted as Son)	(63)	(4)	(1/ 15.8)	(3)	(1/ 21)	(75)
(D. Departure)	(63)	(6)	(1/ 10.5)	(4)	(1/ 15.8)	(66.6)
Book IV						
On the Way to Pelrapeire	58	8	1/ 7.3	0	0/ 58	–
Arrival at Pelrapeire	156	17	1/ 9.2	5	1/ 31.2	29.4
Meeting with Condwiramurs	112	7	1/ 17.4	5	1/ 22.4	71.4
Relief through Cousins	38	1	1/ 38	0	0/ 38	–
Night Visit and Plea	143	10	1/ 14.3	6	1/ 23.8	60
Battles Kingrun	103	2	1/ 51.5	0	0/ 103	–
Lord of Pelrapeire	110	6	1/ 18.3	4	1/ 27.5	66.6
Readying to Fight Clamide	83	2	1/ 41.5	2	1/ 41.5	100
Kingrun at Arthur's Court	29	1	1/ 29	0	0/ 29	–
Fights Clamide	271	10	1/ 27.1	8	1/ 33.9	80
Clamide at Arthur's Court	185	11	1/ 16.8	7	1/ 26.4	63.3

Passage Topic	Lines	Images	Image/Line	Metaphors	Metaphor/Line	Metaphors %
Peace at Pelrapeire	35	1	1/ 35	1	1/ 35	100
Leaves to Find Herzeloide	16	0	0/ 16	0	0/ 16	–
Wandering Aimlessly	30	1	1/ 30	0	0/ 30	–
Meets the Fisher-King	39	1	1/ 39	0	0/ 39	–
Arrival at Grail Castle	103	6	1/ 17.1	1	1/ 103	16.6
Dinner with Grail Company	386	28	1/ 13.7	15	1/ 25.7	53.6
(A. General Narrative)	(198)	(7)	(1/ 28.3)	(5)	(1/ 39.6)	(71.1)
(B. Grail Ceremony)	(158)	(12)	(1/ 13.2)	(5)	(1/ 31.6)	(41.7)
(C. Wolfram's Apology)	(30)	(9)	(1/ 3.3)	(5)	(1/ 6)	(55.5)
In Parzival's Bed-Chamber	88	10	1/ 8.8	6	1/ 14.7	60
(A. The Service to Him)	(72)	(6)	(1/ 12)	(3)	(1/ 24)	(50)
(B. The Nightmare)	(16)	(4)	(1/ 4)	(3)	(1/ 5.3)	(75)
Abandoned at Munsalvaesche	90	7	1/ 12.9	5	1/ 18	71.4
Sigune Again, Learns Error	234	6	1/ 39	3	1/ 78	50
Reconciles Orilus-Jeschute	463	23	1/ 20.1	11	1/ 42.1	47.8
The Reconciliation	67	3	1/ 22.3	3	1/ 22.3	100
Orilus-Jeschute, Arthur's Court	180	4	1/ 45	2	1/ 90	50
Book VI						
Arthur Seeks Red Knight	39	1	1/ 39	0	0/ 39	–
Parzival and Drops of Blood	717	58	1/ 12.4	43	1/ 16.6	74.1
(A. Source of Trance)	(74)	(4)	(1/ 18.5)	(3)	(1/ 24.6)	(75)
(B. Discovery by Page)	(36)	(1)	(1/ 36)	(1)	(1/ 36)	(100)
(C. Segramors Begs to Fight)	(54)	(2)	(1/ 27)	(1)	(1/ 54)	(50)
(D. Segramors vs. Parzival)	(99)	(9)	(1/ 11)	(6)	(1/ 16.5)	(66.6)
(E. Keie Fights Parzival)	(102)	(13)	(1/ 7.8)	(11)	(1/ 9.3)	(84.6)
(F. Complaint to Vrou Minne)	(88)	(11)	(1/ 8)	(9)	(1/ 9.8)	(81.8)
(G. Wolfram Defends Keie)	(47)	(3)	(1/ 15.6)	(1)	(1/ 47)	(33.3)

Passage Topic	Lines	Images	Image/Line	Metaphors	Metaphor/Line	Metaphors %
(H. Gawan Fetches Parzival)	(217)	(15)	(1/ 14.5)	(11)	(1/ 19.7)	(73.3)
Parzival Received by Arthur	205	11	1/ 18.6	7	1/ 24.6	63.6
Cundrie	228	38	1/ 6	28	1/ 8.1	73.7
(A. Her Arrival)	(69)	(13)	(1/ 5)	(4)	(1/ 17.3)	(30.7)
(B. The Denunciation)	(120)	(21)	(1/ 5.7)	(20)	(1/ 6)	(95.2)
(C. Plea for Captive Queens)	(20)	(1)	(1/ 20)	(1)	(1/ 20)	(100)
(D. Court's Grief for Parzival)	(19)	(3)	(1/ 6.3)	(3)	(1/ 6.3)	(100)
Kingrimursel vs Gawan	205	7	1/ 29.3	6	1/ 34.1	85.7
Reactions to Cundrie's News	256	8	1/ 32	7	1/ 36.5	87.5
(A. Clamide-Cunne. Betroth.)	(46)	(0)	(0/ 46)	(0)	(0/ 46)	–
(B. News of Feirefiz)	(30)	(3)	(1/ 10)	(2)	(1/ 15)	(66.6)
(C. Attempts to Comfort Parzival)	(60)	(3)	(1/ 20)	(3)	(1/ 20)	(100)
(D. Parzival Leaves to Seek Grail)	(90)	(2)	(1/ 45)	(2)	(1/ 45)	(100)
(E. Knights to Schast. Marv.)	(30)	(0)	(0/ 30)	(0)	(0/ 30)	–
Gawan, Clamide, etc. Depart	60	1	1/ 60	1	1/ 60	100
Epilog: Kindness to Women	30	3	1/ 10	2	1/ 15	66.6
Book VII						
Introd. to Gawan Episodes	30	3	1/ 10	2	1/ 15	66.6
Great Unknown Army	98	4	1/ 24.5	2	1/ 49	50
Squire's Explanation	229	9	1/ 25.4	5	1/ 45.8	55.5
(A. Identifies Army)	(62)	(2)	(1/ 31)	(1)	(1/ 62)	(50)
(B. Quarrel, Meljanz-Obie)	(124)	(6)	(1/ 20.7)	(4)	(1/ 31)	(66.6)
(C. Concluding Details)	(43)	(1)	(1/ 43)	(0)	(0/ 43)	–
Gawan to Bearosche	126	5	1/ 25.2	5	1/ 25.2	100
Battle Preparations	82	2	1/ 41	0	0/ 82	–
Vesperie	100	3	1/ 33.3	3	1/ 33.3	100

Passage Topic	Lines	Images	Image/Line	Metaphors	Metaphor/Line	Metaphors %
Gawan's Involvement	367	26	1/ 14.1	21	1/ 17.5	80.7
(A. Obie's Hostility)	(73)	(1)	(1/ 73)	(1)	(1/ 73)	(100)
(B. Scherules' Courtesy)	(72)	(7)	(1/ 10.3)	(3)	(1/ 24)	(43)
(C. Discourse: Obie–Love)	(32)	(3)	(1/ 10.6)	(3)	(1/ 10.6)	(100)
(D. Lippaot Asks for Help)	(67)	(1)	(1/ 67)	(1)	(1/ 67)	(100)
(E. Obilot Wins Gawan)	(123)	(14)	(1/ 8.8)	(13)	(1/ 9.5)	(92.8)
Obilot's Token for Gawan	108	2	1/ 54	2	1/ 54	100
Night Preparations	64	2	1/ 32	1	1/ 64	50
Battle at Bearosche	296	15	1/ 19.7	6	1/ 49.3	40
(A. General Survey)	(56)	(8)	(1/ 7)	(2)	(1/ 28)	(25)
(B. Gawan)	(112)	(2)	(1/ 56)	(2)	(1/ 56)	(100)
(C. Red Knight)	(22)	(1)	(1/ 22)	(1)	(1/ 22)	(100)
(D. Gawan Captures Meljanz)	(46)	(1)	(1/ 46)	(0)	(0/ 46)	–
(E. Lippaot)	(21)	(0)	(0/ 21)	(0)	(0/ 21)	–
(F. Gawan Unhorses Meljacanc)	(39)	(3)	(1/ 13)	(1)	(1/ 39)	(33.3)
Red Knight's Dispensations	71	1	1/ 71	1	1/ 71	100
Conflict Resolved	229	4	1/ 57.3	3	1/ 76.3	75
Book VIII						
Gawan Arrives, Schampfanzun	54	5	1/ 10.8	2	1/ 27	40
Vergulaht Hunting; Invitation	142	7	1/ 20.3	3	1/ 47.3	42.8
Gawan with Antikonie	284	13	1/ 21.8	8	1/ 35.5	61.6
(A. Attempted Seduction)	(83)	(5)	(1/ 16.6)	(3)	(1/ 27.6)	(60)
(B. Under Attack)	(114)	(6)	(1/ 19)	(3)	(1/ 38)	(50)
(C. Rescue by Kingrimursel)	(29)	(0)	(0/ 29)	(0)	(0/ 29)	–
(D. Truce)	(58)	(2)	(1/ 29)	(2)	(1/ 29)	(100)
Arguments, Right vs Wrong	145	8	1/ 18.1	8	1/ 18.1	100
(A. Antikonie)	(38)	(3)	(1/ 12.6)	(3)	(1/ 12.6)	(100)
(B. Kingrimursel)	(38)	(3)	(1/ 12.6)	(3)	(1/ 12.6)	(100)

Passage Topic	Lines	Images	Image/Line	Metaphors	Metaphor/Line	Metaphors %
(C. Liddamus)	(24)	(0)	(0/ 24)	(0)	(0/ 24)	–
(D. Kingrimursel's Reply)	(45)	(2)	(1/ 22.5)	(2)	(1/ 22.5)	(100)
Liddamus' Discourse: Fights	96	8	1/ 12	2	1/ 48	25
The Evening Truce	128	8	1/ 16	6	1/ 21.3	75
(A. Ordered by Vergulaht)	(18)	(1)	(1/ 18)	(0)	(0/ 18)	–
(B. In Antikonie's Chamber)	(47)	(4)	(1/ 11.8)	(3)	(1/ 15.6)	(75)
(C. Vergulaht's Council)	(63)	(3)	(1/ 21)	(3)	(1/ 21)	(100)
The Morning of Judgment	201	8	1/ 25.1	7	1/ 28.7	87.5
(A. Antikonie Escorts Gawan)	(51)	(5)	(1/ 10.2)	(4)	(1/ 12.7)	(80)
(B. Vergulaht's Offer: Grail)	(29)	(0)	(0/ 29)	(0)	(0/ 29)	–
(C. Gawan–Company Reunion)	(51)	(1)	(1/ 51)	(1)	(1/ 51)	(100)
(D. Gawan Leaves for Grail)	(70)	(2)	(1/ 35)	(2)	(1/ 35)	(100)

Book IX

Passage Topic	Lines	Images	Image/Line	Metaphors	Metaphor/Line	Metaphors %
Transition Back to Parzival	61	5	1/ 12.2	4	1/ 20.3	80
(A. Vrou Aventiure)	(40)	(2)	(1/ 20)	(1)	(1/ 40)	(50)
(B. Parzival's Interim Wandering)	(21)	(3)	(1/ 7)	(3)	(1/ 7)	(100)
Sigune in Hermit Cell	234	14	1/ 16.7	11	1/ 21.3	78.5
Parzival vs. Grail Knight	95	5	1/ 19	0	0/ 95	–
Good Friday Pilgrims	152	2	1/ 76	1	1/ 152	50
Horse Goes to Trevrizent	58	1	1/ 58	1	1/ 58	100
Discovery of Grail Story	84	3	1/ 28	3	1/ 28	100
Reception by Trevrizent	153	5	1/ 30.6	5	1/ 30.6	100
Instruction about God	201	31	1/ 6	29	1/ 6.9	93.5
Instruction about Grail	214	2	1/ 107	1	1/ 214	50
Kinship Guilt Revealed	98	5	1/ 19.6	4	1/ 24.5	80
Story of Anfortas	210	7	1/ 30	6	1/ 35	85.7
Trevrizent's Hospitality	90	7	1/ 12.8	1	1/ 90	14.3

Passage Topic	Lines	Images	Image/Line	Metaphors	Metaphor/Line	Metaphors %
Parzival's Confession	20	0	0/ 20	0	0/ 20	–
Trevrizent's Response	31	7	1/ 4.4	7	1/ 4.4	100
Other Grail Phenomena	171	6	1/ 28.5	4	1/ 42.7	66.6
Trevrizent's Youth	120	1	1/120	0	0/120	–
Repentance Begun	66	2	1/ 33	1	1/ 66	50
Titurel	15	0	0/ 15	0	0/15	–
Final Lessons, Parting	27	3	1/ 9	3	1/ 9	100
Book X						
Introduction	4	0	0/ 4	0	0/ 4	–
Summary, Gawan's Release	32	0	0/ 32	0	0/ 32	–
Lady and Wounded Knight	114	6	1/ 19	4	1/ 38.5	66.6
Meets Orgeluse de Logrois	145	13	1/ 11.2	11	1/ 13.2	84.7
Gets Horse; Bare Acceptance	135	6	1/ 22.5	4	1/ 33.7	66.6
Encounter with Malcreatiure	128	7	1/ 18.3	4	1/ 32	57.1
(A. Description of Malcreatiure)	(20)	(3)	(1/ 6.6)	(0)	(0/ 20)	–
(B. Cundrie and Malcreatiure)	(62)	(2)	(1/ 31)	(2)	(1/ 31)	(100)
(C. Quarrel with Malcreatiure)	(46)	(2)	(1/ 23)	(2)	(1/ 23)	(100)
Gawan's Horse Stolen	80	1	1/ 80	1	1/ 80	100
Story of Urjans and Gawan	158	0	0/158	0	0/158	–
Gawan & Malcreatiure's Nag	74	4	1/ 18.5	4	1/ 18.5	100
Amor and Cupido	68	6	1/ 11.3	6	1/ 11.3	100
Arrive, Schastel Marveile	61	0	0/ 61	0	0/ 61	–
Fights Lischois Gwelljus	230	6	1/ 38.3	5	1/ 46	83.3
Ferryman Gets Lischois	93	3	1/ 21	1	1/ 93	33.3
Ferryman's Hospitality	178	9	1/ 19.8	7	1/ 25.4	77.7
Book XI						
Gawan Inquires about Ladies	287	6	1/ 47.8	5	1/ 57.4	83.3

Passage Topic	Lines	Images	Image/Line	Metaphors	Metaphor/Line	Metaphors %
(A. Early Morning Curiousity)	(20)	(0)	(0/ 20)	(0)	(0/ 20)	–
(B. Ferryman's Daughter)	(70)	(0)	(0/ 70)	(0)	(0/ 70)	–
(C. Ferryman Plipalinot)	(197)	(6)	(1/ 32.8)	(5)	(1/ 39.4)	(83.3)
Merchant at Castle Gate	65	2	1/ 32.5	0	0/ 65	–
Enters Schastel Marveile	48	5	1/ 9.6	2	1/ 24	40
Chamber of the Lit Marveile	224	12	1/ 18.7	4	1/ 56	33.3
(A. The Bed)	(64)	(7)	(1/ 9.1)	(2)	(1/ 32)	(28.5)
(B. The Stones and Arrows)	(39)	(1)	(1/ 39)	(1)	(1/ 39)	(100)
(C. The Churl)	(37)	(2)	(1/ 18.5)	(1)	(1/ 37)	(50)
(D. The Lion)	(84)	(2)	(1/ 42)	(0)	(0/ 84)	–
Nursed by Ladies and Arnive	276	5	1/ 55.2	5	1/ 55.2	100
Book XII						
Introd.; Gawan Oppressed, Love	64	7	1/ 9.1	4	1/ 16	57.1
Vrou Minne, Discourse	70	3	1/ 23.3	3	1/ 23.3	100
Suffering for Orgeluse	46	0	0/ 46	0	0/ 46	–
Tower of Magic Pillar	163	8	1/ 20.4	4	1/ 40.7	50
(A. Pillar and Windows)	(70)	(3)	(1/ 23.3)	(1)	(1/ 70)	(33.3)
(B. Four Captive Queens)	(40)	(2)	(1/ 20)	(2)	(1/ 20)	(100)
(C. Orgeluse and Turkoite)	(53)	(3)	(1/ 17.6)	(1)	(1/ 54)	(33.3)
The Turkoite	150	5	1/ 30	4	1/ 37.5	80
(A. Gawan Prepares to Fight)	(90)	(0)	(0/ 90)	(0)	(0/ 90)	–
(B. They Fight)	(32)	(3)	(1/ 10.6)	(3)	(1/ 10.6)	(100)
(C. Orgeluse Taunts Gawan)	(28)	(2)	(1/ 14)	(1)	(1/ 28)	(50)
Chasm & Wreath, Last Test	143	6	1/ 23.8	5	1/ 28.6	83.3
Gramoflanz and Gawan	210	2	1/ 105	1	1/ 210	50
Gawan Wins Orgeluse	134	13	1/ 10.3	11	1/ 12.2	84.6

Passage Topic	Lines	Images	Image/Line	Metaphors	Metaphor/Line	Metaphors %
Orgeluse and Anfortas	43	3	1/ 14.3	3	1/ 14.3	100
Orgeluse and Klingsor	41	0	0/ 41	0	0/ 41	–
Orgeluse and Parzival	40	0	0/ 40	0	0/ 40	–
Triumphant Return to Sch. M.	156	1	1/ 156	1	1/ 156	100
Messenger Sent to Arthur	60	0	0/ 60	0	0/ 60	–
Book XIII						
Arnive and Gawan's Secret	18	0	0/ 18	0	0/ 18	–
Lischois & Turkoite Freed	107	4	1/ 26.7	1	1/ 107	25
Gawan-Itonje re Gramoflanz	159	7	1/ 22.7	5	1/ 31.8	71.4
Banquet and Dance	166	10	1/ 16.6	9	1/ 18.4	90
Gawan's Night with Orgeluse	71	6	1/ 11.8	6	1/ 11.8	100
Gawan's Messenger	320	11	1/ 29.1	10	1/ 32	90
(A. Ginover's Counsel)	(105)	(6)	(1/ 17.5)	(6)	(1/ 17.5)	(100)
(B. Reception at Court)	(138)	(3)	(1/ 46)	(2)	(1/ 69)	(66.6)
(C. Return to Gawan)	(77)	(2)	(1/ 38.5)	(2)	(1/ 38.5)	(100)
Gawan Learns of Klingsor	184	11	1/ 16.7	6	1/ 30.7	54.5
Arthur's Court Arrives	146	9	1/ 16.2	7	1/ 20.8	77.7
Gawan Prepares to Meet Him	138	1	1/ 138	0	0/ 138	–
Reunion with Arthur	62	0	0/ 62	0	0/ 62	–
Arthur and Orgeluse	60	2	1/ 30	2	1/ 30	100
Preparations for Duel	116	1	1/ 116	1	1/ 116	100
(A. Keie as Poor Friend)	(29)	(1)	(1/ 29)	(1)	(1/ 29)	(100)
(B. Other Details)	(87)	(0)	(0/ 87)	(0)	(0/ 87)	–
Parzival Re-enters Story	13	5	1/ 2.6	5	1/ 2.6	100
Book XIV						
Gawan and Stranger Fight	61	6	1/ 10.1	5	1/ 12.2	83.3

Passage Topic	Lines	Images	Image/Line	Metaphors	Metaphor/Line	Metaphors %
Gramoflanz's Entourage	69	0	0/ 69	0	1/ 69	–
Arthur's Messengers with Gr.	143	2	1/ 71.5	2	1/ 71.5	100
Belated Recognition, Ga.-Par.	72	4	1/ 18	4	1/ 18	100
Duel Set, Gawan-Gramoflanz	75	3	1/ 25	3	1/ 25	100
Parzival's Offer to Fight Refused	20	2	1/ 10	2	1/ 10	100
Vrou Bene Scolds Gramoflanz	29	4	1/ 7.3	4	1/ 7.3	100
Joy, Trouble Intermingled	115	2	1/ 57.5	2	1/ 57.5	100
(A. Parzival as Gawan's Guest)	(80)	(0)	(0/ 80)	(0)	(0/ 80)	–
(B. Itonje's Plight)	(35)	(2)	(1/ 17.5)	(0)	(0/ 35)	–
P.'s Honor Restored, Rnd. Tab.	70	3	1/ 23.3	3	1/ 23.3	100
2nd Offer to Fight Refused	46	0	0/ 46	0	0/ 46	–
Parzival Fights Gramoflanz	212	5	1/ 42.4	3	1/ 70.6	60
Arthur Helps Itonje	577	11	1/ 52.4	9	1/ 64.1	81.8
Peace Established All Around	37	0	0/ 37	0	0/ 37	–
Marriage Festivities	64	0	0/ 64	0	0/ 64	–
Parzival Slips Away	60	1	1/ 60	1	1/ 60	100
Book XV						
Wolfram Promises to Finish	34	4	1/ 8.5	4	1/ 8.5	100
Parzival-Feirefiz Fight	290	18	1/ 16.1	16	1/ 18.1	88.8
Relationship Discovered	156	4	1/ 39	2	1/ 78	50
Brothers Speak of Gahmuret	90	2	1/ 45	2	1/ 45	100
Invitation to See F.'s Army	24	0	0/ 24	0	0/ 24	–
Feir. Invited to See Arthur	34	1	1/ 34	1	1/ 34	100
Events in Parzival's Absence	31	1	1/ 31	1	1/ 31	100
P. and F. as Gawan's Guests	319	7	1/ 45.6	4	1/ 79.7	57.1
Arthur and Feirefiz	100	2	1/ 50	1	1/ 100	50
Listing of Knights	92	0	0/ 92	0	0/ 92	–

Passage Topic	Lines	Images	Image/Line	Metaphors	Metaphor/Line	Metaphors %
Court Marvels at Feirefiz	42	0	0/ 42	0	0/ 42	–
Round Table Honors Feirefiz	120	0	0/ 120	0	0/ 120	–
Cundrie Proclaims Parzival King	138	6	1/ 23	3	1/ 46	50
Parzival's Joy: Prepares to Go	120	1	1/ 120	1	1/ 120	100
Book XVI						
Anfortas Pleading for Death	63	1	1/ 63	1	1/ 63	100
Time of Greatest Pain	96	3	1/ 32	3	1/ 32	100
Cundrie, P. and F. Arrive	77	1	1/ 77	1	1/ 77	100
Parzival Releases Anfortas	61	2	1/ 30.5	1	1/ 61	50
Rides to Condwiramurs	76	1	1/ 76	1	1/ 76	100
Reunion with Condwiramurs	87	2	1/ 48.5	2	1/ 48.5	100
Kardeiz King of Parzival's Lands	50	0	0/ 50	0	0/ 50	–
Parz. & Cond. Bury Sigune	47	3	1/ 15.6	1	1/ 47	33.3
Condwiramurs' Reception	53	3	1/ 17.6	0	0/ 53	–
Grail Ceremony and Banquet	82	1	1/ 82	1	1/ 82	100
Feirefiz Smitten by Repanse	96	2	1/ 48	2	1/ 48	100
Baptism Need Explained	82	4	1/ 20.5	4	1/ 20.5	100
F.'s Baptism, Marries Repan.	83	1	1/ 83	1	1/ 83	100
All New Roles Defined	67	0	0/ 67	0	0/ 67	–
Feirefiz, Repanse to India	70	0	0/ 70	0	0/ 70	–
Lohengrin's Fate	110	1	1/ 110	1	1/ 110	100
Epilogue to Epic	30	0	0/ 30	0	0/ 30	–

Notes

(1)   Singer also points out the counterpart to this fabel in Rabelais' long-tailed
        mare that not only kills flies but knocks down the entire forest with her tail.
        (Gargantua, Book I, Chapter VI). Op.cit., Wiener Sitzungsberichte, 13-14.

(2)   Lachmann's punctuation would seem to make better sense here. He shows a
        period at the end of line 15 and no parenthesis in line 16. The implication
        would be that after Vergulaht orders Antikonie to take Gawan and Kingrimur-
        sel with her, he asks the others to go with him and give him advice. He would
        not be asking Antikonie for advice in the Lachmann version. Hence her re-
        mark comes unsolicited and seems to gain in irony through the pun she makes
        on the word "waegest", taking it in its literal connotation, not the figurative
        one Vergulaht obviously intended.

(3)   In current German slang the molting of a falcon still carries the implication
        of exaggerated preening or "dolling up." See "sich mausig machen" in Heinz
        Kupper, Wörterbuch der deutschen Umgangssprache, Bd. 1 (4. Aufl., Ham-
        burg: Claassen, 1965), 345.

(4)   I have followed the Lachmann punctuation, which emphasizes the contrast
        between "trueben jehe" and "lûter prîs". The Leitzmann punctuation is in-
        dicated in parenthesis.

CHAPTER IV

THE DISTRIBUTION OF IMAGERY IN
TERMS OF THE GENERAL STRUCTURE OF THE EPIC

The nature and effect of Wolfram's use of imagery, rather than the source or construction of specific images, is the primary concern of this study. This raises the question of style characteristics and perhaps of artistic intent, although style can be analyzed without knowledge of the latter. Passages which are distinguished by an unusually frequent resort to imagery are compared with others which are conspicuous by the lack of it in an attempt to establish valid correspondences between image frequency and other literary features. The measuring stick of frequency is Wolfram's practice within Parzival as a whole, that is, the average image frequency for the entire epic is taken as a norm against which specific passages are judged to be high or low in imagery.

Before making a closer examination of given passages, it may be of value to see what relationships can be observed between image frequency and some of the broader aspects of the epic. Because of the very extensiveness of the passages concerned in these broader aspects it is assumed that while some style characteristics pertaining to the frequency of imagery may be revealed, they would be artistically unconscious or accidental, that is, they would be beyond the probable scope of the author's awareness and control.

The particular comparisons to be made here are: 1) the various books compared with the epic averyages and with one another; 2) the first six books contrasted collectively with the following ten; 3) the books which could have been based upon Cretien's Perceval in contrast to those which had to have another source; and 4) the episodes of the three heroes, Gahmuret, Parzival, and Gawan, compared with one another.

The Books of Parzival Compared

Since the books vary in length from 900 lines in Book XI (Gawan's Ordeal in the Schastel Marveile) to 2100 lines in Book IX (the Trevrizent book), comparisons of image frequency can be made most meaningfully in terms of a ratio between the number of images in a given book and its number of lines. Thus, Table III (page 177) shows a ratio for Book I of an average of one image for every 19.4 lines, for Book II an average of one image for each 22 lines, and so on. On this basis the frequency of image occurrence is said to be slightly higher in Book I than in Book II. Table III also shows what percent of the images in a given book are considered to be metaphors and gives a ratio representing the average frequency of metaphor occurrence within each book.

The figures for the entire epic show 1117 images for the 24,810 lines. Of these 759, or 67.9 %, are metaphors. The frequency of occurrence comes to an average of one image for each 22.2 lines and one metaphor for every 32.7 lines. The range on either side of these averages extends from the highest image frequency of 1 per 13.7 lines for Book VI (which concludes with Cundrie's curse on Parzival and Kingrimursel's indictment of Gawan's honor) to the lowest frequency of 1 image per 49 lines in Book XVI, the final book. These two books also show the highest and lowest metaphor frequency respectively, from 1:18.5 to 1:64.7. These books which are polar opposites in image and metaphor frequency resemble one another closely in the proportion of metaphor among the total imagery in each book: 74 % in Book VI and 76 % in Book XVI, both exceeding the average figure of 67.9 % for the epic.

Only two other books maintain the same rank in both image and metaphor frequency. (See Table IVA-B, page 178.) These are Book XII (in which Gawan finally wins Orgeluse) ranking twelfth in these frequencies among the sixteen books; and Book XV (Parzival's encounter with Feirefiz), ranking fourteenth in both.

While most books rank very similarly in both their frequency of imagery in general and the frequency of metaphoric imagery in particular, there are a few notable exceptions. Book IV, with its many non-metaphoric images of hunger at besieged Pelrapeire, is second among the sixteen in the frequency of image occurrence but only tenth in the frequency of metaphor. In Book V, as Wolfram follows Parzival's first encounter with Anfortas and the grail mysteries, he applies simile and other forms of direct comparison almost as often as he uses metaphor. As a result, Book V stands only ninth in terms of metaphor frequency but fourth in total imagery. This situation is nearly reversed in Book IX where non-metaphoric imagery is very rare. Book IX is second among the sixteen in the frequency of metaphor and fourth in the proportion of metaphor to other images but only seventh in the over-all frequency of images. A glance at Table IVa-b will show other such discrepancies.

Looking at the books in the order of metaphor percentage one notes that, while the average for the epic is 67.9 %, nine books exceed a 70 % proportion of metaphor. Book XIV goes as high as 88.3 %. This book has very few images of any kind (1 for every 38.4 lines), but non-metaphoric imagery is almost non-existent, only 5 of the 43 images occurring in the book. Book VII, the first of the Gawan books, is almost exactly at the epic average, having a 67 % proportion of metaphor, and Book II, the conclusion of the Gahmuret episodes, is close to the epic average at 65.4 %. None of the five remaining books shows a majority of non-metaphoric imagery, and only in Book IV does it equal metaphor in frequency. Clearly, Wolfram's preference in imagery is for metaphor, whether in imitation of the literary taste of his time or from personal habit of thought. This predominance would be even more striking if all instances of personification had been included in the study as a special form of metaphoric transference.

Table IVB (page 179) reveals another phenomenon in regard to the metaphor percentages. There seems to be almost an inverse relationship between a book's rank in image occurrence and its rank in metaphor percentage. That is, a book with a particularly high image frequency may have a particularly low percentage of metaphor among the images and vice versa. Three of the five books with the least image frequency, Books XIV, XV, and XVI, are among the five highest in proportion of metaphor in their imagery. This is not true for the other two among the five, so the pattern is not wholly consistent, Book XI being among the five lowest in both image frequency and metaphor percentage and Book XII near the median in metaphor proportion, ranking seventh. Nonetheless, the pattern seems significant. The converse comparison is nearly as remarkable: three of the five books with the highest image frequency, Books I, IV, and V, are among the lowest five in metaphor proportion. Surveying the data given for the books in order of their appearance in the epic rather than by rank (Table III) will confirm this observation. Where Wolfram's use of imagery is relatively less frequent, metaphor tends to form a greater percentage than usual of the imagery which does occur. This seems to support the conclusion made above that Wolfram had a marked preference for metaphor above other forms of imagery. Exceptions to the tendency of inverse relationship between image frequency and metaphor proportion are Books VI and IX where both factors are higher than average for the epic, and Book XI where both are lower than average.

Metaphor is exceptionally abundant in Books VI and IX, with 94 instances in the former and 81 in the latter. Of the other books in the epic only Books III, with a metaphor for every 27.5 lines, and VIII, with one for every 29.1 lines, even approach this richness, a fact which will be noted again below in the comparison of the Gahmuret, Parzival, and Gawan books.

Books I-VI Compared Collectively with VII-XVI

It is generally assumed from allusion in Wigalois that the first six books of Parzival were known to Wolfram's contemporaries as a unit before he finished the rest of the epic. Following upon this assumption is the one that Wolfram paused in the work of composition at this point. If a considerable intermission did occur between Book VI and Book VII, it seems strange that he makes no reference to this when he begins the Gawan episode, prone as he was to interject his personal circumstances into the narrative. The points of reference external to Parzival which give some idea of the times before which certain books could not have been written do not of themselves make the assumption of a pause between Books VI and VII compelling. Allusions made to Hartmann's Erec in Books II and III and to Iwein in Book V set the earliest possible dates of their writing as 1190 and 1203 respectively. Reference in Book VII to the fighting near Erfurt between King Philip of Swabia and Hermann of Thuringia establishes that it could not have been written before 1203. There is nothing in this, however, which precludes the possibility that the composition of Books V, VI, and VII proceeded smoothly one after the other.

Nevertheless, the division of the epic into two parts with the line drawn between Books VI and VII persists as a literary impression. Wolfram's epilogue to Book VI is the most obvious support for such an impression. He summarizes the fates of the heroines of the epic thus far, appears to have made his peace with the angry court ladies he had talked about at the end of Book II, and suggests that he'll continue the story only if a certain person (assumed to be a woman) asks him to, but that he would be willing to let anyone else take up the task "der âventiure prüeven kan / und rime künne sprechen, / beidiu samenen und zebrechen" (P337, 24-26); all of which sounds like a man who feels he has reached a goal and is ready to stop. All of these aspects of the epilogue could just as well be mere rhetoric, however. Both Curtius' and Singer's studies in comparative medieval literature show too many instances of similar rhetoric to allow us to take Wolfram's comments here at face value without reservations.

A change of style which is subtly felt as one reads on into Book VII and beyond may be a more significant support of the impression of a literary dividing line after Book VI. A certain decrease of liveliness or vitality in the narration seems to occur. The contrasts to be drawn here from the data on image occurrence may be particularly helpful in examining the possible validity of such a literary division.

The ratios of image frequency differ markedly between the two parts of the epic. If image occurrence is one criterion of wit, the reader's general impression that Wolfram expended more wit on the first six books than he did thereafter finds statistical support. Table V (page 179) shows that the first six books, with only 40.7 % of the epic, contain 50 % of its images. The ratio for frequency of image occurrence is 1 image per 18 lines in Books I-VI compared with 1 per 26.3 lines for the rest of the epic. Both the image frequency and the metaphor frequency in the first six books is slightly higher than the average for the epic as a whole: 1 per 18 and 1 per 19.05 respectively, compared with the epic averages of 1 per 22.2 and 1 per 32.7. The image frequency and metaphor frequency of the following ten books taken collectively are less than the epic average: 1 per 26.3 and 1 per 35.8.

The collective figures for the two parts do not do full justice to their differences. Looking at the breakdown of all the books in Table III, one notices still greater contrasts in image frequency between the first six books and the last six books, omitting for the moment the middle books, VII, VIII, IX, and X. None of the last six books has as high an image frequency as any of the first six, and only Book II among the first six has a ratio of less than one image in 20 lines (1:22). Four of the last six books have such ratios as one image per 30 lines, one per 34.6, 38.4, and 49 line lines. (1)

The contrast between Book VI with its high ratio of one image for every 13.7 lines and Book VII with only one for every 23.7 lines is particularly abrupt. Wolfram recovers his form in the Gawan-Antikonie episodes in Book VIII (1:18.4) and maintains it with a ratio of 1 per 19.8 lines in Book IX (although, as has been seen, the frequency of imagery varies tremendously within this book). In Book X, however, with only one image for every 24.6 lines, he falls even below the imagery lull of

Book VII, and he never again equals the level he maintained in the first six books. Book XIII, which includes Gawan's long yearned-for reward from Orgeluse, the Klingsor story, Arthur's arrival at Schastel Marveil, and Parzival's re-entry into the narrative, makes enough of a recovery of image frequency to stand out conspicuously among the latter half of the epic (1:23.6), but even so, it does not quite equal the average ratio for the epic as a whole.

It is clear that Wolfram used less and less imagery as the epic went on and that Book VI is indeed the turning point.

Books with Cretien de Troyes as Source Compared with Non-Cretien Books

Cretien de Troyes' Perceval le Galois or Li Contes del Gral begins with Parzival and Herzeloide in the wilderness and ends, unfinished, at about the point of Gawan's final conquest of Orgeluse's favor. This corresponds in story line to the events beginning with Book III of Wolfram's version, ending at a point midway through Book XIII. It does not have the Gahmuret episodes, the conclusion of Gawan's adventures at the Schastel Marveil, or the outcome of Anfortas' suffering and Parzival's quest. It also lacks a great amount of elaboration added by Wolfram. Cretien's version is contained within 9234 lines, while in Wolfram's epic the corresponding part of the whole has been expanded to over 15,800 lines.

In view of the large number of studies and discussions which have had Wolfram's originality as their focus, it seems strange that none exist which compare his imagery with Cretien's. It is to be hoped that this omission in Parzival scholarship will soon be remedied. However, it is not within the scope of this study. The comparison here is not of Wolfram with Cretien, but rather of Wolfram composing under one situation with Wolfram composing under another. The former is Wolfram with Cretien's work as stimulus and source material, the latter, Wolfram working either solely from his own imagination or from the hypothetical Kyot source. If one were to assume that Wolfram rejected Cretien as a source entirely, the comparison made here would make no sense at all. In the absence of any Kyot document, however, and with Wolfram's acknowledged familiarity with Cretien's version, that would be an adventurous assumption which this study does not make. (2)

Book XIII is omitted from the comparison because part of its story can be assumed to derive from Cretien and part extends into events beyond Cretien's narration. Rather than try to divide the book validly, it has been assumed that whatever may be significant in regard to Wolfram's use of imagery will appear from a comparison of Book III through XII with Books I-II and XIV-XVI. (See Table VI, page 180.)

With Book XIII thus omitted, the Cretien category contains about twice as many lines as the non-Cretien books, 65.9 % of the 23,250 lines involved in the comparison. It accounts for 768 or 73 % of the 1051 images in the two categories.

As would be assumed from this, the ratio of image frequency is higher in the Cretien category than in the other, approximately one image for every 21 lines compared with one for every 28 lines in the books not based upon Cretien. The metaphor ratios hold nearly the same proportional difference: one metaphor for each 29.8 lines in the Cretien books, one for each 41 lines in the non-Cretien books. The proportion of metaphoric to non-metaphoric imagery is 66.9 % in the former and 68.2 % in the latter category.

Any significance which could be attached to the collectively higher image frequency in the books which are based upon Cretien's story becomes very questionable when it is observed that the two Gahmuret books in the non-Cretien category compare very favorably with several of the books based upon Cretien. Book I's image ratio exceeds that of six of the ten books in the Cretien group, Book II's ratio is higher than four of them. The difference in the average image frequency of the two categories seems due more to the fact that three of the five books in the non-Cretien group come at the end of the epic than to their lack of relationship to Cretien. They merely reflect the general trend noted earlier toward the decreasing use of imagery after Book VI. As long as the data here are the criterion, it must be concluded that whether or not Wolfram was working from Cretien as a source, this had no influence upon how often he used imagery.

The Gahmuret, Parzival, and Gawan Books Compared

The Gahmuret story forms the chief content of Books I and II. Since the prologue of Book I is actually a prologue to the epic as a whole and not just to the Gahmuret episodes, it is not included in the calculations of image frequency relating to Gahmuret in contrast to Gawan and Parzival. For these purposes, then, the term "Gahmuret Books" really means Book I beginning with line 4, 27 and all of Book II.

It could be argued that the epilogue to Book II should also be excluded from consideration here, since it is wholly unrelated to Gahmuret. The reason for not doing so is that similar short intrusions upon the narrative by Wolfram of a similarly personal nature occur also in the Gawan and Parzival books. This seems to be a stylistic idiosyncrasy which occurs generally in Parzival, and nothing is to be gained by excluding such passages when the books of the three main protagonists are to be compared.

The Gawan books cover three main episodes which can be defined according to the women because of whom his various adventures occur. In Book VII, which shows him on his way to Ascalon to defend his honor against Kingrimursel's indictment, these women are the sisters Obie and Obilot, the latter still a child. At Ascalon in Book VIII the heroine is the lovely Antikonie, sister to King Vergulaht. From Book X through Book XIV it is Gawan's relationship to Orgeluse de Logrois which runs as a connecting thread through numerous jousts, ordeals, discoveries, and states of mind, from the depths of depression to ecstatic heights of triumphant love. It is through her that he comes to the Schastel Marveil and also to the encounter with Gramoflanz.

The resolution of the conflict with Gramoflanz is the central plot of Book XIV, which must, therefore, be included among the Gawan books. This book, however, also finds Parzival again an active protagonist from his inadvertent duel with Gawan at the very beginning right through to the end. Since over 700 of the 1650 lines are taken up with Arthur's role as peace-maker between Gawan and Gramoflanz, Book XIV could also be called the Arthur book of the epic, if one wished to single Arthur out for particular consideration. The larger part of the book, however, is fairly evenly divided between Gawan and Parzival, including the 213 lines in which they are co-protagonists. Because of this interweaving, Book XIV has been included among both the Gawan books and the Parzival books in the calculations here.

The term "Gawan books" refers, therefore, to Books VII and VIII, and X through XIV. The Parzival books are Books III through VI, Book IX, and Books XIV through XVI. He appears or is referred to briefly in several of the Gawan books and, of course, also at the end of the Gahmuret books where his birth is described, but the books specified here are the ones in which he is clearly a major carrier of the action.

With the three categories thus defined, the Gahmuret books include 3338 lines, the Gawan books 9780 lines, and the Parzival books 13,226 lines. The data of Table VII (page 181) show the ratios of image frequency to be one occurrence for every 24.5 lines in the Gahmuret books, one for every 25.7 in the Gawan books, and one for every 21.6 in the Parzival books. This is about a three-line difference between Parzival and Gahmuret and a four-line difference between Parzival and Gawan, neither a very striking contrast. The four-line difference between Parzival and Gawan remains in metaphor frequency with a ratio of 1:31.5 for the former and 1:35.4 for the latter. Between Parzival and Gahmuret the contrast becomes greater in regard to metaphor frequency, amounting to more than a seven-line difference.

If Book XIV is omitted from consideration entirely, the average image frequency of the Gawan books is almost identical with that of the Gahmuret episodes: 1:24.1 compared with 1:24.5. This may be a more valid picture of the correspondence between the occurrence of imagery and Gawan as protagonist than is gained by including Book XIV where both Arthur and Parzival figure so prominently. The effect of its omission on the average figures for Parzival is very slight. It increases the average image frequency from one for every 21.6 lines to one per 20.3 lines.

The contrast between the Parzival books and those of Gawan and Gahmuret in either case is much less than might have been expected, if one had assumed some partiality on Wolfram's part for the figure of Parzival and had also assumed that this attitude would be reflected in a livelier treatment of his story as compared with Gawan or Gahmuret. Both of these assumptions are stated unequivocally as fact by Wolff, who claims:

> Die innere Beteiligung als der eigentliche Quell (der Bilder) spiegelt
> sich schon in der Verteilung wider; in den Büchern, die von Parzival
> handeln, sind sie weit häufiger als in den Gawanbüchern. . . (3)

This is an impression with which few readers of Parzival would disagree, but the
actual data seem to contradict it to the extent that they render the contrast relatively insignificant.

The source of the erroneous impression becomes clear as soon as the comparison between Wolfram's treatment of Parzival and Gawan is based solely upon
Books III through VI of the Parzival episodes, and if the last two books of the epic,
which are unquestionably Parzival books, are left out of the picture. The average
image frequency for Books III-VI is one for every 16.9 lines, compared with Gawan's ratio (omitting Book XIV) of one for each 24.1 lines. Also, as has been point-
ed out earlier, the drop of image frequency from Book VI to Book VII, the first of
the Gawan books, is a striking change from 1:13.7 to 1:23.7. To attribute these
differences to the change of protagonist, however, is faulty logic, for Gawan's loss
compared with the first four of the Parzival books is more than offset by his gain
in contrast to the last two Parzival books. There the image frequency is a mere
1:39.7, far lower than any of the Gawan books, if Book XIV is excepted. The final
Parzival book, in fact, has the lowest image ratio in the entire epic, only 1:49.

The fact that, collectively, the Parzival books show a slightly higher frequency of imagery than the Gawan books seems best explained by the coincidence
that four of the seven Parzival books come among the first six books of the epic,
where Wolfram's style was much livelier in general than it became later. The comparison with the Gahmuret books, therefore, which also occur among the first six,
becomes relatively more important than the contrast with Gawan. Using only the
data from these six books, the contrast of image frequency between Parzival and
Gahmuret is that of 1:16.9 compared with 1:24.5. This difference may be due to
the difference in Wolfram's interest in his protagonists, but it may also support
the assumption held by Mustard and Passage, among others, that the Gahmuret episodes were a later addition to the epic. (4) If this was the case, the Gahmuret passages may merely show the effect of Wolfram's general tendency to use less and
less imagery as he went along.

More remarkable than any contrasts between Parzival books and Gawan books
are the contrasts to be observed between some Parzival books and others and between some Gawan books and others. Within the Gawan category the Antikonie episode, Book VIII, stands out for its high image frequency. Its ratio of one for each
18.4 lines is exceptionally high for the epic as a whole, comparing very favorably
with the first four Parzival books. In fact, its style more closely resembles the
early Parzival episodes than any of the other books of the epic. Among the Parzival
books, III and IX have nearly the same frequency of metaphor and a far higher frequency than any of the other Parzival books, with the single exception of Book VI
(which is exceptional for the entire epic in image frequency as well). Of the rest of

the epic the Antikonie episode most closely resembles them in metaphor frequency. If there is an explanation for these observable facts it must be sought in other correspondences than the mere coincidence of protagonist. The data seen here do not show Wolfram's inclination to use imagery to have been significantly influenced by the identity of the protagonist with whom he was involved, at least as far as this compares Gahmuret, Gawan, and Parzival. The data suggest, on the other hand, that the Gahmuret episodes were composed later than the early Parzival books, perhaps at about the same time as the first six Gawan books.

Summary

    Four broad structural features of Parzival have been examined from the perspective of image frequency to see whether or not any valid correspondences could be discovered. Two of these comparisons have proven fruitful.

    The data on image frequency, metaphor frequency, and the percentage of imagery which is metaphoric when contrasted between the individual books and the epic's collective averages establishes Wolfram's marked preference for metaphor above other forms of imagery. This preference shows itself both absolutely and relatively: absolutely in the consistently higher percentage of metaphor occurrence in each book and in the epic averages, and relatively in the tendency of metaphoric imagery to persist where non-metaphoric imagery declines.

    The comparison of the first six books with the remainder of the epic reveals that the sense of literary division into these two groups can be validly supported on the basis of a changing style as far as the frequency of imagery is concerned. It can be seen that following Book VI Wolfram tended to use less and less imagery as the epic progressed, with only a temporary recovery of his former style in Books VIII and IX.

    The remaining two points of comparison have had negative results. Neither the fact that he was dealing with material which could have been based upon Cretien de Troyes nor the fact that he was dealing with Parzival instead of Gahmuret or Gawan seems to show a significant correspondence to the degree to which Wolfram did or did not use imagery.

Notes

(1)   These statistics support Zwierzina's assumption (based on diction analysis) of a pause in the composition after Book VI but not his conclusions of pauses also after Books VIII and XIV; neither do they support Panzer's deductions (from diction and rhyme analysis) of a major break between Books XIII and XIV. Their thesis, also followed by Matz, seems unconvincing; namely, that the reappearance of a word or Formel indicates Wolfram's return to composition after a pause following the last book in which the word had been missing. See Elsa-Lina Matz, Formelhafte Ausdrücke in Wolframs Parzival, (Diss., Kiel, 1907), 103 ff.; and Konrad Zwierzina, "Beobachtungen zum Reimgebrauch Hartmanns und Wolframs," in Festgabe für Richard Heinzel, (1898), 437-511.

(2)   Three major works illuminating Wolfram's relationship to Cretien are: Joachim Bumke, Die romanisch-deutschen Literaturbeziehungen im Mittelalter. Ein Ueberblick, (Heidelberg: Carl Winter Universitätsverlag, 1967); Hildegard Emmel, Formprobleme des Artusromans und der Graldichtung, (Bern: Francke, 1951); and Bodo Mergell, Wolfram und seine französische Quellen, II. Band, Wolframs Parzival, (Münster: Aschendorff, 1943).

(3)   Ludwig Wolff, "Vom persönlichen Stil Wolframs in seiner dichterischen Bedeutung. Ein Versuch," in Kleinere Schriften zur altdeutschen Philologie, (Berlin: de Gruyter, 1967), 268. Jensen's thesis along this line has been discussed previously (page 29 ff.).

(4)   Helen M. Mustard and Charles E. Passage, "Introduction" in Parzival, A Romance of the Middle Ages, (New York, Random House, 1961), ix.

THE DISTRIBUTION OF IMAGERY

Table III: Summary of Data for the Books of Parzival

Book	Lines	Images	Image per Line	Meta-phors	Meta. per Line	Meta-phor %
I	1736	91	1/ 19	50	1/ 34.7	54.9
II	1718	78	1/ 22	51	1/ 34.3	65.4
III	1898	98	1/ 19.4	69	1/ 27.5	70.4
IV	1338	76	1/ 17.6	38	1/ 35.2	50
V	1680	89	1/ 18.9	46	1/ 35.2	51.7
VI	1740	127	1/ 13.7	94	1/ 18.5	74
VII	1800	76	1/ 23.7	51	1/ 35.3	67
VIII	1050	57	1/ 18.4	36	1/ 29.1	62.8
IX	2100	106	1/ 19.8	81	1/ 25.9	76.4
X	1500	61	1/ 24.6	47	1/ 31.9	77
XI	900	30	1/ 30	16	1/ 56.2	53.3
XII	1320	48	1/ 27.5	36	1/ 36.6	75
XIII	1560	66	1/ 23.6	52	1/ 30	78.8
XIV	1650	43	1/ 38.4	38	1/ 43.4	88.3
XV	1590	46	1/ 34.6	35	1/ 45.4	76
XVI	1230	25	1/ 49	19	1/ 64.7	76
Epic	24810	1117	1/ 22.2	759	1/ 32.7	67.9

Table IV: Rank of Books in Image Frequency, Metaphor Frequency,
and Metaphor Percent

A)   BOOKS IN SEQUENCE

Book	Image Frequency	Metaphor Frequency	Metaphor %
I	5th (1/ 19)	8th (1/ 34.7)	13th (54.9)
II	8th (1/ 22)	7th (1/ 34.3)	11th (65.4)
III	6th (1/ 19.4)	3rd (1/ 27.5)	9th (70.4)
IV	2nd (1/ 17.6)	10th (1/ 35.2)	16th (50)
V	4th (1/ 18.9)	9th (1/ 35.2)	15th (51.7)
VI	1st (1/ 13.7)	1st (1/ 18.5)	8th (74)
VII	10th (1/ 23.7)	11th (1/ 35.3)	10th (67)
VIII	3rd (1/ 18.4)	4th (1/ 29.1)	12th (62.8)
IX	7th (1/ 19.8)	2nd (1/ 25.9)	4th (76.4)
X	11th (1/ 24.6)	6th (1/ 31.9)	3rd (77)
XI	13th (1/ 30)	15th (1/ 56.2)	14th (53.3)
XII	12th (1/ 27.5)	12th (1/ 36.6)	7th (75)
XIII	9th (1/ 23.6)	5th (1/ 30)	2nd (78.8)
XIV	15th (1/ 38.4)	13th (1/ 43.4)	1st (88.3)
XV	14th (1/ 34.6)	14th (1/ 45.4)	5-6th (76)
XVI	16th (1/ 49)	16th (1/ 64.7)	5-6th (76)

Table IV

B)   BOOKS BY RANK ORDER

Rank	Image Frequency	Metaphor Frequency	Metaphor %
1st	VI	VI	XIV
2nd	IV	IX	XIII
3rd	VIII	III	X
4th	V	VIII	IX
5th	I	XIII	XV, XVI
6th	III	X	XV, XVI
7th	IX	II	XII
8th	II	I	VI
9th	XIII	V	III
10th	VII	IV	VII
11th	X	VII	II
12th	XII	XII	VIII
13th	XI	XIV	I
14th	XV	XIII	XI
15th	XIV	XI	V
16th	XVI	XVI	IV

Table V: Books I-VI Compared Collectively with VII-XVI

Books	Lines	Images	Image per Line	Meta-phors	Meta. per Line	Meta-phor %
I-VI	10,110	559	1/ 18	348	1/ 29.1	62
VII-XVI	14,700	558	1/ 26.3	411	1/ 35.8	73.6

. . . .

Books	% of Epic	% of Epic Images	% of Epic Metaphors
I-VI	40.7	50.04	45.9
VII-XVI	59.3	49.9+	54.1

179

Table VI: Books with Cretien as Source Versus Non-Cretien Books

Cretien as Source

Book	Lines	Image Ratio	Meta. Ratio	Meta. %
III	1898	1/ 19.4	1/ 27.5	70.4
IV	1338	1/ 17.6	1/ 35.2	50
V	1680	1/ 18.9	1/ 35.2	51.7
VI	1740	1/ 13.7	1/ 18.5	74
VII	1800	1/ 23.7	1/ 35.3	67
VIII	1050	1/ 18.4	1/ 29.1	62.8
IX	2100	1/ 19.8	1/ 25.9	76.4
X	1500	1/ 24.6	1/ 31.9	77
XI	900	1/ 30	1/ 56.2	53.3
XII	1320	1/ 27.5	1/ 36.6	75

Other Source

Book	Lines	Image Ratio	Meta. Ratio	Meta. %
I	1736	1/ 19	1/ 34.7	54.9
II	1718	1/ 22	1/ 34.3	65.4

XIII Omitted from the comparison as belonging partially in both categories

Book	Lines	Image Ratio	Meta. Ratio	Meta. %
XIV	1650	1/ 38.4	1/ 43.4	88.3
XV	1590	1/ 34.6	1/ 45.4	76
XVI	1230	1/ 49	1/ 64.7	76

Collective Averages	Total Lines	Images	Metaphors	Image Ratio	Meta. Ratio	Meta. %
Cretien as Source	15,326	768	514	1/ 21.1	1/ 29.8	66.9
Other Source	7,924	283	193	1/ 28.1	1/ 41	68.2

Table VII: Gahmuret, Gawan, Parzival Books Compared

	Lines	Images	Image Ratio	Meta-phors	Meta. Ratio	Meta. %
GAHMURET						
I (4, 27 -)	1620	58	1/ 27.9	35	1/ 46.3	60.3
II	1718	78	1/ 22	51	1/ 34.3	65.4
Totals	3338	136	1/ 24.5	86	1/ 38.8	63.2
GAWAN						
VII	1800	76	1/ 23.7	51	1/ 35.3	67
VIII	1050	57	1/ 18.4	36	1/ 29.1	62.8
X	1500	61	1/ 24.6	47	1/ 31.9	77
XI	900	30	1/ 30	16	1/ 56.2	53.3
XII	1320	48	1/ 27.5	36	1/ 36.6	75
XIII	1560	66	1/ 23.6	52	1/ 30	78.8
XIV	1650	43	1/ 38.4	38	1/ 43.4	88.3
Totals	9780	381	1/ 25.7	276	1/ 35.4	72.4
PARZIVAL						
III	1898	98	1/ 19.4	69	1/ 27.5	70.4
IV	1338	76	1/ 17.6	38	1/ 35.2	50
V	1680	89	1/ 18.9	46	1/ 35.2	51.7
VI	1740	127	1/ 13.7	94	1/ 18.5	74
Subtotal:						
III-VI	6656	392	1/ 16.9	247	1/ 26.1	63
IX	2100	106	1/ 19.8	81	1/ 25.9	76.4
XIV	1650	43	1/ 38.4	38	1/ 43.4	88.3
XV	1590	46	1/ 34.6	35	1/ 45.4	76
XVI	1230	25	1/ 49	19	1/ 64.7	76
Subtotal:						
XV-XVI	2820	71	1/ 39.7	54	1/ 52.2	76
Totals	13226	612	1/ 21.6	420	1/ 31.5	68.6

Gawan, excluding Book XIV

	Lines	Images	Image Ratio	Meta-phors	Meta. Ratio	Meta. %
Totals:	8130	338	1/ 24.1	238	1/ 34.1	70.4

Parzival, excluding Book XIV

	Lines	Images	Image Ratio	Meta-phors	Meta. Ratio	Meta. %
Totals:	11576	569	1/ 20.3	382	1/ 30.3	67.1

CHAPTER V

CONSISTENT PATTERNS OF HIGH IMAGE FREQUENCY

In the previous chapter the frequency of imagery was correlated with divisions of the epic which were so extensive in definition that conscious choice by the poet as to whether or not to use imagery was excluded as a determining influence of any significance. In the analysis which follows this can no longer be ruled out. Here the scope of the focus narrows to passages in which Wolfram's artistic awareness of stylistic detail is the more plausible assumption. In each book the two thematic passages with the highest degree of image frequency and the two with the lowest frequency have been singled out for particular examination. In general only passages of thirty lines or longer have been considered, but two exceptions will be noted in Table VIII (page 210) where the data is summarized. These are the short thirteen-line passage at the end of Book XIII which brings Parzival back into the story as a main protagonist after nearly four books of Gawan, and the relatively short passage (29 lines) in Book XIV in which Itonje's lady-in-waiting, Vrou Bene, scolds Gramoflanz for his hostility to Gawan, Itonje's lord and brother. Both of these passages are by far the fullest of imagery in their respective books so they have been included in spite of their shortness. To avoid a possible distortion of Wolfram's pattern by this, a third passage of highest frequency has also been taken into account for each of these books. This has been done, too, where the two highest or lowest passages for a book have an identical image ratio. In such cases the next highest or lowest passage has been included in the analysis. The question is, of course, whether or not any consistent patterns can be demonstrated in Wolfram's inclusion or omission of imagery in a text.

Imagery being an important rhetorical device, one might naturally expect it to be particularly prominent in prologues, epilogues, and other passages which are similarly more persuasive or interpretive than narrative. The validity of this expectation is born out by the data of Table IX (page 215). There all but three of the rhetorical passages show an image ratio which is significantly higher than the average ratio for the epic as a whole (1: 22.37). Of the three exceptions, one is the introduction to Book IX in which Vrou Aventiure leads Wolfram back to Parzival's affairs. Most of this passage is actually a summary of narrative events and is included among the rhetorical passages only because of the stylistic device of dialogue with a Muse. A second exception is that part of the introduction to Book XII in which Wolfram addresses himself wholly to Vrou Minne without reference to Gawan's particular suffering of the moment. The image ratio there, while higher than that book's average, is about equal to the average for the epic as a whole. Most of the imagery which does occur in this introduction is to be found in the Gawan parts in which his feelings demonstrate triuwe(1) for Orgeluse. The final exception to the rule that discursive passages are particularly high in imagery is the epilogue to the epic. No imagery at all occurs within these thirty lines. The passage is straight-forward and dignified. It is totally lacking in the wittiness (often irreverant) found in the earlier books of the epic.

CONSISTENT PATTERNS OF HIGH IMAGE FREQUENCY

Many of the discursive, primarily rhetorical, passages listed in Table IX need to be examined in detail in respect to thematic aspects of Parzival. For, though it is true that discursive passages tend to maintain a higher ratio of image frequency than narrative passages in general, still, some narrative passages are the ones of highest image frequency in their books while some rhetorical passages are not. Therefore, it would seem that the dichotomy between story-telling and rhetoric is not sufficient to account for the varying frequency with which Wolfram uses imagery.

One of the effects of the omission of imagery is to move the narrative along with a minimum of digression. In such passages the reader encounters a series of events or actions: he did this, she said that, then this happened. The narrative here is not necessarily colorless, but the descriptions are given in detailed enumeration of what actually was, without reference to anything outside of the story. How graphic a description may be in this unadorned style can be seen from the account of Gahmuret's parade and the sights that meet his eyes as he enters the city at Zazamanc, of dark-skinned people, wounded men, damaged shields and weapons. Yet, only four images occur here within 230 lines of story, and they are simple ones indeed. Two compare the color of the residents of Belacane's land with that of the night and ravens. The third describes Belacane as "sweetness without falsity", and the fourth calls Gahmuret "love's reward", both stereotyped phrases of courtly poetry. Some such flattering phrase seems to have been stylistically mandatory, in fact, whenever a hero or heroine appeared on the stage, judging from how regularly Wolfram provides these commonplaces.

If one had expected a positive correlation between the presence of imagery and the importance of a passage within the structure of the epic, a glance at the themes of the lowest image frequency listed in Table VIII must show some surprises. Among them is Parzival's fateful first encounter with knighthood; his second meeting with Sigune in which he learns of the shame he has incurred for not asking about Anfortas' suffering; and Trevrizent's unfolding of the grail mysteries in Book IX. Their image ratios are 1:44, 1:39, and 1:107, respectively. The trend toward less frequent imagery as the epic progresses doubtless plays a role in the great difference between the Trevrizent episode and the other two. Passages with the low image ratio of Parzival's encounter with the knights or his second meeting with Sigune are not at all remarkable in the later books. For Books III and V, however, they are conspicuously low. The Trevrizent passage is particularly interesting because of its counterpart, the instruction he gives Parzival about God. This occurs in 201 lines which precede closely the 214 lines of grail instruction. Thirty-one images are to be found there compared with only two in the grail instruction, an image ratio contrast of 1:6.5 to 1:107.

Another observation which may seem surprising is that several scenes with a potential for strong emotionality are among those of lowest image frequency. The account of Gahmuret's death, for instance, proceeds in a quite unadorned style. That Wolfram's imagery does very effectively enhance his listener's emotional involve-

184

ment in the Herzeloide passage which follows it is obvious, pointing up all the more the relatively dry style here.

Gahmuret's death is described with only two images in 114 lines, neither of which has to do with heightening the listener's sense of grief, pity, or indignation. The squire Tampanis, who tells Herzeloide and the court what has happened, once uses the expression "the one who is painted as the lamb with the cross in his hoof" in place of the name Christ and once refers to the killer's deed with the ironic pun "he rewarded my lord with death", apparently a commonplace. The righteous indignation which could have been expected over the treachery which had rendered Gahmuret vulnerable to his enemies is wholly absent, the deed evoking no stronger reference than "gunêrtiu heidensch witze." The grief of the people of the Baruch of Baghdad, in whose service he had fallen, appears only in two dry lines: "vor jâmer wart vil liuten wê" and "sîn tôt tet Sarrazînen wê." The grief of Gahmuret's people at home receives one only slightly more vivid line: "Wâleise man vil weinen sach." When the focus shifts to Herzeloide in the succeeding passage (in which Parzival is born), Wolfram's treatment becomes far more graphic and emotionally arousing. Most of the effect stems from the behavior he describes and the direct words of grief which he puts in her mouth without figurative adornment. The intensity of her weeping, however, and of the inner conflict between joy and sorrow is condensed at the end of this moving portrayal of Herzeloide in three metaphoric descriptions, all the more effective for reinforcing one another in their close succession in these final eight lines:

> sich begôz des landes vrouwe
> mit ir herzen jâmers touwe:
> ir ougen regenden ûf den knaben.
> si kunde wîbes triuwe haben:
> beidiu siufzen unde lachen
> kunde ir munt vil wol gemachen.
> si vreute sich ir suns geburt:
> ir schimph ertranc in riuwen vurt.
> (113, 27 - 114, 4)

One of Wolfram's most empathic and warmly human scenes is the episode of lowest image frequency in Book VIII. This is the reunion of Gawan's pages and squires with their lord after having been captured and imprisoned while Gawan, unarmed, was fighting for his life against the crowd led by the outraged King Vergulaht. Having feared for his death, their joy is great and tearful when all turns out well. The picture Wolfram draws of Gawan's teasingly tender concern for them and their devotion to him is thoroughly convincing and succeeds without any aid of imagery. He carries it out entirely through their conversation and a few simple descriptions as, for example:

> dô in diu kint ersâhen,
> dâ wart grôz ummevâhen.

> ieslîchez sich weinde an in hienc:
> daz weinen iedoch von liebe ergienc.
> (429, 13-16)

In the middle of the scene Wolfram digresses to name a few of the boys. The only image in the 51-line episode occurs in this digression and adds nothing to the drama. A boy is described with a Minnesang commonplace: "sîn munt, sîn ougen und sîn nase / was rehte der minne kerne."

Two other passages of great joy and gladness are to be found among those of lowest image frequency: Gawan's triumphant return with Orgeluse de Logrois to the Schastel Marveil, and Parzival's reception of Cundrie's miraculous news of his naming to the grail with a second chance to free Anfortas and undo his old shame. Each episode contains one image, giving a ratio of 1:156 for Gawan's and 1:120 for Parzival's scene.

The Gawan passage culminates three books of nearly incessant suffering from unrequited love for the disdainful and arrogant Orgeluse. Her beauty was so exceptional that at first his devotion had been understandable:

> eine alsô klâre vrouwen,
> die er gernde muoste schouwen,
> aller wîbes varwe ein bêâ flûrs.
> âne Condwîrâmûrs
> wart nie geborn sô schoener lîp:
> mit klârheit süeze was daz wîp,
> wol geschicket und kurtois.
> si hiez Orgelûse de Lôgrois.
> ouch saget uns diu âventiur von ir,
> si waere ein reizel minnen gir,
> ougen süeze âne smerzen
> und ein spansenewe sherzen.
> (508, 19-20)

Her behavior toward him, however, was so insulting and so utterly unbecoming of a fair lady and heroine that soon Wolfram feels moved to apologize for her. He begs his listeners to withhold judgment until they know the full story:

> swer nû des wil volgen mir,
> der mîde valsche rede gein ir.
> niemen sich verspreche,
> er enwizze ê waz er reche,
> unz er gewinne künde
> wiez um ir herze stüende.
> ich kunde ouch wol gerechen dar
> gein der vrouwen wol gevar,
> swaz si hât gein Gâwân

in ir zorne missetân
oder daz si noch getuot gein im:
die râche ich alle von ir nim.

(516, 3-14)

Eventually she is revealed as the counterpart to Sigune in grieving loyalty, for all her harshness stems from sorrow for the husband killed by Gramoflanz and for Anfortas' suffering from the wound incurred in service to her. Where Sigune's triuwe leads to devotional martyrdom, however, Orgeluse's expresses itself in an unrelenting quest to avenge her beloved husband against Gramoflanz. As a possible tool to this end, Gawan's mettle is tested again and again: "dem golde ich iuch geliche, / daz man liutert in der gluot: / als ist geliutert iuwer muot." (614, 12-14). His final ordeals in her service are undertaken while he is still weak from the wounds received in the chamber of the Lit Marveile, and all who watch him ride out to fight the Turkoite despair for him. Now, after that battle, a terrible fall on Gringuljete into an abyss, and a near drowning in full armor in the swift waters of the Sabine, he returns with Orgeluse riding at last docilely and lovingly at his side and is welcomed as their new lord by all of Klingsor's army at the Schastel Marveile. In winning Orgeluse, freeing the 400 captive queens, and becoming lord of the Castle of Marvels, Gawan's honor forms the worldly parallel to Parzival's winning of Condwiramurs, freeing Anfortas, and becoming lord of Munsalvaesche. The Gawan scene in question bears some structural similarity to Parzival's welcome by the grail army when he returns to Munsalvaesche with Cundrie and Feirefiz, but the main theme in it is the change in Orgeluse's behavior toward Gawan, from hostility to devotion. This it is which evokes Wolfram's sole image in the 156 lines of description. When Orgeluse offers Gawan a goblet from which she has already drunk it is said:

sô wart im niuwe vreude kunt,
daz er dâ nâch solde trinken.
sîn riuwe begunde hinken
und wart sîn hôchgemüete snel.

(622, 24-27)

All other evidence of joy, whether Gawan's or the joy of those who see him return safely contrary to all their fears, is presented in an unadorned style.

Much of the scene at the end of Book XV following Cundrie's announcement of the grace which has befallen Parzival is taken up with the details of his choosing Feirefiz as his companion for the journey to Munsalvaesche, of Feirefiz's generosity in farewell to his new friends at Arthur's court, and of their departure with Cundrie. The one image in the passage occurs at the beginning, before Parzival's reply to Cundrie: tears, "the well-spring of the heart", flow for joy. That this is his first reaction rather than pride in his new honor testifies to the profound changes which have occurred in him since his last encounter with Cundrie, as does even more so the humble and forgiving tone of his words to her:

dô sprach er: 'vrouwe, solhiu dinc,
als ir hie habet genennet,
bin ich vor gote erkennet,
sô daz mîn sündehafter lîp
und hân ich kint, dar zuo mîn wîp,
daz diu des phlihte suln hân,
sô hât got wol ze mir getân.
swar an ir mich ergetzen meget,
dâ mite ir iuwer triuwe reget.
iedoch hete ich niht missetân,
ir hetet mich zornes etswenne erlân.

(783, 4-14)

Parzival's entire response has a natural sincerity which is very moving in its simple dignity. One does not feel a need for anything more to vivify the emotional impact of Cundrie's message.

Many of the scenes of lowest image frequency are relatively devoid of emotional significance. Some simply fill in background detail for the personal history of the characters (Gawan's story of Urjans, Trevrizent's story of his youth). Others turn loose-ended or unresolved fates of secondary figures into happy endings (betrothal of Clamide and Cunneware, marriage of Feirefiz to Repanse, the Lohengrin story). Many carry the details of the narrative further, accounting for the movements of the protagonists, getting them out of one situation and into the next (Gahmuret's travels to Zazamanc, to Spain, to Kanvoleis; preparations for the duel between Parzival and Clamide and between Gawan and Gramoflanz; Parzival's departure from Arthur to seek the grail, Gawan's departure from Vergulaht on the same mission). A few describe hospitality in a routine fashion (Parzival as Gawan's guest on the plain before Rosche Sabins, the Round Table festivities in honor of Feirefiz). These passages have almost the tone of reportage: factual, clear, informative, somewhat dry. In them Wolfram doesn't create any of the warmth of human interest that he does in the scene between Gawan and his young retinue or between Parzival and Cundrie. These latter scenes, and others of low image frequency (Orilus' anger with Jeschute, Parzival's duel with Kingrun, Obie's hostility toward Gawan), clearly demonstrate that Wolfram could indeed convey an emotional impact without recourse to imagery when he chose to do so. Through the content and naturalness of the direct discourse employed and through the particular details of behavior he describes, so vivid a picture is created that no further incitement to participation in the feelings of his characters or to concern for their fate is needed. Why, then, the abundance of imagery in other passages? What function does it seem to serve? What is its effect?

Episodes in which grief is a main theme are as full of imagery as those of joy and gladness are devoid of it. It is typical of these episodes that Wolfram is dealing with the feelings of one person rather than of a group, ie., with Herzeloide rather than with Gahmuret's mourners collectively. The protagonists of the main grief scenes, in order of their appearance in the epic are:

1) Gahmuret's brother and mother when he leaves home;
2) Belacane when he abandons her pregnant with Feirefiz;
3) Gahmuret himself, longing later for Belacane and then hearing of his brother's death;
4) Herzeloide, both at Parzival's birth and when he departs to become a knight;
5) Sigune, in three scenes with Schionatulander's corpse before her own death;
6) Ginover lamenting Ither;
7) Gurnemanz grieving the loss of Parzival after already losing three sons through death;
8) Cundrie's grief for Anfortas (and for Gahmuret's disgrace in having such a son as Parzival);
9) Trevrizent, responding to the news of Ither's death and then to Parzival's confession about Anfortas;
10) Orgeluse in her account of Zidegast's death and Anfortas' wound.

A comparison with the highest image frequency passages in Table VIII shows seven of these instances included there. Even though the others do not rank that high in their respective books, all do contain imagery.

Examination of this imagery reveals the rather surprising fact that relatively little of it has to do with the feeling of grief itself. Instead, the images emphasize the worthiness of a person to evoke grief and whether or not a mourner grieves well. In other words, Wolfram's use of imagery in these passages has more to do with propriety in such situations than with the emotions involved in death or other loss and regret. Sigune's words to Parzival, when he offers to avenge Schionatulander, seem to give the key: "dû bist geborn von triuwen / daz er dich sus kan riuwen." Triuwe, not jamer, is the real theme in these scenes. The eulogistic images of the mourned person so prominent here are evidence of the mourner's ability to show triuwe. Thus, when Ginover laments the killing of Ither, three of the six images Wolfram puts in her speech extol his virtues: he was "vor wildem valsche zam" and "ein sloz ob dem prise", his heart was "ob dem sloze ein hantveste." A fourth image shows her concern for Arthur, also triuwe:

ouwê unde heiâ hei!
Artûses werdekeit enzwei
sol brechen noch diz wunder.
(160, 3-5)

The remaining two speak of the grief good women now must feel:

ein berndiu vruht al niuwe
ist trûrens ûf diu wîp gesaet.
ûz dîner wunden jâmer waet.
(160, 24-26)

Similarly, when Orgeluse's resistance to Gawan dissolves and she confides in him the cause of her wretched behavior, seven of the twelve images in the passage eulogize Zidegast, two express their devotion to one another while he lived, one claims her distress to be greater than Gawan's, and the other two relate to her treatment of him.(2)

Signe's scenes are instructive. Her function in Parzival's enlightenment on these three occasions and the images she uses to praise him and Herzeloide are of no concern here, only Signe as the embodiment of loyal grief.(3) In this role one image in her first appearance bespeaks grief: "ein vrouwe ûz rehtem jâmer schrei: / ir was diu wâre vreude enzwei" (138, 13-14). One in the scene of the hermit cell relates grief and triuwe explicitly:

> wîplîcher sorgen urhap
> ûz ir herzen bluete alniuwe
> und doch durch alde triuwe.
> (435, 16-18)

Six of the seven other images referring to Signe's own situation play primarily upon either the triuwe theme or upon propriety, including two disparaging allusions to Hartmann's Vrou Lunete.(4) With the first of these Wolfram gives the real key to Signe: "ir leben was doch ein venje gar." Penitence, more than grief, is her motivation. It is not Schionatulander's death and her loss which so distresses her as her failure to reward his devotion properly. This ordering of values is sharply demonstrated in her reaction to the news that Parzival has seen Anfortas without asking a question. Anfortas' misery draws no outcry from her, at best the words:

> iuch solde iuwer wirt erbarmet hân,
> an dem got wunder hât getân,
> und hete gevrâget sîner nôt.
> (255, 17-19)

Her whole emotion is outrage at Parzival's dishonorable behavior, for which Wolfram uses a strong metaphor:

> ouwê was woldet ir zuo mir her,
> gunerter lîp, verbluochet man!
> ir truoget den eiterwolves zan,
> dâ diu galle in der triuwe
> an iu bekleip sô niuwe.
> (255, 12-16)

The bitterness of Signe's attack is matched by Cundrie in her denunciation of Parzival before Arthur and all his court, a marvel of invective sustained for 120 lines, much of it in figures which help give this passage one of the highest image ratios in the entire epic, 1:5.7.(5) Four of the 21 images there praise Gahmuret, held up in scornful contrast to Parzival; the last one says of Cundrie that she "was selbe sorgens phant"; the remaining 16 deal with Parzival's disgrace and its reflection upon his host Arthur. Unlike Sigune, real grief, not merely propriety, seems to underlie Cundrie's outrage in her first direct words to Parzival:

> her Parzivâl, wan saget ir mir
> und bescheidet mich einer maere,
> dô der trûrege vischaere
> saz âne vreude und âne trôst,
> war umbe ir in niht siufzens hât erlôst?
> er truoc iu vur den jamers last...
>
> (315, 26 - 316, 1)

Real grief is also revealed in her parting behavior as she leaves the dismayed company:

> diu maget trûrec, niht gemeit,
> âne urloup dannen reit,
> al weinde si dicke wider sach.
> nû hoeret wie si ze jungest sprach:
> 'ei Munsalvaesche, jâmers zil!
> wê daz dich niemen troesten wil!'
>
> (318, 25-30)

The explicit bond between jamer und triuwe is also present in the Cundrie scene:

> al weinde si die hende want,
> daz manec zaher den andern sluoc.
> grôz jâmer si ûz ir ougen truoc:
> die maget lêrte ir triuwe
> wol klagen ir herzen riuwe.
>
> (318, 6-10)

The Gurnemanz passage is unique among these episodes of grief in that all of its imagery speaks of his suffering.(6) The triuwe element is limited to the one line of stereotyped praise of a hero: "dô sprach der vürste ûz triuwe erkorn." As Parzival's tutor in the manners and ethics of knighthood Gurnemanz's triuwe and sense of propriety must be assumed to be irreproachable. Nevertheless, the didacticism implied in Wolfram's treatment of the other scenes discussed seems truly subdued here, the social rule yielding to simple humanness in a father's grief for his dead sons. One is tempted to see Wolfram's own commentary in the bitter sigh: "sus lont iedoch diu ritterschaft: / ir zagel ist jamerstricke haft."

This examination of scenes of grief has led us to one main key to the passages of highest image frequency in Parzival, the theme of triuwe. As will be seen, this appears in four guises: triuwe demonstrated in jamer, triuwe in minne, triuwe between living knights (based upon a variety of ethical principles), and triuwe between Man and God. The other key is wit. It may be well to turn from the triuwe theme for a moment to look at Wolfram's wit.(7)

Wit plays a part in all imagery, whether as imagination, inventiveness, humor, or a sense for the appropriate application of stock images or allusions. It seems to dominate Wolfram's style in those passages of highest image frequency where the triuwe element is slight or lacking. Wolfram's pleasure in wittiness for its own sake is especially clear in the involved and prolific imagery of the Prologue. Triuwe is a theme there, to be sure, but a theme very nearly drowned in the flood of fanciful play with words and concepts. When he says "diz vliegende bîspel ist tumben liuten gar ze snel" that sounds like a boast, not an apology. In the epilogue to Book II wit again emerges more importantly than the theme of triuwe. (8) It continues beyond the topic of Wolfram's relationship to women, touches deftly upon his pride as a knight, comes forward with his much-debated disclaimer to literacy and a written source for his tale, ending with the inelegant joke:

> ê man si hete vür ein buoch,
> ich waere ê nacket âne tuoch,
> sô ich in dem bade saeze,
> ob ich squesten niht vergaeze.

When he pauses in the description of events at Munsalvaesche to tell his audience that they must wait until later for the right point in the epic to learn all the details about Anfortas, wit carries him off into twenty-three lines of uninterrupted fancifulness which produces one of the highest image frequencies in the entire epic, one variation on the bow-string-arrow image for every three lines in thirty. The entire theme of the imagery is narrative style, merely (but not simply!) that:

> ich sage die senewen âne bogen.
> diu senewe ist ein bîspel.
> nû dunket iuch der boge snel:
> doch ist sneller daz diu senewe jaget.
> ob ich iu rehte hân gesaget,
> diu senewe gelîchet maeren sleht:
> diu dunkent ouch die liute reht.
> swer iu saget von der krümbe,
> der wil iuch leiten ümbe.
> swer den bogen gespannen siht,
> der senewe er der slehte giht,
> man welle si zer biuge erdenen
> sô si den schuz muoz menen.
> swer aber dem sîn maere schiuzet,
> des in durch nôt verdriuzet
> (wan daz hât dâ ninder stat
> und vil gerûmeclîchen phat
> zeinem ôren în, zem andern vür),
> mîn arbeit ich gar verlür,
> ob den mîn maere drünge:
> ich sagete oder sünge,

daz ez noch baz vernaeme ein boc
oder ein ulmeger stoc.
(241, 8-30)

Wolfram loses his way in the grammar toward the end and has to leap from the third
person swer to an ich in the same breath, but that seems a pardonable slip in an
otherwise virtuoso display of mental agility. One can almost imagine his audience
bursting into applause at the conclusion, unless they were purists like Gottfried. (9)
Wolfram likes this bow image so well he refers to it again near the end of the epic,
when Parzival and Condwiramurs begin the last part of their journey together to
Munsalvaesche: "ez ist niht krump alsô der boge, /diz maere ist war unde sleht,"
(805, 14-15).

As imagery in general becomes less frequent in the later books, so, too,
are such displays of sheer cleverness greatly reduced. Wit is harnassed more
completely to narrative purposes. The introduction to Book XV comes closest to
these earlier passages in its initial tone of rhetorical cleverness, but very soon it
becomes a logical, non-digressive bridge from the last previous grail book (IX) to
the concluding events in Parzival's fate. The last two of the four images in its
thirty-four lines build suspense twoard the dangerous fight with Feirefiz which follows at once. (10)

Of the seven Gawan passages which have little to do with triuwe but which
nevertheless rank among the highest in their books in image frequency, two are
particularly enhanced by Wolfram's wit in the narration. One is Gawan's first meeting with Orgeluse, the other is the scene of the night in which he at last receives
from her the reward he has earned so arduously through nearly 2800 intervening
lines of kummer. Imagery in the other five scenes adds to the vividness of the portrayal but is not otherwise notable: 1) the general view of the battle at Bearosche;
2) Gawan's arrival at Schampfanzun; 3) his first view inside the Schastel Marveile;
4) his ordeal on the Lit Marveile; and 5) the festival at Schastel Marveile after
Klingsor's army has become his and the captive queens are rescued. (See Table
VIII, page 210 .)

The humor in the night scene with Orgeluse lies in Wolfram's tongue-in-
cheek manner of saying that they made love while pretending not to be so indiscrete.
He prepares the scene with Queen Arnive's instructions to Orgeluse on taking good
care of the wounded Gawan, including such encouraging details as:

ob der helfe an iu ger,
iuwer helfe habet ir êre.
ich ensage iu nû niht mêre,
wan daz sîne wunden
mit kunst sô sint gebunden,
er möhte nû wol wâpen tragen.
(642, 16-21)

In contrast to Arnive's discrete words, Wolfram's comment which follows seems a burlesque of discretion. He says that if they knew how "to steal love" at that point, he can conceal the fact quite firmly, but that he would say "yes, it happened" except that "man dem unvuoge ie jach, / der verholniu maere machte breit." Having claimed to avoid doing what he has just done, he then adds chastely: "zuht sî des slôz ob minne site", and proceeds to describe the therapy Orgeluse gave Gawan with her feminine companionship:

> er vant die rehten hirzwurz,
> diu im half, daz er genas,
> sô daz im arges niht enwas:
> diu wurz was bî dem blanken brûn.
>
> (643, 28 - 644, 1)

One wonders how much plainer Wolfram could have spoken within the bounds of zuht. To no other love scene in the epic does he devote so much witty attention.

The wit in the first scene with Orgeluse is expressed in their repartee. Gawan woos with conventional minne-phraseology to which she replies first with blunt indifference:

Gawan:	"mîn lîp muoz ersterben sô, daz mir nimmer wîp gevellet baz."
Orgeluse:	"daz ist et wol: nû weiz ich ouch daz."

(509, 8-10)

Her indifference soon turns to sarcasm:

Gawan:	"mîn prüeven lât iuch doch niht vri: ir sît mînem herzen bî."
Orgeluse:	"verre ûzerhalp, niht drinne."

(509, 26-28)

The humor then fades into mere cleverness at applying a variation of the stock images of cupid's dart and the "prisoner of love":

Orgeluse:	"maneger sîniu ougen bolt, er möhte si ûf einer slingen ze senfterm wurfe bringen, ob er sehen niht vermîdet, daz im sîn herze snîdet."
Gawan:	". . . vrouwe, ir saget mir wâr. mîn ougen sint des herzen vâr: die hânt an iuwerm lîbe ersehen, daz ich mit wârheit des muoz jehen daz ich iuwer gevangen bin. kêrt gein mir wîplîchen sin.

swies iuch habe verdrozzen,
ir habet mich in geslozzen:
nû loeset oder bindet.
(510, 2-23)

Of the other images in the passage, one describes Orgeluse's castle, three her
excellent worthiness for Gawan's love, and a fifth her prideful discrimination toward men.

At first glance two of the Parzival passages of highest image frequency may
seem relatively divorced from the theme of triuwe: the description of Pelrapeire
under siege with its many similes and allusions to stress from hunger, and the
scene in Parzival's bed-chamber at Munsalvaesche after the grail ceremony. (11)
Four of the ten images in the latter passage describe his nightmare of arduous
struggle, a premonition of the troubles to follow upon his failure to ask the question.
However, since Sigune, Cundrie, and Trevrizent all later refer to this failure in
terms of defective triuwe, the implications of the nightmare for this theme becomes
obvious. (12) Prior to the nightmare images one describes the elegant bed, four extol his beauty and its effect upon the young ladies who serve him, and another plays
upon his modesty in their presence. These aspects, too, are not unrelated to triuwe,
as will soon be seen. As for the scene at Pelrapeire, the entire motivation for the
suffering there is the triuwe displayed by its inhabitants toward Condwiramurs.

One should probably not consider the two scenes of Gawan and Orgeluse as
divorced from the triuwe element, either. While it is not mentioned in them it is
implicit in any scene which touches upon a minne-relationship and also in every
instance in which the noble qualities of a knight or lady are praised. The ability to
do the latter well would demonstrate not only Wolfram's skills as a poet but also
his zuht as a knight. It should not be surprising, then, to discover that eulogy forms
the bulk of the imagery in many of the high frequency passages (in addition to those
with a jâmer theme). When Antikonie escorts the captive Gawan to King Vergulaht
to hear his judgment (Book VIII), all five images in the fifty-one lines extol her pris
and staete, both of which had been impugned by her brother's suspicions. When Gawan fights Orgeluse's mighty Turkoite (Book XII), the only images are of praise for
the two warriors, none show concern by Wolfram for Gawan's weakened condition
as might have been expected. Most of the images in the scene of Gahmuret's abandon-
ment of Belacane are in eulogy of the unborn Feirefiz. The highest frequency of
eulogistic imagery in the epic occurs in the brief passage at the end of Book XIII
which announces Parzival's reentry into the main narrative action, just before his
erroneous fight with Gawan:

(Gawan) sach einen ritter halden
bi dem wazzer Sabîns.
den wir wol möhten heizen vlins
der manlîchen krefte,
er schûr der ritterschefte,
sin herze valsch nie underswanc.

> er was des lîbes wol sô kranc
> swaz man heizet unprîs
> daz entruoc er nie deheinen wis
> halbes vingers lanc noch spanne.
> von dem selben werden manne
> muget ir wol ê hân vernomen:
> an den rehten stam diz maere ist komen.
>
> (678, 18-30)

By contrast it seems strange that no images praise Condwiramurs in the scene of her welcome at Munsalvaesche (one of the two scenes with the most imagery in Book XVI). Only three images occur at all in the fifty-three lines of this passage, one describing the brightness of the candles burning there ("rehte ob brünne gar der walt", 805, 21), the other two praising the slenderness of maidens waiting to receive her ("swankel als ein ris", 806, 18; and "als ein âmeize gelenket", 806, 26). The image ratio of this passage, 1:17.6, though high at this end of the epic would have been only average for Book IV (1:17.8). The passage can thus be said actually to represent Wolfram's unadorned narrative style. The account of Condwiramurs' reception is very vivid in detail. There is also an amusingly realistic touch in the child Lohengrin's shyness in front of his strangely colored uncle, and a more contrived humor in Wolfram's wishing he could relieve the weary Condwiramurs of her duty in kissing Repanse and the others at the court. All of these effects, while showing some wit, are produced without imagery. It would seem that by Book XVI, with its image ratio of only one in forty-nine lines, nothing had as much influence on Wolfram's use of imagery as his eagerness to finish his task. To this end imagery was of little use. Its relationship to scenes of triuwe, as both the Condwiramurs reception and the burial of Sigune and Schionatulander (the second "high" image frequency passage in Book XIV) could be considered, has become minimal here, and wit, too, is less abundant.

With the fight between Gawan and Parzival the triuwe theme is more sharply focused than in any of the passages mentioned above. As Wolfram warns just before the duel begins:

> wênec gewunne, vil verlorn
> hât, swer behaldet dâ den prîs:
> der klagetz doch immer, ist er wîs.
>
> (680, 4-6)

Their battle is a serious violation not only in that both are knights of the Round Table, but more importantly, they are blood relatives: "gein ein ander stuont ir triuwe" (680.7). The sixty-one lines of narration prior to their belated recognition are quite dull compared with the later account of the fight between Parzival and Feirefiz. Wolfram does little to build up suspense as to the outcome other than to say twice (once with an image) that no one can win joy from it. He expresses anxiety about Gawan but excludes Parzival from his worries because, after all, he was a "one-man army" (679, 5-7). None of the other images are particularly interesting for either strength or novelty. Parzival's outer garment and his horse's gear are "redder than a ruby." Up to now the triuwe between the two heroes "dürkel scharten nie emphienc" (680, 9). Both have an equal birthright to knighthood, being born "ûz der tjoste geslehte." They fought hard with their swords until "schildes schirben und daz grüene gras / ein gelîchiu temperte was" (680, 25-26). In the scene of belated recognition two rather more arresting images occur, when Parzival laments "sus sint diu alden wâpen mîn / ê dicke und aber worden schîn" (689, 1-2), thinking of his earlier offense in killing Ither, also a kinsman: and Gawan replies, granting him the superiority in battle:

> nû lâ dirz durch uns beide sîn leit:
> dû hâs dir selben ane gesiget,
> ob dîn herze triuwen phliget.
> (689, 30 - 690, 2)

A similar but fuller image of the oneness of men in the bonds of familial triuwe appears in the Feirefiz scene:

> man mac wol jehen, sus striten sie,
> der si beide nennen wil ze zwein.
> si wâren doch beide niht wan ein:
> min bruoder und ich daz ist ein lip,
> als ist guot man und des guot wip.
> (740, 26-30)

Although the Feirefiz-Parzival passage has a lower image ratio than the Gawan fight scene (1:16.1 compared with 1:10.1), its imagery is more interestingly appropriate and very thoughtfully situated in the stream of narration to emphasize a point or heighten the suspense. Wolfram has taken more pains in this situation to create a very effective episode by the interweaving of style and content. By comparison, the style of the Gawan scene appears mechanical. He also gives the Feirefiz scene much more space in the epic (290 lines) as befits its dramatic role, and also, of course, because of the need to give enough substance to the characterization of the latecomer Feirefiz to make him sufficiently important in the listener's mind. His great prîs must be substantiated.

The suspense begins with the introduction to Book XV, as has already been mentioned: whatever trouble Parzival's hand had previously encountered, "daz was mit kinden her getan" (734, 19); his life was now to be confronted by a stranger who was "ob allem strîte ein voget" (734, 30). The great wealth apparent on the unknown heathen is then described, wealth surpassing anything to be found in "any of the lands serving Arthur." Most of the precious stones and fabrics he wore were gifts from women, for he was valiant in the service of minne. About forty-five lines are thus occupied, with one image, the Arthur comparison, among them. Fifteen more lines account for his presence where Parzival meets him, nine bring Parzival into focus again, and then the heart of the matter, their actual encounter, begins.

CONSISTENT PATTERNS OF HIGH IMAGE FREQUENCY

Imagery increases at once, three within the following thirty-five lines. (13)
They are eulogizing images, standard practice in every combat scene. The way in
which their themes are interwoven by the particular sequence in which they appear
is unusual, however. Wolfram seems to increase the significance of each one
through its interaction with the other two. The first establishes the two point of
praise reinforced by the others, kiusche and boldness:

> hie wellent ein ander vâren,
> die mit kiusche lemmer wâren
> und lewen an der vrecheit.
> (737, 19-21)

The second adds to the first motif a new twist in the suspense by introducing the s
suspicion that untriuwe is unwittingly involved in this combat, stating the paradox
of "intimate strangers":

> die lûtern truopheite vrt,
> ieweder des andern herze truoc:
> ir vremde was heimlîch genuoc.
> (738, 8-10)

The third combines elements of each of the first two by enlarging upon the lion image
and also by suggesting a common paternal experience as the source of their boldness:

> den lewen sîn muoter tôt gebirt:
> von sîns vater galme er lebendec wirt.
> dise zwêne wâren ûz krache erborn . . .
> (738, 19-21)

The connection to Gahmuret is not made explicit until 100 lines further (742, 14).
The image could be taken simply as emphasis of their birthright to knightly combat,
similar to one in the Gawan-Parzival fight ("ûz der tjoste geslehte / wâren si beide
samt erborn") though far more colorful. Nevertheless, for listeners who had begun
to suspect the identity of the mighty heathen, remembering information given by
Cundrie and the visiting heathen queen at Arthur's court in Book VI, the lion image
must have been very pleasing. They must wait through some detailed description of
the combat (with two evenly-spaced, relatively unimportant descriptive images) for
clearer confirmation of their hunch. The fighting has become very serious, Feirefiz's helmet is well-dented, the horses have grown over-heated and been abandoned,
and a mighty blow has brought Parzival to his knees, when the untriuwe danger is
sounded again, more loudly and clearly than before:

> man mac wol jehen, sus striten sie,
> der si beide nennen wil ze zwein.
> si wâren doch beide niht wan ein:
> si wâren doch beide niht wan ein:
> mîn bruoder und ich daz ist ein lîp,
> als ist guot man und des guot wîp.
> (740, 26-30)

The exact relationship has finally been given for the enlightened to perceive but for the less perceptive it is still hidden in generalities: brothers, husbands, wives, family somehow. There follows digression to more description of Feirefiz's rich gems and his coat-of-arms from Queen Sekundille, then reiteration of the problem: "da streit der triuwen lûterheit, / grôz triuwe aldâ mit triuwen streit" (741, 21-22). Three images stressing the intensity of the fight follow in close succession: Feirefiz was a "stranger to defeat" (742, 8), "viurs blicke ûz helmen sprungen" and "von ir swerten gienc der sûre wint" (742, 12-13). Then, at last, Wolfram specifies their common bond to Gahmuret in a pious wish for God's intervention to save them both:

> got ner dâ Gahmuretes kint.
> der wunsch wirt in beiden,
> dem getouften und dem heiden:
> die nande ich ê vür einen.
> sus begunden siz ouch meinen,
> waeren si ein ander baz bekant:
> si ensazten niht sô hôhiu phant.
> ir strît galt niht mêre
> wan vreude, saelde und êre.
> swer dâ den prîs gewinnet,
> ob der triuwe minnet,
> werltlîche vreude er hât verlorn
> und immer herzen riuwe erkorn.
> (742, 14-26)

The entire problem is now clear to the listener but not yet to the combatants, so the suspense regarding the outcome continues until Wolfram brings them to a truce about sixty lines later. Just before the truce occurs, the last two images in the combat scene reiterate the concept of divine intervention. One does it obliquely by saying that Feirefiz "mit strûche venje suochte" (744, 13) instead of saying simply that he fell to his knees from Parzival's blow. The last one is explicit:

> zurteile stêz in beiden
> vor der hoesten hende
> daz diu ir sterben wende!
> (744, 22-24)

The truce begins, anxiety ends, suspense changes to pleasant anticipation of the protagonists' amazement and joy when they learn what the listener already knows.

It has seemed worthwhile to delineate this long scene in stylistic detail because it affords an excellent example of Wolfram's use of imagery at its best from a modern point of view, that is, when it is the least mechanical or "merely rhetorical."(14) As Parzival's third and most serious encounter with the test of familial triuwe its dramatic role is obvious.(15) That disaster seems to be averted this time by divine intervention instead of not at all as in Ither's case or by human intervention as in Gawan's case seems a prefiguring of the final grace about to be announced by Cundrie later in the same book. All of this could account for the special care Wolfram has given to the composition of the episode, but, as has been noted before, skilled narration and the use of imagery do not always go together in his style. The fact that this scene is by far the richest in imagery for Book XV apparently has to do less with the scene's general importance than with its triuwe theme.

In this regard it is of interest to note that a triuwe scene of far less general importance, involving a very minor character with Gawan and of no significance to the epic as a whole, is nonetheless one of the two highest ranking scenes in Book VII in image frequency. This is the passage (divided into two parts by Obie's misbehavior) which depicts the courtesy offered by the knight Scherules to the strange knight, Gawan.(16) When first Obie and then even her noble father seem willing to abuse the fair stranger, their liegeman takes it upon himself to preserve courtly ethics:

> Scherules der lobes gehêrte
> sprach als in sîn triuwe lêrte:
> 'sît ez sich hât an mich gezoget,
> ich bin vor vlust nû iuwer voget.'
> (362, 9-12)

To his own lord's ungenerous intentions toward Gawan, a peaceful guest at their gates, Scherules boldly asserts:

> swer im dar über tuot gewalt,
> waerez mîn vater oder mîn kint,
> alle die gein im in zorne sint,
> mîne mâge oder mîn bruoder,
> die müesten diu strîtes ruoder
> gein mir ziehen: ich wil in wern.
> (364, 4-9)

Scherules is the most striking example in the epic of the ideal of triuwe on the basis of sheer knightly courtesy, unrelated to either a family or a minne relationship.

Keie's behavior by contrast, especially in the episode of Parzival's trance outside Arthur's encampment, is indeed crude and curiously mixed in quality. His zealously faithful service to Arthur is a model of triuwe. This it is which motivates him to fight the unrecognized Parzival here, as it had been when he treated Cunneware so harshly. Yet, he seems unable to carry out any action with true nobility of soul.(17) The Keie incident evokes more imagery than any other part of the long trance episode in Book VI, though only very slightly more than Wolfram's complaint to Vrou Minne there.(18) Only the Cundrie scenes in this book rank higher in image frequency.

The function of the trance scene, of course, is to demonstrate the great strength of Parzival's triuwe toward Condwiramurs. This demonstration reaches its highest point in the Keie passage, hence, apparently, the greater concentration of imagery there. Three verbal insults from Keie as well as physical abuse and two images of Keie's ardor for combat testify to the risks to both life and pris Parzival must endure for his triuwe. They are as nothing, however, compared to the suffering "der valscheitswant" (296,1) has inflicted upon him by minne itself. So absorbed is he in this suffering that nothing Keie can do is of any concern to him. The counterpart to this scene occurs for Gawan at the beginning of Book XII where all the pain of his wounds from the ordeal on the Lit Marveile and from the battle with the lion is nothing compared with his suffering from love of Orgeluse (587, 15-30).

A variation on the theme of minne-triuwe is the distress Vrou Bene feels for her mistress Itonje when Gramoflanz's hostility to Gawan puts her into sharp conflict between two different triuwe obligations. When Bene thinks the conflict is between minne-triuwe and triuwe to Gawan as her lord, her distress for Itonje expresses itself to Gramoflanz in anger in a play on two meanings of herz:

> . . . ir ungetriuwer hunt!
> iuwer herze in sîner hende liget,
> dar iuwer herze hazzes phliget.
> (693, 22-24)

Anger deepens to grief when she learns that Gawan is brother as well as lord:

> dô zugen jâmers ruoder
> in ir herzen wol ein vuoder
> der herzenlîchen riuwe.
> (694, 13-15)

Vrou Bene seems the feminine counterpart to Scherules. This scene of her triuwe to her mistress actually receives more colorful treatment from Wolfram than the scenes of Itonje's own distress, possibly because in the former three triuwe motifs meet: minne, family, and loyalty to a lord or mistress.

Situations of jâmer from death or jâmer from longing for a beloved woman are those Wolfram uses most often to depict ideal triuwe. It seems to be the test of great distress which most clearly shows the strength of the triuwe. Minne's relationship to triuwe is an ambivalent one, however. On the one hand it is the twin of triuwe in the noble person and is therefore of positive value (532, 7-10). In another guise it is a power for ill. It is the negative aspect which Wolfram develops and chastises in the discourse which weaves in and out of Keie's attack upon Parzival in the trance. Wolfram's complaint begins with protest over the ill treatment Vrou Minne is permitting to befall her loyal subject whom she has dubbed with "ir krefte rîs" and ends on the same note:

> vrou Minne, hie seht ir zuo:
> ich waene manz îu ze laster tuo,
> wan ein gebûr spraeche sân:
> 'mînem herren sî diz getan.'
> (294, 21-24)

Between these two points he catalogues all of the powerful lady's faults. She has played him so false with foolish promptings that he can no longer trust her. All of her deeds are "hâlscharlîcher vâr", she obstructs good sense as a "slôz ob dem sinne", she "phleget untriuwen" by causing good women to lose their prîs and by disrupting all kinds of triuwe relationships. With her power she is very unkind to her subjects, loading their hearts with "swaeren soum", as Parzival's heart is here oppressed:

> sîn pensieren umbe den grâl
> und der künegîn gelîchiu mâl,
> iewederz was ein strengiu nôt.
> an im wac vür der minnen lôt.
>
> (296, 5-8)

The similar discourse on Amor, Cupido, and Venus in the early part of Gawan's painful relationship to Orgeluse draws a distinction between the negative and positive aspects of minne. One must learn to discriminate between that which comes from cupid's darts, the "ungehiure minne", and that which comes from real triuwe:

> swâ liep gein liebe erhüebe
> lûter âne trüebe,
> der enwederz des verdrüzze
> daz minne ir herze slüzze
> mit minne von der wanc ie vlôch,
> diu minne ist ob den andern hôch.
>
> (533, 25-30)

The important point for the purposes of this analysis is that Wolfram stresses the inseparableness of both suffering and minne from triuwe, even though triuwe may be lacking from minne:(19)

> swem herzenlîchiu triuwe ist bî,
> der wirt nimmer minnen vrî,
> mit vreude, etswenne mit riuwe.
> reht minne ist wâriu triuwe.
>
> (532, 7-10)

Every passage in which minne is the particular theme is among those of highest image frequency for their respective books. This is true even of the scene where Parzival experiences the first stirrings of its power as he thinks unhappily of the lovely Liaze he has left behind with Gurnemanz.

The fourth aspect in which Wolfram examines the subject of triuwe is in the relationship between Man and God. This is the explicit subject of Trevrizent's long lecture on theology (460, 28-467, 18): "der ist ein durchluhtec lieht / und wenket siner minne niht" (466, 3-4). Parzival is admonished to persevere in his triuwe to God "âne allez wenken, / sît got selbe ein triuwe ist" (462, 18-19). Following the tale of Adam and of God's incarnation as Man, Trevrizent repeats the theme of his instructions:

> sit sin getriuwiu mennescheit
> mit triuwen gein untriuwe streit,
> ir sult ûf in verkiesen.
>> (465, 9-11)

The bitter despair of God's triuwe with which Parzival opens this episode in some of the most arresting images of the epic lifts toward hope at the end of Trevrizent's lecture. If God truly lets nothing go unaccounted for ("ungelônet"), neither misse-wende nor tugent, he feels that he must have some good coming his way, for as he tells Trevrizent, he has suffered constantly through triuwe for both the grail and his wife:

> ich hân mit sorgen mine jugent
> alsus brâht an disen tac,
> daz ich durch triuwe kummers phlac...
>> (467, 16-18)

The variety and fancifulness of the imagery in this whole passage, as well as its effectiveness, often has little bearing on the main theme. Eight of the thirty-one images in it express Parzival's suffering when he comes to Trevrizent. Another nine have to do with God's power to see a person's thoughts. Seven play with the idea of the earth being Adam's mother, the "virgin" earth violated by Cain when he killed Abel. Several others were probably stock phraseology in homilies of the time with which Wolfram could be exprected to be familiar. (20)

The exact nature of his imagery here is not the point of particular interest for this study but rather its plentifulness. This scene not only has the second highest image frequency for Book IX, it also ranks sixth among all of the episodes in the entire epic. The significance of this is highlighted by comparison with the image ratios of the passages which surround it in the same book, especially the lecture on the grail which immediately follows it. The two lecture episodes are very similar in length, the former occupying 201 lines, the latter 214, but there the similarity ends. The image ratio drops from a high of 1:6.48 to one of the lowest ratios in the epic, only one image for each 107 lines.

In seeking an explanation for this extreme difference the comparison which seems the most pertinent is not the thematic contrast of God or grail, or perhaps "Christian doctrine versus grail myth", but rather a contrast in Wolfram's purpose in the two passages. The grail passage tells a story, it satisfies some of the curiosity aroused previously in the epic. That is its whole purpose: it fills gaps in the listener's understanding of the objective aspects of the story. As we have noted before, most of Wolfram's passages of lowest image frequency serve this function. He does not seem to find imagery necessary in order to "tell a good story." The purpose of the preceding lecture on God, however, is not to tell a story so much as to show what Parzival learned from Trevrizent about triuwe in relationship to God. Wolfram's pattern of image use holds true here as in all the other scenes in which triuwe is of major relevance: the frequency of imagery increases.

Trevrizent's response to Parzival's confession about the question error is the other high point in image frequency in Book IX, and it, too, concerns triuwe, even though the imagery speaks of youth trying to become wise, of the importance of old men not being foolish, and of faded tugent becoming green again (489, 5-10). Parzival has begged him for help on the basis of triuwe: "mîn triuwe hât doch gein iu vluht", he says, "ir sult mit râtes triuwe / klagen mîne tumpheit" (488, 14-15). His great fault was a fault in triuwe towards Anfortas:

> "wie was dîn triuwe von in (your senses) bewart
> an den selben stunden
> bî Anfortases wunden? "

asks the dismayed Trevrizent (488, 28-30). The consoling hope with which Trevrizent concludes his response to the shocking confession is the assurance of God's triuwe: "got selbe dich niht lieze: / ich bin von gote dîn râtes wer" (489, 20-21).

Assuming, then, that Wolfram deliberately wanted to emphasize triuwe, its importance, its problematic nature, and the appropriate forms of its expression in his society, what function does mere quantity of imagery serve, irrespective of the theme of the images themselves? The most plausible answer seems to be that it arrests the attention of the listener. It can do this through bafflement or delight or any number of other reactions. The important thing is to elicit his heightened, more conscious attention, so that he dwells upon what he is hearing. Images interrupt the narrative flow. They digress, however slightly, and digression can either please or annoy, but in either case it is hard to overlook, it causes thought, it focuses a drifting mind.

Imagery also calls attention to the author. As the story events recede slightly into the background relative to the sudden prominence of such non-events as ideas, allusions, or comparison, the objective narrative becomes more patently subjective. Imagery is one obvious illustration of an author's wit. Especially in those passages where his cleverness or mental agility come to the fore so much that all concern for triuwe seems secondary, one hears him saying: "ich bin Wolfram von Eschenbach / und kan ein teil mit sange" (114, 12-13). By holding his audience's attention longer or more closely upon passages with strong triuwe implications, Wolfram also indicated his own high regard for this virtue. (21)

The images in the triuwe episodes are less digressive than they are in those passages where his humor takes the lead. In the former they retain a clear connection with the narrative situation, elaborating upon it in some way, sometimes very artfully as in the combat scene between Parzival and Feirefiz. If Wolfram's images had been fairly evenly distributed throughout his narrative passages, there would have been little reason to question their function. It is only the extremely uneven distribution there, by virtue of which images become conspicuous also by their absence, which has raised the question of artistic intent. Pursuit of this question leads to the discovery that artistic intent and ethical intent coalesce on the common ground of triuwe.

Summary

In this chapter the distribution of imagery has been examined in those passages which ranked among the two highest or the two lowest in image frequency in their respective books in an attempt to establish patterns of relationship between image occurrence and other literary features.

No significant relationship has been found to exist with the effects of graphic vividness, dignity, excitement, or of convincing naturalness in human interaction. Wolfram's style quite frequently produces these effects independently of imagery. Many of the most effective narrative scenes are among those of lowest image occurrence.

On the other hand, discursive passages such as prologues and epilogues, or digressions such as discourses on minne or defenses of his own style tend to show a higher ratio of image frequency than narrative passages in general. Many of the discursive, primarily rhetorical passages listed in Table IX (page 215) have been discussed in respect either to triuwe or to Wolfram's wit. Those which were not discussed did not rank among the highest two passages for image frequency in their respective books. The five Gawan scenes which are among those of highest image ratios while being neither triuwe episodes nor particularly witty (page 193) are exceptional among the thirty-five highest passages in the epic in that Wolfram applied more wit or fancy in straight description than usual.

Since some narrative passages have been found to be the passages of highest image frequency in their books while some rhetorical passages are not, the dichotomy between rhetoric and story-telling has been rejected as the most significant factor in accounting for Wolfram's variations in the use of imagery. Those literary features which have been found to bear the most consistent relationship to high image frequency are humor (or a playful pleasure in being clever) and the theme of triuwe. This theme finds expression in four aspects: 1) triuwe in relationship to grief; 2) triuwe in relationship to minne; 3) triuwe demonstrated in courtly courtesy and ethics; and 4) triuwe in the relationship between Man and God. It has been seen that Wolfram regularly focuses attention upon such passages by increasing his use of imagery. The images themselves do not always speak directly to the theme of triuwe. Their main function seems to be to interrupt the narrative flow in order to hold the listener's mind upon these scenes and thereby to create a sense of their prominence or special importance. A secondary purpose may be to point to the author's own careful observation of the virtue of triuwe. Egotism is unquestionably present in the passages of great wittiness where the opportunity to show off his agility with words and concepts seems to give Wolfram great pleasure.

The passages of highest image frequency given in Table VIII (page   ) can be catalogued according to these five aspects (the triuwe aspect being divided into four parts) as follows:

Wit

Prologue
Epilogue to Book II, 114, 5 - 116, 4
Apology for the delay of clarification, Book V, 241, 1-30
Gawan meets Orgeluse, Book X, 508, 1 - 512, 25
Gawan's night with Orgeluse, Book XIII, 642, 1 - 644, 11
Introduction to Book XV, 734, 1 - 735, 4
General view of Bearosche, Book VII, 378, 5 - 379, 30
Arrival at Schampfanzun, Book VIII, 398, 1 - 399, 24
Entering the Schastel Marveile, Book XI, 564, 23 - 566, 10
Ordeal on the Lit Marveile, Book XI, 566, 11 - 568, 14
Festival at Schastel Marveile, Book XIII, 636, 15 - 641, 30

Triuwe in Grief

Conclusion in Zazamanc, Book I, 53, 15 - 58, 26
Birth of Parzival, Book II, 109, 2 - 114, 4
Grief for Ither, Book III, 159, 13 - 161, 8
Departure from Gurnemanz, Book III, 177, 10 - 179, 12
Cundrie, Book VI, 312, 2 - 319, 19
Gawan wins Orgeluse, Book XII, 611, 7 - 615, 20
Sigune's burial, Book XVI, 804, 1 - 805, 17

Triuwe in Minne

On the way to Pelrapeire, Book IV, 179, 13 - 181, 10
Keie attacks Parzival, Book VI, 290, 3-30; 293, 19 - 294, 20; 295, 1 -
        296, 12
Discourse on Amor and Cupido, Book X, 532, 1 - 534, 8
Gawan oppressed by love, XII, 583, 1 - 585, 4
Vrou Bene scolds Gramoflanz, Book XIV, 693, 21 - 694, 19

Triuwe in Courtly Courtesy and Ethics

Parzival's bed-chamber at Munsalvaesche, Book V, 242, 19 - 245, 16
Antikonie escorts Gawan, Book VIII, 426, 10 - 427, 30
Gawan fights the Turkoite, Book XII, 597, 14 - 598, 15
Parzival reenters the narrative, Book XIII, 678, 18-30
Parzival fights Gawan, Book XIV, 679, 1 - 681, 1
Belated recognition of Gawan and Parzival, Book XIV, 688, 4 - 690, 15
Parzival fights Feirefiz, Book XV, 735, 5 - 744, 24
Condwiramurs received at Munsalvaesche, Book XVI, 805, 18 - 807, 10

CONSISTENT PATTERNS OF HIGH IMAGE FREQUENCY

Triuwe between Man and God

      Trevrizent's instruction on God, Book IX, 460, 28 - 467, 18
      Trevrizent's response to the confession, Book IX, 488, 21 - 489, 21

Notes

(1)   In this and the concluding chapter the Middle High German terms triuwe and minne will be used without further italicizing. The concepts they signify have no equivalent terminology in English so the MHG terms will be used as loan words in English.

(2)   See the Table of Images, "Gawan Wins Orgeluse,", page 132.

(3)   The pietà typos suggested by Sigune with Schionatulander in her first meeting with Parzival is discussed by Julius Schwietering, "Typologisches in mittelalterlicher Dichtung," in Vom Werden des deutschen Geistes (Ehrismann Festschrift), Paul Merker, Wolfgang Stammler, editors, (Berlin: de Gruyter, 1925), 49.

(4)   See the Table of Images, "Sigune in the Hermit Cell," page 110.

(5)   See Table of Images, "The Denunciation," p. 90 ff.

(6)   See Table of Images, "Parzival's Departure,", 67 ff.

(7)   For fuller treatment of Wolfram's humor see: 1) Karl Kant, Scherz und Humor in Wolframs von Eschenbach Dichtungen (Heilbronn: Henninger, 1878); 2) Christian Starck, Die Darstellungsmittel des Wolframschen Humors, (Diss., Rostock, 1879); 3) Max Wehrli, "Wolframs Humor," in Wolfram von

Eschenbach, Heinz Rupp, ed., (Darmstadt: Wissenschaftliche Buchgesellschaft, 1966), 104-124; and 4) Hans J. Bayer, "Zu Besonderheiten des Stils
Wolframs von Eschenbach," Untersuchungen zum Sprachstil weltlicher Epen
des deutschen Früh- und Hochmittelalters, (Berlin: Erich Schmidt, 1962),
199-226.

(8)   Mackensen's assertion that Wolfram's feelings were more sincerely involved
in this passage than in the Prologue may be true, but I find the feeling conveyed to be much the same in both places, only with more of a playfully teas-
ing quality here. (See page 33.)

(9)   For a more serious significance to the bow metaphor see Groos, footnote 40,
page 21.

(10)   See Table of Images, "Wolfram Promises to Reveal the End," page 145.

(11)   See Table of Images, "Arrival at Pelrapeire," page 69, and "In Parzival's
Bed-Chamber," page 79.

(12)   Sigune: "ir truoget den eiterwolves zan,/dâ diu galle in der triuwe / an iu
bekleip sô niuwe" (255, 14-16); Cundrie: "ir vil ungetriuwer gast, / sîn nôt
iuch solde erbarmet hân" (316, 2-3); Trevrizent: "wie was dîn triuwe von in
(your senses) bewart / an den selben stunden / bî Anfortases wunden?"
(488, 28-30).

(13)   See the Table of Images, "Parzival Encounters Feirefiz," page 146.

(14)   Compare the following description of a passage in Shakespeare by Wolfgang
Clemen, op.cit., 82-83: ". . . the audience has pricked up its ears; upon the
imagination a very definite image has impressed itself for a brief moment,
and this will come to life again later on when reality demands it. Here we
see Shakespeare's peculiar technique which is to develop more and more in
the great tragedies. By means of such delicate touches and hints, . . .
he succeeds in gradually preparing for something to come, . . . a residue of
doubt remains, at once disturbing and a source of enhanced concentration."

(15)   The most thorough discussion of the role of familial triuwe in Parzival is
probably by Julius Schwietering, Die deutsche Dichtung des Mittelalters,
(Potsdam: Akademische Verlagsgesellschaft Athenaion, 1932), 160-172.

(16)   Table of Images, "Scherules' Courtesy,", page 98.

(17)   Wolfram is unwilling to deny Keie's good qualities. See the apology he inter-
jects following this scene (296, 13 ff.).

(18)   Table of Images, "Parzival Entranced," page 84 ff.

(19)   This is one of the main theses in two very interesting analyses: James F.
Poag, Heinrich von Veldeke's minne; Wolfram von Eschenbach's liebe und
triuwe," Journal of English and Germanic Philology, 61 (1962), 721-735;
"Wolfram von Eschenbach's Metamorphosis of the Ovidian Tradition, "Monatshefte, 57 (1965), 69-76.

(20)   The influence of sermon literature is discussed in chapter I, page 16 ff.

(21)   The pervasive subjectivity of the poet in Parzival (which Bayer considers a
particularly effective technique for maintaining rapport with a listening
audience) is viewed by Böckmann as a fact of Wolfram's individualizing, per-
sonalizing manner of thought. He holds this to be a departure from medieval
form and sees Wolfram as representing a stylistic middle ground between
the old medieval "Sinnbildsprache" and the coming, modern "Ausdruckssprache." His imagery is remarked as a clear illustration of that trend: "Aus
dem Gegensatz von Bild und Sinn bricht ein subjektiver Schein auf, so dass
in der Sinnbildgestaltung eigentümliche Brechungsverhältnisse entstehen, die
auf die Individualität des Dichters zurückweisen. Noch in alle ernste Be-
trachtung kann diese Eigenwilligkeit des Vergleichs eindringen, so dass die
Metaphorik ein seltsames Eigenleben gewinnt und besondere Aufmerksamkeit
fordert (my italics) ... Bild und Bedeutung verknüpfen sich auf eine eigenwil-
lige, zum Nachdenken anregende Weise (my italics), so dass dadurch die
Subjektivität in die Darstellung fühlbar eindringt." Böckmann, op.cit., 149.

Table VIII: Passages of Highest and Lowest Image Frquencies per Book

Thematic Topic	Image Ratio	Lines	Images	Meta-phors	Meta. Ratio	Meta. %
BOOK I (Image Ratio 1/19)						
Prologue	1/ 3.5	116	33	15	1/ 7.7	45.4
Conclusion of Adventures in Zazamanc	1/ 14.7	162	11	8	1/ 20.3	72.5
....						
Gahmuret Goes to Zazamanc	1/ 57.5	230	4	2	1/115	50
Gahmuret, New Lord of Zazamanc	1/ 71	284	4	1	1/284	25
BOOK II (Image Ratio 1/22)						
Epilogue	1/ 8.6	60	7	6	1/ 10	85.7
Birth of Parzival	1/ 11.8	153	13	12	1/ 12.8	92.3
....						
Gahmuret in Spain, to Kanvoleis	1/ 46	92	2	0	–	–
Gahmuret's Death Described	1/ 57	114	2	0	–	–
BOOK III (Image Ratio 1/19.4)						
Grief Over Ither	1/ 9.3	56	6	6	1/ 9.3	100
Parzival's Departure from Gurnemanz	1/ 10.5	63	6	4	1/ 15.8	66.6
....						
Parzival Meets the Knights	1/ 44	264	6	4	1/ 66	66.6
Orilus and Jeschute	1/ 78	156	2	1	1/156	50
BOOK IV (Image Ratio 1/17.6)						
Parzival on Way to Pelrapeire	1/ 7.3	58	8	0	–	–
Arrival and Reception at Pelrapeire	1/ 9.2	156	17	5	1/ 31.2	29.4
....						

Table VIII

Thematic Topic	Image Ratio	Lines	Images	Meta-phors	Meta. Ratio	Meta. %
Preparations for Battle with Clamide	1/ 41.5	83	2	2	1/ 41.5	100
Parzival Battles Kingrun	1/ 51.5	103	2	0	-	-
BOOK V (Image Ratio 1/18.9)						
Apology for Delay of Clarification	1/ 3.3	30	9	5	1/ 6	55.5
Parzival's Bed-Chamber, Munsalvaesche	1/ 8.8	88	10	6	1/ 14.7	60
....						
Parzival Meets the Fisher-King	1/ 39	39	1	0	-	-
Sigune Again; Parzival Learns of Error	1/ 39	234	6	3	1/ 78	50
Orilus, Jeschute at Arthur's Court	1/ 45	180	4	2	1/ 90	50
BOOK VI (Image Ratio 1/13.7)						
Cundrie	1/ 6	228	38	28	1/ 8	73.7
Keie Fights Parzival	1/ 7.8	102	13	11	1/ 9.3	84.6
....						
Betrothal, Clamide-Cunneware	0/ 46	46	0	0	-	-
Parzival Leaves to Seek Grail	1/ 45	90	2	2	1/ 45	100
Departures of the Others	1/ 60	60	1	1	1/ 60	100
BOOK VII (Image Ratio 1/23.7)						
Battle at Bearosche, General View	1/ 7	56	8	2	1/ 28	25
Scherules Courtesy to Gawan	1/ 10.3	72	7	3	1/ 24	43
....						
Red Knight's Dispensations	1/ 71	71	1	1	1/ 71	100
Obie's Hostility to Gawan	1/ 73	73	1	1	1/ 73	100

Table VIII

Thematic Topic	Image Ratio	Lines	Images	Meta-phors	Meta. Ratio	Meta. %
BOOK VIII (Image Ratio 1/18.4)						
Antikonie Escorts Gawan to Vergulaht	1/ 10.2	51	5	4	1/ 12.7	80
Gawan Arrives at Schanpfanzen	1/ 10.8	54	5	2	1/ 27	40
....						
Gawan Leaves on Grail Quest	1/ 35	70	2	2	1/ 35	100
Gawan Reunited with his Retinue	1/ 51	51	1	1	1/ 51	100
BOOK IX (Image Ratio 1/19.8)						
Trevrizent's Response to Confession	1/ 4.4	31	7	7	1/ 4.4	100
Trevrizent Instructs about God	1/ 6.5	201	31	29	1/ 6.9	93.5
....						
Trevrizent Instructs about Grail	1/107	214	2	1	1/214	50
Trevrizent Tells about his Youth	1/120	120	1	0	-	-
BOOK X (Image Ratio 1/24.6)						
Gawan Meets Orgeluse	1/ 11.2	145	13	11	1/ 13.2	84.7
Discourse on Amor and Cupid	1/ 11.3	68	6	6	1/ 11.3	100
....						
Arrival at Schastel Marveile	0/ 61	61	0	0	-	-
Gawan Tells Story of Urjans	0/158	158	0	0	-	-
BOOK XI (Image Ratio 1/30)						
Gawan's Ordeal on the Lit Marveile	1/ 9.1	64	7	2	1/ 32	28.5
Gawan Enters the Schastel Marveile	1/ 9.6	48	5	2	1/ 24	40
....						

Table VIII

Thematic Topic	Image Ratio	Lines	Images	Meta-phors	Meta. Ratio	Meta. %
The Lion	1/ 42	84	2	0	-	-
Gawan Nursed by the Ladies	1/ 55.2	276	5	5	1/ 55.2	100
BOOK XII (Image Ratio 1/27.5)						
Intro., Gawan Oppressed by Love	1/ 9.1	64	7	4	1/ 16	57.1
Gawan Wins Orgeluse	1/ 10.3	134	13	11	1/ 12.2	84.6
Gawan Fights the Turkoite	1/ 10.6	32	3	3	1/ 10.6	100
....						
Gramoflanz and Gawan Talk	1/105	210	2	1	1/210	50
Triumphant Return to Schastel Marveil	1/156	156	1	1	1/156	100
BOOK XIII (Image Ratio 1/23.6)						
Parzival Re-enters the Narrative*	1/ 2.6	13	5	5	1/ 2.6	100
Gawan's Night with Orgeluse	1/ 11.8	71	6	6	1/ 11.8	100
Banquet and Dance, Schastel Marveile	1/ 16.6	166	10	9	1/ 18.7	90
....						
Preparations for Duel, Gawan-Gramoflanz	1/116	116	1	1	1/116	100
Gawan Prepares to Meet Arthur	1/138	138	1	0	-	-
BOOK XIV (Image Ratio 1/38.4)						
Vrou Bene Scolds Gramoflanz for Itonje*	1/ 7.3	29	4	4	1/ 7.3	100
Gawan and Parzival Fight Unawares	1/ 10.1	61	6	5	1/ 12.2	83.3
Belated Recognition of Gawan by Parzival	1/ 18	72	4	4	1/ 18	100
....						

*These passages shorter than the thirty-line limit generally observed in the selection.

Table VIII

Thematic Topic	Image Ratio	Lines	Images	Meta-phors	Meta. Ratio	Meta. %
Arthur's Messengers with Gramoflanz	1/ 71.5	143	2	2	1/ 71.5	100
Parzival as Gawan's Guest	0/ 80	80	0	0	-	-
BOOK XV (Image Ratio 1/34.6)						
Intro., Wolfram Promises to Finish	1/ 8.5	34	4	4	1/ 8.5	100
Parzival and Feirefiz Fight	1/ 16.1	290	18	16	1/ 18.1	88.8
· · · · · · · · ·						
Round Table Honors Feirefiz	0/120	120	0	0	-	-
Parzival's Joy; Prepares to go with Cundrie	1/120	120	1	1	1/120	100
BOOK XVI (Image Ratio 1/49)						
Parzival and Condwiramurs bury Sigune	1/ 15.6	47	3	1	1/ 47	33.3
Condwiramurs Received at Munsalvaesche	1/ 17.6	53	3	0	-	-
· · · · · · · · ·						
Feirefiz' Baptism, Marries Repanse	1/ 83	83	1	1	1/ 83	100
Summary of Lohengrin's Fate	1/110	110	1	1	1/110	100

Table IX: Passages Primarily Rhetorical, Non-Narrative

Type of Passage	Image Ratio	Lines	Images	Meta-phors	Meta. Ratio	Meta. %
PROLOGUES						
Book I	1/ 3.5	116	33	15	1/ 7.7	45.4

Table IX

Type of Passage	Image Ratio	Lines	Images	Meta-phors	Meta. Ratio	Meta. %
Book III	0/ 10	10	0	0	-	-
Book VII	1/ 10	30	3	2	1/ 15	66.6
Book IX (Vrou Aventiure)	1/ 20	40	2	1	1/ 40	50
Book X	0/ 4	4	0	0	-	-
Book XII (Gawan and Love)	1/ 9.1	64	7	4	1/ 16	57.1
Book XV	1/ 8.5	34	4	4	1/ 8.5	100
EPILOGUES						
Book II	1/ 8.6	60	7	6	1/ 10	85.7
Book VI	1/ 10	30	3	2	1/ 15	66.6
Book XVI	0/ 30	30	0	0	-	-
ADDRESSES TO VROU MINNE						
Book VI 291, 1 - 293, 18; 294, 21-30	1/ 8	88	11	9	1/ 9.8	81.8
Book X (Amor and Cupid) 532, 1 - 534, 9	1/ 11.3	68	6	6	1/ 11.3	100
Book XII 585, 5 - 587, 14	1/ 23.3	70	3	3	1/ 23.3	100
DEFENSE OF WOLFRAM'S STYLE						
Prologue, 1, 15 - 4, 8	1/ 3.8	84	22	14	1/ 6	63.6
Epilogue, Book II	1/ 8.6	60	7	6	1/ 10	85.7
Book V (Bow Image) 241, 1-30	1/ 3.3	30	9	5	1/ 6	55.5
Book IX 453, 1-10	0/ 10	10	0	0	-	-
Book XV 734, 1-9	1/ 4.5	9	2	2	1/ 4.5	100
Book XVI Epilogue	0/ 30	30	0	0	-	-

Table IX

Type of Passage	Image Ratio	Lines	Images	Meta-phors	Meta. Ratio	Meta. %
DISCOURSES						
In Defense of Keie, 296, 13 - 297, 29	1/ 15.6	47	3	1	1/ 47	33.3
On Obie and Love, 365, 1 - 366, 2	1/ 10.6	32	3	3	1/ 10.6	100
Liddamus on Fighting 418, 26 - 422, 1	1/ 12	96	8	2	1/ 48	25
On Friendship 675, 16-28	1/ 13	13	1	1	1/ 13	100

CHAPTER VI

CONCLUSIONS: A THEORY FOR IMAGERY IN <u>PARZIVAL</u>

The emergence of triuwe as a principle theme in an analysis of <u>Parzival</u> is in no way surprising, but that this should happen through an analysis of the distribution of imagery alone may well be startling and was completely unexpected at the outset of this study.

Most discussions of triuwe in the literature naturally proceed either from an examination of specific narrative situations or from consideration of the broader philosophical implications of the work, in other words, from content.(1) Of the previous studies of Wolfram's style, only Mackensen attempts to relate the frequency and type of imagery to thematic situations, but, curiously enough, although he considers the themes of grief and minne, triuwe is not mentioned. My own expectation was that image frequency might be related to strong emotionality, such as Clemen remarks in Shakespeare's works:(2)

> Are there particular events which more than other occasions call
> forth imagery? We find that in the presence of death Shakespeare's
> characters always use metaphorical language. The incomprehensible
> mystery of death, transcending the compass of human understanding,
> demands language different from the common and direct speech of
> every day.

Yet, the actual data for Wolfram refused to support this thesis. Grief scenes were often among those of most frequent imagery, to be sure, but the imagery itself never dealt with death per se, nor even primarily with the emotions of the grieving person. Eulogy was its chief theme. More important was the fact that many other scenes which conveyed high feeling (such as Orilus' anger with Jeschute), or strong vividness (as in Gahmuret's arrival in Zazamanc), or great importance for the course of the epic (as when the child Parzival encounters knights for the first time) did so with little or no imagery.(3) Mackensen's theory of the lack of a need for emphasis through imagery beyond that provided by the action of such scenes might be a reasonable intuition. On the other hand, many of those scenes of the highest image frequency which were not associated with grief were of a very mild feeling-quality, and often even of little apparent epic importance. What was the common denominator, or was there one at all? A solution was first suspected in reflecting upon the most dramatic contrast in image frequency in the epic, that between Trevrizent's two lectures, the one on God and the other on the grail, scenes of nearly equal length but showing one image for every 6 lines in the first, while only one for every 107 lines in the other. The puzzle seemed to resolve itself with the key of triuwe.

Reexamining all the other passages of highest and lowest image frequency in this light confirmed such an insight. There could be no question but that images, used quantitatively, stressed the theme of triuwe in <u>Parzival</u>. Their very presence in unusual number, combined with the slightly digressive quality of all imagery, slows down the narrative flow and arrests the attention of the audience upon the passage in which this happens. The images themselves are only infrequently didactic, but their use collectively seems to serve a didactic purpose in the areas in which they are most plentiful. Sometimes, as seen in the combat between Parzival and Feirefiz, they also serve very effectively to heighten suspense, but this is not generally the case. Their more common function is merely to attract special attention to particular passages in which triuwe, or the lack of it, is exemplified.

The triuwe lessons thus emphasized divide roughly into four relationships: triuwe in grief, triuwe in minne, triuwe in ethical relationships and courtly courtesy (with familial triuwe included among the former), and triuwe between Man and God. The didactically emphatic function of imagery occurs too regularly to doubt that it reflects Wolfram's intent. It hardly seems possible that it could have occurred this way either unconsciously or spontaneously. The implications for his manner of composing are obvious and agree closely with Bayer's general conclusions based upon analysis of his oral literature techniques, namely, that Wolfram was a very conscious stylist who skillfully directed his audience's attention where he wanted it. (4) Another of Bayer's observations deserves mention here, that is, that most of Wolfram's imagery is not the obscure type for which he is famous. Those images which Singer finds similar to the Provencal trobar clus actually form a small part of the imagery in its entirety. In fact, from the point of view of a modern taste in metaphor, much of Wolfram's imagery is quite trite and even dull, both in content and in its decorative function, its lack of inherent necessity for poetic meaning. The conspicuousness of the exceptions to this rule has unduly colored general impressions about the imagery in Parzival. It would doubtless be a mistake, however, to assume that the metaphoric commonplaces which abound in the epic, or their frequently decorative application, were held by his contemporaries in the low regard that modern taste assigns to them. On the contrary. They may well have been very pleasing to the ears of his audience, having the comfortable ring of propriety and courtesy, as Parry suggests was the case with the traditional metaphor in Homer's time and in certain highly stylized periods of English literature. (5)

Following upon the observation of the decorative nature of much of the imagery even in the triuwe scenes, it is not surprising to note that most of the passages which can be considered more rhetorical than narrative in their attempts to persuade or their dalliance with ideas also contain much imagery. Didacticism is obvious here, too, for example in the Prologue or in the discourse with Vrou Minne, but equally obvious in a number of them is wit, apparently for its own sake. The passage of highest image frequency in any book is not always one of the rhetorical or discursive passages; their imagery is often exceeded by a narrative passage that illustrates triuwe. But those passages of highest image frequency which are not clearly triuwe passages all have the common bond of wit. This is the second stylistic key to Wolfram's usage of exceptionally plentiful imagery. It often expresses itself in a playful delight in metaphoric pyrotechnics (as in the bow image, for example, P241, 1-30). This side of Wolfram has been too little appreciated. Even the studies of his humor tend toward a serious interpretation, seeing it as a philosophical attitude, a response to the recognition of life's bitter paradoxes, even as destructive.(6) Perhaps so, but despite the seriousness of his themes Wolfram had a gift for play, not unrelated, surely, to his empathy for children. Here and there in Parzival the poet engages in sheer fun, a tendency which nearly disappears, however, in the latter parts of the epic. It seems a mistake that some of his critics have hailed this as an improvement.

The decline in wit is accompanied by a decline in imagery following Book VI, as Parzival and Gawan depart on their respective missions. By the beginning of Book XVI neither triuwe nor wit evoke much of it. These two books are polar opposites in the epic in image frequency, the former showing an image for every 14 lines approximately, the latter only one for every 49 lines. Both of these are books in which clearly Parzival, not Gawan, is the protagonist, it should be noted. The common impression that Wolfram shows a marked partiality for Parzival over his more worldly counterpart through the use of imagery simply does not bear out from the point of view of image frequency. Whether or not other kinds of evidence could establish such a partiality as a fact, I cannot say, but such an assertion as the following must be judged erroneous:(7)

> Die innere Beteiligung als der eigentliche Quell (der Bilder) spiegelt sich schon in der Verteilung wider; in den Büchern die von Parzival handeln, sind sie weit häufiger als in den Gawanbüchern.

It is an easy error to fall into, if one's basis for judgment is Books III through VII. Three of the first four Parzival books, IV-VI, are full of imagery, fuller than any other part of the epic. The first of the Gawan books, VII, is conspicuously low in imagery in contrast. Indeed, the drop from the frequency in Book VI (the highest in the epic) to Book VII is a striking change, from an average of one image in 14 lines to one in 24. The analysis must not stop there, however, to be accurate. The rest of the epic shows that none of the Gawan books is as low in imagery as the last two Parzival books (or the last three, if Book XIV is considered more properly assigned to Parzival than to Gawan), while the Antikonie book (VIII) has slightly more imagery even than the first Parzival book, Book III, enchanting though the latter is. Furthermore, Book IX, with all of its importance, has less imagery than the Gawan book preceding it. Both resemble the early parts of the epic in style more closely than any of the other books following Book VI.

The trend toward decreasing imagery which seems to set in with Book VII (Gawan and Obilot) is very marked, and may support the theory of a pause in the composition after Book VI. The hypothesis that the Gahmuret books were composed later than the rest of the first six finds some support in the statistics here, too. Assuming the Prologue to have been composed independently of the Gahmuret episodes and excluding its great quantity of imagery from consideration, therefore, the image frequency in the Gahmuret scenes averages one for each 24 lines, notably less than the norm for the epic through Book VI, more like the books which follow.

CONCLUSIONS: A THEORY FOR IMAGERY IN PARZIVAL

The decline in both imagery and wit as the epic progresses past Book VI is easier to demonstrate than to explain. Was Wolfram influenced to a more sober, less fanciful treatment of his subject by Gottfried's criticism (and the criticism of others of which we have no evidence)? Was it loss of enthusiasm for his task which made him want to tell his tale with as little effort as possible? Surely it takes more effort to elaborate with imagery than to simply tell a story. Was the interruption between Books VI and VII, and perhaps again after Book IX, so long that Wolfram's own poetic nature had changed? Were his life circumstances so altered that he no longer had as much time to compose? All of these seem possible and none are provable.

The one aspect of his imagery which did not change, however infrequent imagery became, was his preference for metaphor over other forms. Mackensen's apparent certainty that simile exceeded metaphor in Parzival is puzzling. (8) Since he did not list the images from which he drew this conclusion, there is no way to account for the discrepancies in our findings. In the statistics here, however, of the 1117 images found in the epic (excluding only instances where personification is the sole figurative element), 67.9 % are metaphors. In the present study a narrow distinction was drawn for metaphors. An image was called a metaphor only where two conditions were fulfilled: first, the expression needed to violate common sense logic about reality (ie., a human face is not a pan of milk and cannot really have a layer of Rahm on it - P. 1, 22); and secondly, no other figurative element, whether pun or symbol, could be present. A metaphor which was also a pun was classified as a pun, one which was a symbol (such as the use of black in an ethical sense) was considered a symbol, and both were catalogued as "other" or non-metaphoric imagery. Hence, it may be assumed that the percentage for metaphoric imagery (67.9) is a conservative figure.

The persistence of metaphor as a form in Wolfram's style may perhaps most clearly be seen by again comparing Books VI and XVI, those two which are at the opposite extremes in general image frequency. In each case the proportion of metaphor is nearly the same: 74 % for Book VI and 76 % for Book XVI. Book IX, which ranks seventh in the epic in terms of total image frequency, is second in the ratio of metaphor to lines and has also a 76 % proportion of metaphor over other forms. Book XIV, which ranks fifteenth in total image frequency, has the highest proportion of metaphor to other images of any book in the epic, 88.3 %. The conclusion based on the summary of such detail is that, in Parzival, as imagery decreased, the greatest amount of decrease was in the non-metaphoric forms, so that as the actual quantity of imagery declined in the later books of the epic, that portion which remained was more and more predominantly metaphor.

This finding could have various implications, all of which must remain speculation at this point for lack of sufficient evidence. It may reflect a deliberate stylistic ideal of Wolfram's, an assumption of the superiority of metaphor, an assumption supported by classical rhetorical tradition. (9) It would be helpful to know whether or not Wolfram's practice was typical of his time and what the proportion of metaphor is in the works of Gottfried, Hartmann, or Veldeke. Or in Cretien, too, for that matter. Although Wolfram extended Cretien's <u>Perceval</u> to almost twice its original length (referring only to the scenes common to both), and although no evidence could be found from the statistics of this study to support the theory that his image frequency was influenced by the source from which he might have been working, we don't really know anything about how his actual imagery, in either choice or form, compares with that of Cretien.

Another possibility is that metaphor came more naturally to his mind than simile or allusion or any other type of imagery, that it was less deliberately ornamental or otherwise rhetorical for him than other forms. If so, then some of the possible reasons for the decline of imagery such as a lack of time for composing or lack of enthusiasm for the task would have had less effect on metaphor than on the other forms for which, presumably, more conscious expenditure of wit was needed.

It is also possible, of course, that the statistics err in including expressions as metaphors which really are not images at all, but merely reflect the standard connotations of the language. Such an error would be more likely to occur with metaphor than with simile or allusion or punning where the poet's intention to provide an image is transparent. If we can assume, however, that increased perception of the standard connotations of MHG words would still leave Wolfram's proportion of metaphor, if not as high as 68 %, at least in a majority, then we would have to agree with Kinzel, Bötticher, Ludwig, and all the others who have stated that the urge to concrete formulation is one of the most notable features of Wolfram's style; for metaphor, more than any other type of imagery, gives an immediacy and a concretely experiential quality to poetic expression. In this regard it may be of interest to note that the frequency of metaphor is about the same in both the Gawan books and the Gahmuret episodes, with Gawan having a slight lead. The Parzival books have more metaphor (in proportion to length) than either of them, though the difference between Parzival and Gahmuret is greater than between Parzival and Gawan. On this basis of more metaphor one could perhaps build a case for Wolfram's deeper personal interest in Parzival even though sheer frequency of imagery in general proves irrelevant.

This study began with two questions: the question of Wolfram's purposes in using imagery and the question of the extent to which these purposes, or at least effects, could be identified and examined from an empirically objective base established from within the epic itself. Of the various findings here, the discovery of Wolfram's quantitative use of imagery to call attention to scenes which form exempla for triuwe are surely the most significant for future Wolfram research. The interweaving of two distinct styles in <u>Parzival</u>, the simple and the adorned (so aptly noted by Bumke), (10) has at least one demonstrable significance for the meaning of the epic as a whole.

The ambitious hope of providing a theory for Wolfram's use of imagery which would best account for all of the data uncovered has been only partially fulfilled.

CONCLUSIONS: A THEORY FOR IMAGERY IN PARZIVAL

Only his practice in the passages of highest and lowest image frequency has been examined. What functions are served in the majority of passages, those where images appear at the average rate for the epic of one in every 22 or 23 lines, has not been discussed. It seems doubtful that statistical treatment there can do more than identify these passages. Nor does it seem likely that it can be of any more use in accounting for the dominance of metaphor than it already has, which is simply to establish the fact.

A complete theory for the functioning of imagery in Parzival might also want to take into account Mackensen's distinctions as to the manner in which an image is expressed, whether as a single word, a phrase, or in more extended form. His selection of examples, however, only 699 for the epic compared with 1117 here, seems insufficient. Concern for the distribution of referential categories apparently adds too little to an understanding of how Wolfram's style works to be of value in the development of a theory of style. A comparison of Wolfram's imagery with that contained in his known French sources might contribute further insight into medieval imagery in general and is surely to be desired. It is not needed, however, to show how imagery functions in Wolfram's own work. For that, hopefully, the empirical groundwork has now been laid from which future research to this end can more fruitfully proceed.

Notes

(1)   In addition to works already cited of Poag, de Boor, Böckmann, and Schwietering, the following should also be mentioned: 1) Vera Vollmer, Die Begriffe der Triuwe und der Staete in der höfischen Minnedichtung, (Diss., Tübingen, 1914); 2) Hermann Heckel, Das ethische Wortfeld in Wolframs Parzival, (Diss., Erlangen, 1939); 3) Gisela Spiess, Die Bedeutung des Wortes 'triuwe' in den mhd. Epen 'Parzival', 'Nibelungenlied' und 'Tristan', (Diss., Heidelberg, 1957); 4) Heinrich Hempel, "Der Eingang von Wolframs Parzival," Kleinere Schriften, (Heidelberg: Carl Winter Universitätsverlag, 1966), 261-276.

(2)   Clemen, <u>op.cit.</u>, 43.

(3)   See page 36. Other scenes of lowest imagery are primarily connections between major events with no other intrinsic importance.

(4)   Bayer, <u>op.cit.</u>, 200 ff. Bumke remarks on some metrical techniques of emphasis (<u>Wolfram von Eschenbach</u>, 14), and Blanka Horacek upon enjambement used similarly: "Die Kunst des Enjambements bei Wolfram von Eschenbach," <u>Zeitschrift für deutsches Altertum und deutsche Literatur</u>, 85 (1954-55), 210-229.

(5)   Milman Parry, "The Traditional Metaphor in Homer," <u>Classical Philology</u>, XXVIII (1933), 30-43.

(6)   Wehrli, <u>op.cit.</u>, 104 ff. Also Bumke, <u>op.cit.</u>, 16.

(7)   Ludwig Wolff, "Vom persönlichen Stil Wolframs in seiner dichterischen Bedeutung," <u>Kleinere Schriften zur altdeutschen Philologie</u>, (Berlin: de Gruyter, 1967), 268.

(8)   See page 33.

(9)   See "Aristotle", page 14, and "Quintilian", page 16.

(10)   See page 17.

BIBLIOGRAPHY

Concerning Medieval Literature

Auerbach, Erich. Literatursprache und Publikum in der lateinischen Spätantike und im Mittelalter. Bern: Francke Verlag, 1958.

_____. Typologische Motive in der mittelalterlichen Literatur. (Schriften und Vorträge des Petrarca-Instituts, Köln) Krefeld: Scherpe, 1953.

Bayer, Hans J. Untersuchungen zum Sprachstil weltlicher Epen des deutschen Früh- und Hochmittelalters. (Philologische Studien und Quellen, Heft 10) Berlin: Erich Schmidt Verlag, 1962.

Böckmann, Paul. Formgeschichte der deutschen Dichtung. I: Von der Sinnbildsprache zur Ausdruckssprache. Hamburg: Hoffmann und Campe Verlag, 1949.

de Boor, Helmut. Geschichte der deutschen Literatur von den Anfängen bis zur Gegenwart. II: Die höfische Literatur: Vorbereitung, Blüte, Ausklang 1170-1250. München: Beck, 1953.

Brinkmann, Hennig. Zu Wesen und Form mittelalterlicher Dichtung. Halle/Saale: M. Niemeyer, 1928.

Bumke, Joachim. Die romanisch-deutschen Literaturbeziehungen im Mittelalter. Ein Ueberblick. Heidelberg: Carl Winter Universitätsverlag, 1967.

Burdach, Konrad. "Nachleben des griechisch-römischen Altertums in der mittelalterlichen Dichtung und Kunst," Vorspiel I. (Address before the Kölner Philologenversammlung, 1895). Halle/Saale: Max Niemeyer, 1925.

Curtius, Ernst Robert. Europäische Literatur und lateinisches Mittelalter. Bern: A. Francke Verlag, 1948.

Ehrismann, Gustav. "Die Grundlagen des ritterlichen Tugendsystems," Zeitschrift für deutsches Altertum, 56 (1918), 137-216.

Emmel, Hildegard. Formprobleme des Artusromans und der Graldichtung. Bern: A. Francke Verlag, 1951.

Frenzen, Wilhelm. Klagebilder und Klagegebärden in der deutschen Dichtung des höfischen Mittelalters. (Bonner Beiträge zur deutschen Philologie, 1). Würzburg: Konrad Triltsch, 1936.

Glunz, Hans H. Die Literarästhetik des europäischen Mittelalters. Frankfurt/Main: Vittorio Klostermann, 1963.

225

BIBLIOGRAPHY

Hempel, Heinrich. "Französischer und deutscher Stil im höfischen Epos," Germanisch-romanische Monatsschrift, 23 (1935), 1-24. (Also in Kleine Schriften, Heidelberg, 1966, 240-260.)

Jackson, W.T.H. "Medieval German Literature," Medieval Literature of Western Europe: A Review of Research 1930-1960, ed. John H. Fisher for the Modern Language Association of America. New York: New York University Press, 1966. Pp. 191-254.

Klaass, Eberhard. Die Schilderung des Sterbens im mittelhochdeutschen Epos. Ein Beitrag zur mittelhochdeutschen Stilgeschichte. PhD. dissertation, Greifswald, 1931.

Kohler, Erika. Liebeskrieg. Zur Bildersprache der höfischen Dichtung des Mittelalters. (Tübinger germanistische Arbeiten, 21) Stuttgart und Berlin: Kohlhammer, 1935.

Kuhn, Hugo. Dichtung und Welt im Mittelalter. Stuttgart: J.B. Metzler, 1959.

_____. "Zur Deutung der künstlerischen Form des Mittelalters," Studium Generale, II (1949), 114-121.

Panzer, Friedrich. "Vom mittelalterlichen Zitieren," Sitzungsberichte der Heidelberger Akademie der Wissenschaften, 35, No. 2 (1949-1950).

Schmuhl, Carl. Beiträge zur Würdigung des Stiles Hartmanns von Aue. Halle: Programm der Lateinischen Hauptschule, 1881.

Schneider, Hermann. "Deutsche und französische Dichtung im Zeitalter der Hohenstaufen," Universitas, 1 (1946).

Schröder, Edward. "Vom Prolog deutscher Dichtungen des 13. Jahrhunderts," Zeitschrift für deutsche Altertumskunde, LXXVI (1940), 301-303.

Schwietering, Julius. Deutsche Dichtung des Mittelalters. Potsdam: Akademische Verlagsgesellschaft Athenaion, 1932. Also Darmstadt: H. Gentner, 1957.

_____. "Die Demutsformel mittelhochdeutscher Dichter," Abh. d. K. G. d. Wissenschaften zu Göttingen, phil.-hist. Kl. N. F., XVII, No. 3 (1921), 43-48, 67-70.

_____. "Typologisches in mittelalterlicher Dichtung," Ehrismann Festschrift: Vom Werden des deutschen Geistes, ed. Paul Merker and Wolfgang Stammler. Berlin: Walter de Gruyter, 1925. Pp. 40-55.

BIBLIOGRAPHY

Singer, Samuel. Sprichwörter des Mittelalters. 2 vols. Bern: Verlag Herbert Lang, 1944, 1946.

Spanke, H. Deutsche und französische Dichtung des Mittelalters. Stuttgart: Kohlhammer, 1943.

Stammler, Wolfgang and Karl Langosch. Die deutsche Literatur des Mittelalters. Verfasserlexikon. 4 vols. Berlin and Leipzig: W. de Gruyter, 1931-1955.

Tubach, Frederic Christian. History of the Exemplum in Germany to 1500. PhD. dissertation, Berkeley, 1957.

Vollmer, Vera. Die Begriffe der Triuwe und der Staete in der höfischen Minnedichtung. PhD. dissertation, Tübingen, 1914.

Wolf, L. Beschreibung des mittelhochdeutschen Volksepos nach seinen grotesken und hyperbolischen Stilmitteln. PhD. dissertation, Göttingen, 1902.

Zingerle, Ignaz V. Die deutschen Sprichwörter im Mittelalter. Wien: Braumuller, 1864.

Metaphor Theory and Rhetoric

Aristotle. Poetics. Translated by Ingram Bywater. New York: Random House Modern Library, 1954.

_____. Rhetoric. Translated by W. Rhys Roberts. New York: Random House Modern Library, 1954.

Armstrong, Edward A. Shakespeare's Imagination: A Study of the Psychology of Association and Inspiration. Lincoln: University of Nebraska Press, 1963. Reprint from 1946.

Barfield, Owen. Poetic Diction: A Study in Meaning. London: Faber and Gwyer, 1928.

Burke, Kenneth. A Grammar of Motives. New York: Prentice-Hall, 1945.

_____. A Rhetoric of Motives. New York: Prentice-Hall, 1950.

Clemen, Wolfgang H. The Development of Shakespeare's Imagery. Revised and augmented version of Shakespeares Bilder. Ihre Entwicklung und ihre Funktion im daramatischen Werk. Cambridge: Harvard University Press, 1951.

BIBLIOGRAPHY

Donatus. The Ars Minor of Donatus. Translated and with an introduction by Wayland Johnson Chase. (Studies in the Social Sciences and History, No. 11) Madison: University of Wisconsin Press, 1926.

Graham, Victor E. The Imagery of Proust. London: Barnes and Noble, 1966.

Hagopian, John V. "Symbol and Metaphor in the Transformation of Reality into Art," Comparative Literature, XX (Winter, 1968), 45-54.

Hastings, Arthur. Psychological and Social Functions of Metaphor. Unpublished article, Stanford University, 1969. 14 pp.

Hayakawa, S.I. Language in Thought and Action. New York: Harcourt, Brace & Co., 1949.

Hornstein, Lillian Herlands. "Analysis of Imagery: A Critique of Literary Method," PMLA, 57 (1942), 638-653.

Langer, Susanne K. Mind: An Essay on Human Feeling, I. Baltimore: Johns Hopkins Press, 1967.

Lausberg, Heinrich. Handbuch der literarischen Rhetorik: eine Grundlegung der Literaturwissenschaft. 2 vols. München: Max Hueber Verlag, 1960.

McKeon, Richard. "Rhetoric in the Middle Ages," Speculum, 17 (Jan., 1942), 1-32.

_____. "Poetry and Philosophy in the Twelfth Century, the Renaissance of Rhetoric," Modern Philology, 43 (May, 1946), 217-234.

Murry, John Middleton. "Imagery and Imagination," Shakespeare, chapter XII. London: J. Cape, 1936.

_____. "Metaphor," Countries of the Mind: Essays in Literary Criticism. Series 2. London: Oxford University Press, 1931. Pp. 1-16.

_____. The Problem of Style. London: Oxford University Press, 1922.

Nohl, Hermann. Stil und Weltanschauung. Jena: E. Diederichs, 1920.

Parry, Milman. "The Traditional Metaphor in Homer," Classical Philology, XXVIII (1933), 30-43.

Perls, Frederick, and R.E. Hefferline, Paul Goodman. Gestalt Therapy: Excitement and Growth in the human Personality. New York: Dell, 1965.

BIBLIOGRAPHY

Pongs, Hermann. Das Bild in der Dichtung. 2 vols. I: Versuch einer Morphologie
der metaphorischen Formen. II: Voruntersuchungen zum Symbol. Marburg:
N.G. Elwert Verlag, 1960, 1963.

Quintilian, Marcus Fabius. Institutes of Oratory: Education of an Orator. Vol. 2.
Translated by John Selly Watson. London: George Bell and Sons, 1876.

Richards, I.A. The Philosophy of Rhetoric. New York: Oxford University Press,
1936.

_____. Practical Criticism: A Study of Literary Judgment. New York: Harcourt,
Brace & Co., 1929.

_____. Principles of Literary Criticism. London: Routledge and Kegan Paul, 1949.
Reprinted from 1924.

Spurgeon, Caroline F.E. Shakespeare's Imagery and What it Tells Us. New York:
Macmillan Co., 1935.

Wellek, Rene, and Austin Warren. Theory of Literature. New York: Harcourt,
Brace & Co., 1956.

Werner, Heinz. Ursprünge der Metapher. (Arbeiten zur Entwicklungspsychologie,
3. Heft, ed. Felix Krueger.) Leipzig: Engelmann, 1919.

Wimsatt, W.K. Jr., and M.C. Beardsley. "The Intentional Fallacy," Essays in
Modern Literary Criticism, ed. Ray Benedict West. N.Y.: Holt, Rinehart,
Winston, 1962. Pp. 174-189.

Wolfram Editions

Lachmann, Karl. Wolfram von Eschenbach. 4th edition. Berlin, 1879.

Leitzmann, Albert. Wolfram von Eschenbach: Parzival. Books I-VI, seventh edition;
Books VII-XVI, sixth edition. Revised by Wilhelm Deinert. Altdeutsche Text-
bibliothek, Nos. 12-14. Tübingen: Max Niemeyer Verlag, 1961-1965.

On Wolfram von Eschenbach

Blamires, David. Characterization and Individuality in Wolfram's Parzival. Cambridge: Cambridge University Press, 1966.

BIBLIOGRAPHY

Bock, Ludwig. Wolframs von Eschenbach Bilder und Wörter für Freude und Leid. Strassburg: Karl Trübner, 1879.

Bötticher, Gotthold. "Ueber die Eigenthümlichkeiten der Sprache Wolframs," Germania: Vierteljahrschrift für deutsche Altertumskunde, XXI, Neue Reihe 9 (1876), 257-332.

Bohner, Jakob G. Das Beiwort des Menschen und der Individualismus in Wolframs Parzival. PhD. dissertation, Heidelberg, 1909.

Bumke, Joachim. Wolfram von Eschenbach. Sammlung Metzler, Realienbücher für Germanisten, Abt. D: Literaturgeschichte. Stuttgart: Metzler, 1964.

Dahms, Friedrich. Die Grundlagen für den Stil Wolframs von Eschenbach. PhD. dissertation, Greifswald, 1911.

Dilthey, Wilhelm. "Wolfram von Eschenbach," Von deutscher Dichtung und Musik. Leipzig und Berlin: Teubner, 1933. Pp. 107-130.

Domanig, Karl. "Die Entstehung von Wolframs Titurel," Die Kultur, XII (1911), 266-286.

Eggers, Hans. "Non cognovi litteraturam (zu Parzival 115, 27)," Festschrift Pretzel. Berlin: Erich Schmidt, 1963. Pp. 162-172.

_____. "Strukturprobleme mittelalterlicher Epik, dargestellt am 'Parzival' Wolframs von Eschenbach," in Wolfram von Eschenbach, ed. Heinz Rupp. (Wege der Forschung, vol. LVII.) Darmstadt: Wissenschaftliche Buchgesellschaft, 1966. Pp. 158-172. Reprinted from Euphorion, 46 (1952), 260-270.

_____. "Wolframforschung in der Krise? Ein Forschungsbericht," Wirkendes Wort, 4 (1953-54), 274-290.

Förster, Paulus Traugott. Zur Sprache und Poesie Wolframs von Eschenbach. PhD. dissertation, Freiburg, 1874.

Götz, Josef. Die Entwicklung des Wolframbildes von Bodmer bis zum Tode Lachmanns in der germanistischen und schönen Literatur. PhD. dissertation, Freiburg, 1940.

Grimm, Wilhelm. "Gleichnisse im Ossian und Parzival," Kleinere Schriften, I. Berlin: 1881. Pp. 48-57.

Groos, Arthur B., Jr. Wolframs Bow Metaphor and the Poetics of 'Parzival'. Unpublished address before the Modern Language Association, New York, 1970.

BIBLIOGRAPHY

Grundmann, Herbert. "Dichtete Wolfram von Eschenbach am Schreibtisch?" Archiv für Kulturgeschichte, IL (1967), 391-405.

Heckel, Hermann. Das ethische Wortfeld in Wolframs Parzival. PhD. dissertation, Erlangen, 1939.

Heffner, R-M. S. (ed.). Collected Indexes to the Works of Wolfram von Eschenbach. Madison: University of Wisconsin Press, 1961.

Hoffman, W. Der Einfluss des Reims auf die Sprache Wolframs von Eschenbach. PhD. dissertation, Strassburg, 1894.

Horacek, Blanka. "Die Kunst des Enjambements bei Wolfram von Eschenbach," Zeitschrift für deutsches Altertum, 85 (1954-55), 210-229.

_____. "Ichne kan deheinen buochstap," Festschrift Dietrich Kralik. Horn, N.-Oe.: Verlag Berger, 1954. Pp. 129-145.

_____. "Wolframprobleme: 750 Jahre Parzival," Wissenschaft und Weltbild, V (1952), 319-324, 371-373.

_____. "Zur Wortstellung in Wolframs 'Parzival'," Oesterreichische Akademie der Wissenschaften, phil.-hist. Kl., Anzeiger, 89 (1952), 270-299.

Jensen, Harro Dewet. Wolfram und sein Werk. Der Stil des Parzival als Ausdruck der Persönlichkeit Wolframs und seiner Anteilnahme am Geschehen der Handlung. PhD. dissertation, Marburg, 1927.

Kant, Karl. Scherz und Humor in Wolframs von Eschenbach Dichtungen. Heilbronn: Henninger, 1878.

Kashiwagi, Motoko. "Zum neuen Stand der Parzivalforschung," Doitsu Bungaku: Die deutsche Literatur, Nos. 27-30 (1961-63), 44-53. (Kyoto, Deutsches Forschungsinstitut.)

Kinzel, Karl. "Zur Charakteristik des Wolframschen Stils", Zeitschrift für deutsche Philologie, V (1874), 1-36.

Klein, Karl Kurt. "Gottfried und Wolfram. Zum Bogengleichnis Parzival 241, 1-30," Festschrift Dietrich Kralik. Horn, N.-Oe.: Verlag Berger, 1954. Pp. 145-154.

_____. "Wolframs Selbstverteidigung," Zeitschrift für deutsches Altertum, 85 (1954-55), 150-162.

BIBLIOGRAPHY

Lippka, Erwin R. "Zum Stilproblem in Wolframs Parzival: Bericht über den Stand der Forschung," Journal of English and Germanic Philology, LXII (1963), 597-610.

Lowet, Ralph. Wolfram von Eschenbachs Parzival im Wandel der Zeiten. (Schriftenreihe des Goethe-Instituts, Band 3.) München: Verlag Pohl and Co., 1955.

Ludwig, Karl. Der bildliche Ausdruck bei Wolfram von Eschenbach. Mies: Programm des K.K. Staats-Obergymnsium, 1889-1890.

Mackensen, Rainer. Das Bild und seine Funktion im Parzival des Wolfram von Eschenbach. PhD. dissertation, Tübingen, 1955.

Matz, Elsa-Lina. Formelhafte Ausdrücke in Wolframs Parzival. PhD. dissertation, Kiel, 1907.

Mergell, Bodo. Wolfram und seine französischen Quellen. II: Wolframs Parzival. Münster: Aschendorff, 1943.

Panzer, Friedrich. Bibliographie zu Wolfram von Eschenbach. Munich: Ackermann, 1897.

Pfeiffer, Franz. "Ueber das Parzival und Wolframs Sprachgebrauch," Germania: Vierteljahrschrift für deutsche Altertumskunde, 6 (1861), 235-243. (Review of Oskar Janicke's PhD. dissertation, De dicendi usu Wolframi de Eschenbach.)

Piderit, Karl Wilhelm. Bilder aus Parzival. Ein Cyclus von Vorträgen. Gütersloh, 1875.

Poag, James F. "Heinrich von Veldeke's 'minne'; Wolfram von Eschenbach's 'liebe' und 'triuwe'," Journal of English and Germanic Philology, LXI (1962), 721-735.

_____. "Wolfram von Eschenbach's Metamorphosis of the Ovidian Tradition," Monatshefte, LVII (1965), 69-76.

Pretzel, Ulrich, and Wolfgang Bachofer. Bibliographie zu Wolfram von Eschenbach. (Bibliographien zur deutschen Literatur des Mittelalters, Heft 2.) Berlin: Erich Schmidt Verlag, 1968.

Reiber, Traugott K. Studien zu Grundlage und Wesen mittelalterlicher höfischer Dichtung. Unter besonderer Berücksichtigung von Wolframs dunklem Stil. PhD. dissertation, Tübingen, 1954.

BIBLIOGRAPHY

Reinecke, O. Das Enjambement bei Wolfram von Eschenbach. PhD. dissertation, Giessen, 1903.

Riemer, G. Die Adjektiva bei Wolfram von Eschenbach stilistisch betrachtet. PhD. dissertation, Halle, 1906.

Rogozinski, Paul. Der Stil in Wolfram von Eschenbachs Titurel. PhD. dissertation, Jena, 1903.

Rupp, Heinz. "Das neue Wolfram Bild," Deutschunterricht, V (1953), 82-90.

_____. (ed.). Wolfram von Eschenbach. Darmstadt: Wissenschaftliche Buchgesellschaft, 1966.

Sacker, Hugh. An Introduction to Wolfram's Parzival. Cambridge: Cambridge University Press, 1963.

Santen, J. von. Zur Beurteilung Wolframs von Eschenbach. Wesel: Fincke und Mallinckrodt, 1882.

Schröder, Walter Johannes. "Grundzüge eines neuen Wolframbildes," Forschungen und Fortschritte, 26 (1950), 174-178.

_____. "Vindaere wilder maere. Zum Literaturstreit zwischen Gottfried und Wolfram," Beiträge zur Geschichte der deutschen Sprache und Literatur, 80 (1958), 269-287.

Schröder, Werner. "Zum gegenwärtigen Stande der Wolfram Kritik," Zeitschrift für deutsches Altertum und deutsche Literatur, XCVI (1967), 1-28.

Schulze, B. Zwei ausgewählte Kapitel der Lehre von der mittelhochdeutschen Wortstellung mit besonderer Rücksicht auf Wolframs Parzival. PhD. dissertation, Berlin, 1892.

Singer, Samuel. Neue Parzival Studien. Zurich und Leipzig: Max Niehaus Verlag, 1937.

_____. "Wolframs Stil und der Stoff des Parzival," Wiener Sitzungsberichte, 180, Abh. 4 (1916), 1-127.

Spiess, Gisela. Die Bedeutung des Wortes 'triuwe' in den mittelhochdeutschen Epen 'Parzival', 'Nibelungenlied' und 'Tristan'. PhD. dissertation, Heidelberg, 1957.

BIBLIOGRAPHY

Springer, Otto. "Etymologisches Spiel im 'Parzival'," Beiträge zur Geschichte der deutschen Sprache und Literatur, 87 (1965), 166-181.

_____. "Playing on Words: A Stilistic Note on Wolfram's 'Titurel'," Research Studies, 32 (1964), 106-124.

Starck, Christian. Die Darstellungsmittel des Wolframschen Humors. Inauguraldissertation der philosophischen Facultät der Universität Rostock. Schwerin: Hofbuchdruckerei von Dr. F. Bärensprung, 1879.

Stavenhagen, Lee. The Science of Parzival. PhD. dissertation, Berkeley, 1964.

Tapp, Henry L. The Use of Imagery in the Works of Wolfram von Eschenbach. PhD. dissertation, Yale, 1954.

Vigl, Hermann. Das Bild als Mittel des Ausdrucks und des Gestaltens bei Wolfram von Eschenbach. Untersuchungen zum sprachlichen Bild in Wolframs Dichtung. PhD. dissertation, Innsbruck, 1953.

Wapnewski, Peter. "Herzeloydes Klage und das Leid der Blancheflur. Zur Frage der agonalen Beziehungen zwischen den Kunstauffassungen Gottfrieds von Strassburg und Wolfram von Eschenbach," Festschrift Ulrich Pretzel. Berlin: Erich Schmidt Verlag, 1963. Pp. 173-184.

Weber, Gottfried. Wolfram von Eschenbach: Seine dichterische und geistesgeschichtliche Bedeutung. I. Frankfurt/Main: Moritz Diesterweg, 1928.

Wehrli, Max. "Wolframs Humor," Wolfram von Eschenbach, ed. Heinz Rupp. (Wege der Forschung, LVII.) Darmstadt: Wissenschaftliche Buchgesellschaft, 1966. Pp. 104-124.

_____. "Wolfram von Eschenbach, Erzählstil und Sinn seines 'Parzival'," Der Deutschunterricht, VI, Heft 5 (1954), 17-40.

Willson, Bernard. "Wolframs Bogengleichnis," Zeitschrift für deutsche Altertumskunde, XCI (1961-62), 56-62.

Wolff, E. Die zusammengesetzten Adjektiva und Adverbia bei Wolfram von Eschenbach. PhD. dissertation, Greifswald, 1913.

Wolff, Ludwig. "Vom persönlichen Stil Wolframs in seiner dichterischen Bedeutung. Ein Versuch," Kleinere Schriften zur altdeutschen Philologie. Berlin: de Gruyter, 1967. Pp. 262-293.

BIBLIOGRAPHY

Wolfram von Eschenbach. Parzival: A Romance of the Middle Ages. Translated and with an introduction by Helen M. Mustard and Charles E. Passage. New York: Random House, 1961.

Zehme, A. Ueber Bedeutung und Gebrauch der Hilfsverba. I: Soln und müezen bei Wolfram von Eschenbach. PhD. dissertation, Halle, 1890.

Zell, H. Das Adjektiv bei Wolfram von Eschenbach, Hartmann von Aue und Gotfrid von Strassburg. PhD. dissertation, Strassburg, 1909.

Zeydel, E.H. "Wolfram von Eschenbach und diu buoch," Euphorion, 48 (1954), 210-215.

Zwierzina, Konrad. "Beobachtungen zum Reimgebrauch Hartmanns und Wolfram," Abhandlungen zur germanischen Philologie, Festgabe für Richard Heinzel. 1898. Pp. 437-511. (Review by Friedrich Panzer, Zeitschrift für deutsche Philologie, 33 (1901), 123-138.

Miscellaneous

Bächtold-Stäubli, Hanns. Handwörterbuch des deutschen Aberglaubens. 10 vol. Berlin and Leipzig: W. de Gruyter, 1927-1942.

Kosch, Wilhelm. Deutsches Literatur-Lexikon. 4 vols. Second edition. Bern: A. Francke, 1949-1958.

Küpper, Heinz. Wörterbuch der deutschen Umgangssprache. Fourth edition. Hamburg: Claassen Verlag, 1965.

Merker, Paul, and Wolfgang Stammler. Reallexikon der deutschen Literaturgeschichte. Revised by Werner Kohlschmidt and Wolfgang Mohr. Berlin: de Gruyter, 1958.